THE WHOLE MANAGER

THE WHOLE MANAGER

Dennis P. Slevin

American Management Association

This book is available at a special
discount when ordered in bulk quantities.
For information, contact Special Sales Department,
AMACOM, a division of American Management Association,
135 West 50th Street, New York, NY 10020.

Library of Congress Cataloging-in-Publication Data

Slevin, Dennis P.
   The whole manager / Dennis P. Slevin.
      p. cm.
   Rev. ed. of: Executive survival manual. c1985.
   Bibliography: p.
   Includes index.
   ISBN 0-8144-5836-X
   1. Management. 2. Executives. I. Slevin, Dennis P. Executive
survival manual. II. Title.
   HD31.S5765 1989
   658.4'09—dc19   88-48033
                                                          CIP

This is a revised edition of Executive Survival Manual, © 1985 Dennis P. Slevin.

Printing number

10 9 8 7 6 5 4 3 2 1

To
Thomas V. Bonoma,

coauthor of the original
Executive Survival Manual,

outstanding scholar, and a good friend

Contents

Preface   ix

1   Harry Thorpe's Mess   1
2   Time Management   9
3   Intolerance as a Response to Noncompliance   40
4   Stress   55
5   Power   82
6   Behavior Modification   116
7   Management by Objectives   130
8   Effective Communications   161
9   Leadership   183
10   Motivation   202
11   Organizational Design   221
12   Negotiation Skills   250
13   Staffing   285
14   Project Management   302
15   Effective Meetings, Teams, and Task Forces   331
16   Entrepreneurship/Intrapreneurship   344

17 Health and Life-Style   366
18 Career Management   381
19 Harry Thorpe—The Survivor   400

Selected Readings   411

Index   417

Preface

The original version of this book was published in 1978 as the *Executive Survival Manual* and coauthored with Thomas V. Bonoma. A significant revision was published in 1985. *The Whole Manager* represents another significant revision, with emphasis on the latest behavioral concepts and pragmatic tools for practicing managers. A variety of diagnostic devices, including surveys, checklists, action plans, and behavioral instruments, are presented. These are combined with the latest concepts to give the reader a practical edge in meeting the management challenges of the 1990s.

I would like to acknowledge a number of people for their assistance in this project. Thomas V. Bonoma was an essential coauthor in the original edition and a supportive advisor in this revision. Betty A. Velthouse provided invaluable conceptual and writing input to the 1985 edition. At the same time, Rosemary Kitch-Bosler proved to be an extremely competent editor. And last, but certainly not least, my wife, Susan, spent countless hours working jointly on the administration, logistics, writing, and editing throughout the entire project.

The Whole Manager is a pragmatic workbook to help you better understand managerial effectiveness, personal satisfaction, and personal growth. In order to implement personal change, you must first have sound concepts; second, you need a good diagnosis of where you stand; and third, you must have an action plan. In my experience, most management texts focus the majority of their efforts on the concept phase. *The Whole Manager* represents an attempt to balance the emphasis among concepts, diagnosis, and action planning.

The concepts presented here are broad based and theoretically sound. Great pains have been taken to make sure that the substantive material in this book is "correct" from a behavioral science perspective. This is not just a book of anecdotes by successful managers.

To help you diagnose your own problems, needs, and options, this book presents more than fifty surveys, exercises, checklists, and forms. The forms are located at the end of each chapter. Some of these are nicely refined psychometrics. Others are a bit less developed but helpful in important areas of self-analysis. Use them to stimulate self-insight so that you can better appreciate where you stand in comparison to other successful managers in a variety of areas.

Finally, action planning is important. In order to receive a return from the use of this book, you must engage in behavior change. You must be able to change your behavior in some effective fashion in order to get a payback for your time spent. A number of action plans have been included to assist you. Use this book as a pragmatic workbook and try to ensure that at least some of your action plans are successfully implemented.

I hope that this book "works for you."

Dennis P. Slevin, Ph.D.

Chapter 1

Harry Thorpe's Mess

Harry thorpe is dying. He doesn't have a fatal physical disease, and he isn't about to have a fatal accident. Nor is he in the middle of an emotional crisis; indeed, others find him quite well balanced. But he is dying and, worse, he will die miserable, frustrated, and confused.

Harry Thorpe is dying because he is failing to survive in a difficult management environment. Like a hiker caught in a sudden snowstorm who frantically walks around in circles, Harry is rapidly expending his vital life energies. His early demise from hypertension, heart disease, or whatever will be of his own making, yet paradoxically it will be out of his control, as is his life.

Harry realizes, usually after midnight, that something is very wrong, but he can't quite put his finger on the problem. All he knows is that he is committed to slugging it out in corporate life. Those who love him and depend upon him most—his family—also see that something is seriously wrong, but they don't know how to help him.

Can we help him and maybe help you, too? That's what this book is about.

Let's look at Harry a little more closely.

PROFILE

Name: Harry M. Thorpe
Age: 43
Personal: Married with 2 children
Position: General manager of a moderate-size subsidiary of a multinational manufacturing company
Sales: Approximately $160 million per year
Total supervised: 1,250 people
Immediate subordinates:

Sales manager: Henry Carothers
Production manager 1: Ralph Kingsley
Production manager 2: Deborah Walters
Manager engineering: Sarah Freeman
Personnel manager: Quentin Hill
Finance and accounting manager: Spencer Bernham

Historical note: Business has been good lately, but recently global and domestic competitive pressures have put added strain on Harry and his staff. Harry was promoted five months ago to his first general management job. Key investments have been made in plant and equipment, and a factory automation project has recently come on line. This year will be his make-or-break year, and he knows it.

Let's look at part of a typical workday, as seen through Harry's eyes.

HARRY THORPE'S TOUGH MONDAY MORNING

7:00 A.M. Alarm rings. Harry didn't get to bed until 1:30 A.M. because he went to a school play and then worked on a quarterly report. He drags out of bed to face the Monday morning work world.

7:30 A.M. Shower completed, Harry grabs a cup of coffee and a slice of toast, and he turns on the *Today Show* to catch the morning news. His stomach, which often gives him trouble, seems knotted and queasy this morning, so he skips the toast and just drinks the coffee. His wife and children are sitting around the table in various states of disrepair, and there is little conversation. Harry rushes out the door after the ritual 5 minutes with his "breakfast" and family. He hopes to make work before 8:00, though it is ordinarily a 35-minute drive.

8:10 A.M. Harry arrives at the office with a renewed conviction that those no-good politicians will keep the roads screwed up forever, and that he is quite possibly the only person in the whole world who can drive a car competently. He wonders how some people survive at all.

8:15 A.M. He feverishly starts on the pile of paper in the in-basket, writing on a yellow pad. He hopes to wade through it before the rest of the staff arrives.

8:25 A.M. Phone call: Carothers (sales manager). He wants to know the cost and delivery date of stampings he's quoting to a special customer. Harry stalls, saying he'll get back to him later in the morning. He has to get Ralph Kingsley (production manager 1) to determine the key information on this and see how the special order can be handled without messing up current production runs.

8:30 A.M. Secretary arrives and waves. Harry is still on the phone to Carothers.

8:32 A.M. Harry begins trying to draft a budget memo to the president, requesting $550,000 for an upgraded inspection facility. Perhaps this will solve some of the quality problems they've been having lately. He knows he really has to justify an expenditure of that size to have any chance of getting it. He wishes that he had more data to go on, but he hopes he can put it together without a costly search.

8:35 A.M. Phone call: Quentin (personnel manager). Wants Harry's approval on a new health and wellness program for the work force. Harry still hasn't had a chance to review the folder, and so he asks Quentin to discuss it at the closing of the staff meeting later in the morning. Quentin agrees, but reminds Harry that this matter is something they really do have to move on quickly.

8:40 A.M. Harry returns to the budget memo. He will have to ask Deborah Walters (production manager 2) about some product-failure rates and piece costs during the staff meeting. Harry still needs about three or four key elements of information to complete his budget request.

8:50 A.M. The secretary brings in six requisition forms for Harry's signature. He glances briefly at each, corrects a typographical error on one, and signs them.

8:52 A.M. Phone call: A union representative wants to meet with Harry to discuss the use of nonunion labor in the exterior maintenance of the plant. Union relations are only fair to moderate, and Harry is concerned. He sets a meeting for Wednesday and makes a mental note to review the company's position with his team before then.

8:57 A.M.   Having given up on the budget memo for the time being, Harry attacks his correspondence. However, he just can't seem to get the first letter out since his mind is on the upcoming budget request.

9:00 A.M.   The staff meeting attended by Harry and his six immediate subordinates begins in the conference room. Harry is less prepared than he would like to be. There is no specific agenda, so Harry spends 10 minutes setting the agenda with the staff.

9:22 A.M.   The staff meeting is interrupted by a phone call: Harrison in Texas. He's got a great opportunity if Harry can deliver a special job in four weeks. Harry tells him that he'll check it out and get back to him that afternoon (this gives Harry until 6:00 P.M. EST). Harry asks Deborah Walters to review the schedule on production line 5 and tell him by 5:00 P.M. if she thinks they can handle it.

9:37 A.M.   Phone call: the president. He is meeting with OSHA tomorrow and wants Harry to brief him by 6:00 P.M. today.

9:45 A.M.   Staff meeting adjourns. Harry resumes working on correspondence with his secretary.

9:55 A.M.   Phone call: A vendor of stamping machines wants to see Harry. Tuesday A.M. meeting is set after Harry checks his appointment book and mentally cancels the last half hour of a meeting with Walters and Kingsley.

10:00 A.M.   Harry gets up to get a cup of coffee and walks through the office. The office staff looks particularly bleary-eyed and unmotivated this morning. However, Priscilla Morgan, Quentin's new administrative assistant, seems organized and efficient. Harry wonders, "What's her secret?"

10:02 A.M.   Quentin meets Harry at the coffee station and says, "Harry, we've got a problem. We must finalize our decision on the new administrative specialist by next week. The three finalists are coming here on Friday to do an in-basket exercise, and I can't find an in-basket that makes sense to me."

"Gee, Quentin," says Harry, who knows quite a bit about the technique, "I'll look through my files and get back to you."

10:05 A.M.   Good progress on correspondence so far. However, Harry stops answering letters to prepare for a Coordination Committee meeting at 10:30 A.M.

10:10 A.M.   Harry shuts his door, requests no more phone calls, and plans his program of attack for his 10:30 meeting. He has got to get the sales force to understand the plant's limitations and the difficulties of meeting the production schedules.

10:30 A.M.   Coordination Committee meeting. In attendance are the president, the executive vice-president, the treasurer of the division, and Harry. The treasurer starts the meeting by throwing Harry a curve: "There is a working capital shortage and we may have to put clamps on additional expenditures for the next six months." Harry's stomach sinks, since this pronouncement may have dire consequences for the proposed quality-control facility he needs so badly. The usual complaints about quality are raised. The president leads the normal weekly cheers for more output and higher quality, which he thinks can be brought about only if they "talk about it." No action steps result from the meeting, and Harry just doesn't have the heart to bring up his quality-control facility proposal at this time.

11:15 A.M.   Visit by Ralph Kingsley (production manager). He wants to know how he and Harry are going to approach the Step 3 grievances that are now pending. Harry really hasn't had a chance to review this problem in sufficient depth, though he knows its outlines. He asks Ralph to use his own judgment in the matter.

11:25 A.M.   Phone call: United Way wants Harry to chair their drive at the plant. He accepts. Top management is very committed, and Harry needs to do well in his "social commitment" area on his annual appraisal.

11:28 A.M.   Harry returns to Ralph Kingsley's office and tells him that, on the Step 3 grievances, they probably should follow a strategy showing negligence on the part of the employees. He requests Ralph to document these negligences more carefully. No reporting system is set up between Harry and Ralph on the project.

11:34 A.M.   Phone call: Miller, in Indiana, wants to know whether Harry can handle the Jameson account, which would amount to $2.5 million total billings. It looks attractive but has stiff quality-control requirements. Harry says he'll call him that afternoon and sets a meeting at 2:00 P.M. with Ralph Kingsley (production manager) and Henry Carothers (sales manager).

11:42 A.M.   Harry phones Clarence Hughes, a personal friend who is a CPA, and asks him if he'll help with the United Way. Clarence says yes, but Harry is skeptical. Clarence has been unreliable in the past, and Harry is concerned that he will end up having to do all the work again.

11:45 A.M.   Secretary brings in the rough drafts of letters that Harry gave her that morning. He corrects an average of two typos per page and returns them for a final draft.

11:56 A.M.   Phone call: A vendor of office equipment calls about a redesign of the inventory-control area. Harry sets a meeting for Thursday afternoon.

11:58 A.M.   Harry gets an urgent phone call from the president. He wants Harry to accompany him to the West Coast that night to close a major deal. Harry, of course, agrees. What choice does he have?

12:08 P.M.   Harry asks his secretary to cancel the Tuesday, Wednesday, and Thursday meetings and to get the plane tickets.

12:17 P.M.   Harry phones his wife at work and asks her to bring him a suitcase to the office by 5:30 P.M. He tells her that he won't make the chamber music concert that they had looked forward to. She reminds him that he'll also miss the open house at their daughter's high school (just like last year). She says, "Harry, when is our life going to get more sane?" But she agrees to help.

12:22 P.M.   Harry asks the secretary to get him a sandwich at the coffee shop to eat at his desk.

12:33 P.M.   Harry closes the door and sits at the desk, staring at the pile of paper in front of him. A tasteless, limp sandwich stares back up at him. He is depressed and anxious. He doesn't feel too well. His stomach hurts. His hands are clammy. A drop of cold sweat rolls down his left side. He knows that the afternoon will probably be even worse.

A doctor might record the following:

Pulse: 92 (20 beats above average)
Blood pressure: 155/95 (hypertensive)
Height/weight: 5'10", 192 pounds (about 20 pounds too much)
Eating habits: Usually small breakfast, either a small or high-calorie business lunch; very large dinner
Drinking habits: Two to three martinis per night. More on weekends and at parties
Exercise: Too little; tennis game every two to three weeks

Career: Rapidly successful to date, currently stationary; could take a nose dive if things don't straighten out

Family: Last meaningful discussion with wife was four weeks earlier during boring company dinner. Last time really talked to kids, seven weeks earlier during Easter vacation visit with grandparents

Diagnosis: Emotions, health, job, life—not enough under control

Prognosis: In the next five years has at least a fifty-fifty chance of suffering one or more of the following:

- Heart attack
- Loss of job
- Divorce
- Serious illness
- Nervous breakdown

IS HARRY'S MESS YOUR MESS?

Why is Harry in such a mess? Because basically he is mismatched to his job. And not only to his job, but to his life. Harry has not taken adequate control of his career and environment. To survive, he needs to be able to manage his time, personal stress, subordinates, and health. He needs, obviously, to do a better job of leading his organization as well as of addressing a variety of specific areas in his management life.

How's your job? Your health? Your life? Maybe you don't have all of Harry's problems, but do you have some?

Are you always rushing to get places? Are you tense all the time? Does your stomach hurt? Do you play with your kids less than once a week? Are you and your spouse drifting apart? Right now, are you in a departure lounge or at your desk or wherever, wondering why you're reading this book instead of doing the fifty other things waiting for you?

Not as bad off as Harry? How many extra years will that buy you? Is it enough?

WHAT THIS BOOK WILL DO FOR YOU

This book is a practical manual for practicing managers. Its purpose is to provide you with the tools for:

- *Survival*—to give you the skills you need not just to hang in there but to prevail in the challenging world of management

- *Managerial effectiveness*—to give you the skills, insights, and new be-haviors to be a truly able and influential executive
- *Personal satisfaction*—to heighten your self-awareness and improve your job success so that you find yourself enjoying life more, both at work and at home
- *Personal growth*—to help you explore your basic goals, values, and objectives in ways that will help you grow as a person

Because our objective is behavior change, the approach here is en-tirely pragmatic. Thus, this book is structured like a workbook, with numerous checklists, forms, exercises, and other practical "how-to" tools to help you change your (and others') behavior. I urge you to use them. If you are an overworked, time-starved practicing manager, you will be better off not reading the book at all than reading it and not taking advantage of the devices I have included for improving managerial be-havior. I would rather accomplish a small element of behavior change, using a simple and straightforward approach, than write a sophisticated treatise that helps no one.

Read and do the exercises in the next chapter. Since each chapter is self-contained, you can then skip around in the book to satisfy your most pressing concerns.

Ready to start taking charge of your life?

BEGIN!

Chapter 2

Time Management

DOES HARRY seem unusual?

He's not.

In fact, the frantic, fever-pitched day he has had so far is quite typical for practicing managers. Although Harry has had thirty-two individual activities and fourteen interruptions this morning, research and consulting experience have shown that this is not unusual, even for very efficient managers. Harry's problem is that he cannot manage his time effectively. If he doesn't learn how, and soon, he is not going to make it, physically or professionally.

How about you? Does time often get away from you? Then read on. Help is on the way. The purpose of this chapter is to help you quickly learn improved time-management skills that you can immediately put into practice.

OBJECTIVES

The objectives in this chapter are pragmatic and straightforward:

1. To save you four hours per week
2. To have you better understand what a manager does

Four hours doesn't seem like much? Assuming you work a forty-hour week (many managers do not, of course; many often work up to sixty hours a week), four hours per week represent:

- Ten percent of your time
- One week of vacation every ten weeks
- Five extra weeks of vacation per year
- Seventeen more hours per month to spend with your family

I have encountered few managers who could not save at least four hours per week by incorporating the skills contained in this chapter.

To begin, it is necessary to ask a few questions.

WHAT DO YOU DO? THE CLASSICAL APPROACH

List below the five key things you do as a manager. Don't hesitate to write in this book. Remember, it was designed as a workbook. What are the five most important things you do?

1. _____
2. _____
3. _____
4. _____
5. _____

Was that a difficult task? Don't be embarrassed. Whenever I ask this question of a group of practicing managers in an executive-development program, a wave of silence washes over the room. After a while, the class begins to give the "classical" answer. Originally formulated by Gulick and Urwick (around 1937), it is popularly known as POSDCORB:[1]

P—Planning involves those activities that broadly outline what needs to be done and how to go about doing it. Planning therefore includes establishing the basic mission of the enterprise, goal setting, and strategic planning.

---

[1]L. H. Gulick, "Notes on the Theory of Organization," in L. H. Gulick and L. Urwick, eds., *Papers on the Science of Administration* (New York: Augustus M. Kelley, 1969).

O—*Organizing* establishes the formal structure of authority—the divisions and subdivisions of the organization. It involves the assignment of teams and their interdependencies.

S—*Staffing* addresses the manager's role in the recruitment, placement, selection, training, orientation, scheduling, and compensation of the labor force.

D—*Directing* is the continuous task of making decisions, instructing, telling, and giving orders. Specifically, it is the translation of the plan into specific behaviors.

CO—*Coordinating* is the process of making sure the interdependent elements work in harmony. Knowing who is doing what and when is essential.

R—*Reporting* refers to all the activities that a manager uses to keep his supervisors and subordinates informed. This includes the use of records, research, and inspection.

B—*Budgeting* is reserved for all the money matters. It includes planning for, allocation of, requests for, accounting of, and control of financial resources.

Does POSDCORB describe what you do? Probably, more or less. The problem is that all of the items on this list are abstract concepts. It is fine to talk about planning, organizing, and so on, but the list doesn't tell you what to do on a day-to-day basis. How do you plan when you are bombarded with crises? Although it is a useful framework, this classical approach is not pragmatic. It does not tell you how to do these tasks effectively.

WHAT DO YOU DO? THE MODERN APPROACH

Since the mid-1950s, behavioral scientists have tried a number of ways to answer this question. First, they asked managers what they did. But observers found that getting answers was harder than they had anticipated.

A scenario like this was not unusual:[2]

---

[2] Adapted from a conversation between observer and executive in C. L. Shartle, *Executive Performance and Leadership* (Englewood Cliffs, N.J.: Prentice-Hall, 1956). Reprinted with permission.

OBSERVER: Mr. R., we have discussed briefly this organization and the way it operates. Will you now please tell me what you do?
EXECUTIVE: What I do?
OBSERVER: Yes.
EXECUTIVE: That's not easy.
OBSERVER: Go ahead, anyway.
EXECUTIVE: As president, naturally I am responsible for many things.
OBSERVER: Yes, I realize that. But just what do you do?
EXECUTIVE: Well, I must see that things go all right.
OBSERVER: Can you give me an example?
EXECUTIVE: I must see that our financial position is sound.
OBSERVER: But just what do you do about it?
EXECUTIVE: Now, that is hard to say . . .

You can imagine, of course, why it was difficult for executives to pin down their exact functions. Managers do a great many specific things to achieve very broad organizational goals; and it is often difficult to verbalize the connection between the two.

The behaviorists then tried a different tack. They followed managers around during the day and recorded their activities, using checkoff forms and logs. The results were quite shocking! The observers found that practicing managers, rather than planning, organizing, and otherwise POSDCORBing in a relaxed, programmed fashion, often made Harry Thorpe look orderly by comparison. Their jobs were characterized by:

- High personal energy level
- Role overload
- Frenetic activity
- Fragmentation
- Superficiality

Managers, they found, had to be personally hard chargers, to be highly energetic; they had many demands on their time from a variety of individuals within and outside the organization. Even though no single demand was unreasonable, the sheer volume of demands could fill a fourteen-hour day—in other words, role overload. The typical manager, they found, engaged in a frenetic sequence of activities—that is, telephoning, dictating, note taking, meeting, reading, and talking—all with many interruptions and with very little time for reflection.

Because of these great demands, managers did things in a fragmented fashion, occasionally resulting in superficiality in managerial decisions. How many times have you regretted making a superficial decision—superficial for the simple reason that there was no more time available in which to make it? You are not alone.

THE AGENDA

The research on practicing managers indicates that they attempt to get things done through the implementation of their "agenda."[3] The agenda is a relatively simple, back-of-the-envelope document that can be a very important short- and long-run guide. Harry Thorpe's typical agenda is shown in Figure 2-1.

As you can see, there are three columns:

1. *Financial*—What sort of monetary and financial goals does the company have?
2. *Business (product/market)*—What business is the company really in? What are its products and services? Who are its customers?
3. *People*—What is being done to hire, retain, and train the personnel? What's the basic organizational structure?

Every manager has a variety of goals that fit these three categories.

The rows in the Figure 2-1 matrix are defined in terms of time. Here I have taken some liberties with Kotter's research on general managers by making the time frames a bit shorter, but the following categories apply in most management situations: zero to six months, six to twelve months, and greater than twelve months.

A practicing manager loads up his agenda and uses it for time management and priority setting. It is a living document and is revised continuously. You can see in Harry's typical agenda an excess of focus on short-run issues. If he really wants to be a success in the long run, he has to make sure that he attends to longer term objectives. Some researchers even suggest that the long term be viewed as a five- to twenty-year period rather than the modest one-year-plus listed here.

Use your agenda. It's simple to construct. You don't need any forms, and you can even use the back of an envelope. However, if you have a basic idea of what your goals are in these three areas and three time frames, you will be substantially more effective in managing your time.

---

[3]John P. Kotter, *The General Manager* (New York: Free Press, 1982).

Figure 2-1. Harry Thorpe's agenda.

	Financial	Business product/market	People
12+ months	Get ongoing Plant Maintenance Fund approved. Reduce overhead (unreasonable) charged by corporate.	Diversify—2 new product lines. Foreign market.	Start up small engineering and R & D departments. Develop an entrepreneurial spirit throughout the organization.
6–12 months	Increase sales to $172 million. Keep net profit before tax >16%.	Get factory project working smoothly. Build $550,000 inspection facility.	Implement wellness program. Union contract. Hire 1 new salesperson in each region.
0–6 months	Stay under operations budget. Keep ROA at >15%. Reduce energy budget by 10%.	Nail down Jameson account. Increase quality (defects <2%). Get 3rd shift stabilized.	Implement staff training project. Hire admin. asst. Talk to Spencer about performance problems.

Source: Adapted from John P. Kotter, *The General Manager* (New York: Free Press, 1982), p. 62.

Figure 2-2. Typical manager's network.

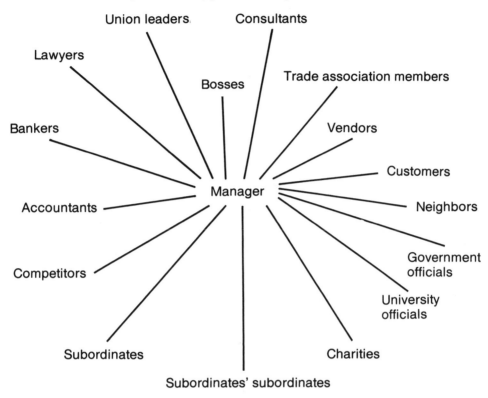

THE NETWORK

Work by Kotter and others has indicated that managers use a far-flung network to implement their agendas. This network may consist of literally thousands of nodes. If you look at a busy manager's Rolodex, you will see hundreds, if not thousands, of names and phone numbers. A typical network is shown in Figure 2-2.

As you can see, the manager's job is not a simple one of arriving at the office and dealing with subordinates and bosses all day; rather, the successful manager moves throughout the organization. A variety of people can be useful in the network. Develop your network. Try to set aside some time each week for the cultivation of your network. Schedule lunches in advance. Busy and successful people often have busy calendars. You may have to do forward planning, but it is through your network both inside the organization and in the community in general that you will implement your agenda.

THE DAILY LOG

The best way to get control of your frantic, fragmented activities is to make a "videotape" of a typical business day, using a daily log as your "camera." By recording work activities in the log, you will discover patterns of interaction and current ways you use your time that will embarrass, enlighten, and amuse you.

An activity is simply any change in what you are doing. Harry, for instance, had thirty-two different activities on Monday morning; each new time entry in his log represented a new activity. These activities included fourteen interruptions. An interruption is any unprogrammed activity initiated by someone else, such as an incoming phone call or an unplanned visit. By logging your activities, both programmed and unprogrammed, you will be able to spot areas that need to be changed.

For example, one manager with whom I consulted found through examining his employees' logs that 30 percent of their work could have been delegated to competent clerical personnel. Using paper, pencil, and calculator, the manager figured that if he could get his employees to delegate just half of that work appropriately, in one branch office alone he could save more than $100,000 per year in employee salaries.

THE TIME MANAGEMENT DAILY LOG

The daily log is your "videotape." It is essential to get a true picture of your time usage. Keep the Time Management Daily Log (Form 2-1) for at least one day, though three days would be better. Begin logging the minute you enter the office in the morning and discontinue logging when you leave. If you continue to work on the train or at home in the evening, don't bother to record these activities; we're interested only in what happens in the office.

The point of this exercise is to show the degree to which your work is characterized by fragmentation, interruptions, and superficiality. Don't be upset that you have listed many small increments of time. The typical manager's day consists of many activities of short duration and lots of interruptions. It is not at all unusual to find:

- Activities: 20–200 per day
- Interruptions: 10–100 per day
- Average duration: 4–30 minutes

Remember that an interruption is also an activity, so your activity total should also include interruptions. In one study of chief executive officers, whom you would expect to be protected from interruptions, it was found that their average desk-work session lasted about 6 minutes. So don't be alarmed at a large number of activities. You are in good company!

MANAGEMENT ACTIVITIES SUMMARY

Read this section only after you have completed at least one day of the Time Management Daily Log. (It wasn't easy, was it? Sometimes there were so many interruptions you almost didn't have time to write down the activity. But you did; that's what's important.) Now you will summarize the data you acquired in assembling your daily log, to give a picture of your overall activities so that you can better analyze the ways to save time.

Using the data contained in your log, complete the Management Activities Summary, shown in Form 2-2.

DIAGNOSIS AND TREATMENT

OK, now you have developed a reasonably clear picture of what a typical business day looks like, you have identified your most effective and least effective incidents, and you have thought about what you'd like to change. That is what we're now concerned about—change—for the key to management is behavior change, and accomplishing that behavior change in the minimum time.

Working with thousands of managers, I have found that the fundamental difference among activities is that effective activities result in behavior change but ineffective activities do not. Some examples of activities typically reported as being effective are those in which managers do the following:

- Delegate tasks to subordinates
- Routinize and systematize repetitive tasks
- Negotiate out of unnecessary tasks

- Get decisions from superiors
- Have staff meetings with agendas and action plans

Examples of ineffective activities are:

- Meetings with no agenda and no action plan
- Unnecessary requests for information
- Meetings with superiors that do not lead to decisions
- Long phone conversations without definite outcomes
- Formal reports that are unnecessary
- Fights with alligators when you should be draining the swamp

How effective are your bit-by-bit managerial activities throughout the day? Giving thought to the information you gathered in your daily log and summarized in the Management Activities Summary, see how you would answer the following questions:

	Yes	No
Lack of planning. Do you program things well in advance?	☐	☐
Poor control systems. Do you get feedback in advance of crises?	☐	☐
No paper-flow system. Do you handle each piece of paper only once?	☐	☐
No daily priorities. Do you use a daily "Do" list?	☐	☐
Failure to develop subordinates. Are your subordinates learning more each month?	☐	☐

Now you have an idea of what your typical day looks like. You have identified effective and ineffective ways in which you are behaving, selected some areas in which you want to change, and assessed yourself in terms of time wasted. You have completed the diagnosis; let's begin the treatment!

FINDING WAYS TO SAVE TIME

More free time = Working faster + doing less

As you can see in Figure 2-3, there are only two basic ways to save time: You can *do less* or *work faster*. Both offer ways of solving some of the difficulties you identified in your diagnosis.

Figure 2-3. Two ways to save time.

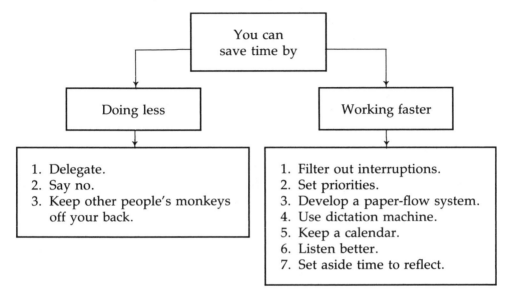

Doing Less

Delegating

The most effective way to do less in your job is to delegate. The only reason corporate heads have other individuals in the company is that they cannot do all of the work themselves. If you were Superman and could run lathes, drive trucks, do accounting, and handle sales and service, all at a blinding speed, you would have no need for an organization. But you can't. Consequently, the better you delegate, the more effective you are going to be. Virtually every manager fails to delegate as effectively as possible.

The experience of a former student is quite typical. After doing a time-management diagnosis, he realized that he was personally completing a routine daily cost report that he had developed two years previously. Delegating it to a subordinate saved him 30 to 40 minutes a day.

You can only delegate if you have subordinates; you will only delegate if you believe that your subordinates can and will do the job well and if you do not believe that the job should be done by you. Some organizations legislate that certain tasks not be delegated, but the most frequent cause of improper delegation is habit.

As you move upward within an organization, you often take on additional responsibilities and more complex tasks without relinquishing old tasks. However, delegating work is probably the single most effective step that you can take to improve time management. There are two added side benefits:

1. Subordinates are more motivated and job satisfied because their jobs have been enriched.
2. You are doing a better job of planning and organizing because delegation forces you to do so.

Effective delegation communication contains two messages: what you expect the subordinate to do, and how much authority the subordinate has to carry out the instructions. In delegating work you tell the subordinate what the task is that he is to carry out, how he is to do it, how long he has to accomplish it, when you will be checking back with him, and how much freedom he has to get the task done. When you delegate to your subordinates, make sure that they fully understand:

• Objectives and task requirements: what you want done, and how
• Decision-making authority: how far they can go in making decisions

Most managers do an adequate job of explaining objectives and approaches to subordinates. However, many fail to provide an explicit idea of the level of decision-making authority the subordinate has. This mistake can be expensive as well as time wasting. An example was reported by the president of a small company:

> The manager of my southern division telephoned me on Wednesday evening to tell me that the company had an opportunity to pick up about $40,000 worth of spare parts at a salvage price of approximately $2,000. "Great," I told him, "I'll look at them when I fly down tomorrow."
>
> The weather was bad and my trip was delayed three days. When I arrived at the southern division, I found that the vendor had sold the parts the night before to a competitor for $1,800.
>
> Opportunity cost to us: $38,200.
>
> Reason: unclear decision authority. My manager should have had budget authorization for amounts as small as this without prior approval.

When you assign tasks to subordinates, also assign one of the following three authority levels:

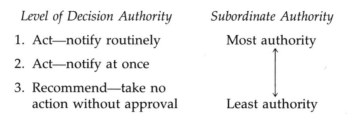

Level of Decision Authority	Subordinate Authority
1. Act—notify routinely	Most authority
2. Act—notify at once	
3. Recommend—take no action without approval	Least authority

Saying No

Next to delegation, the second best way of doing less is to learn to say no. Say it cleanly and quickly. Responses such as "I'll think about it" or "I'll get back to you" simply raise hopes, draw out the decision, and waste time. Most managers find it hard to say no to responsibilities they have the opportunity to assume. It just goes against the grain of an aggressive, ambitious person with a high need for achievement. Still, you can learn to say no to low-priority items for which you don't have time, as perhaps Harry Thorpe should have done to chairing the United Way drive at the plant. It is the habit of saying no to unnecessary and useless tasks that allows you the free time to say yes to those requests that will be personally exciting and helpful to your career.

Keeping Other People's Monkeys off Your Back

An interesting aspect of this "saying no" problem is the concept of "monkeys," developed in 1974 by Oncken and Wass.[4] Using some of their analyses, let's look at another problem that Harry has. Remember when Harry met Quentin, his subordinate, at the coffee station:

10:02 A.M. "Harry, we've got a problem. We must finalize our decision on the new administrative specialist by next week. The three finalists are coming here on Friday to do an in-basket exercise, and I can't find an in-basket that makes sense to me."

"Gee, Quentin," says Harry, who knows quite a bit about the technique, "I'll look through my files and get back to you."

Before Harry and Quentin met, who had the monkey? Right! Quentin. And who has it now? Harry. Quentin either intentionally or un-

---

[4] W. Oncken and D. L. Wass, "Management Time: Who's Got the Monkey?" *Harvard Business Review*, Vol. 52 (November-December 1974), pp. 76–78.

knowingly has allowed one of his monkeys to jump onto Harry's back. He has just successfully delegated upward, and he will now sit back and wait until his boss gets back to him with a solution to his problem. If the subordinate is a good manager himself, he may even "tickle" his boss just to be sure that the boss is completing the subordinate's work on time. If each of Harry's five subordinates execute two monkey leaps a day, at the end of each day Harry will have ten new screaming monkeys weighing him down and howling to be fed.

The moral of this story is: Keep the monkeys on your subordinates' backs! Any delegated responsibilities they have should continue to be their problems and should not be permitted to become your problems. Oncken and Wass maintain that your subordinates will manage to carry as many monkeys as you can effectively feed, and that the feeding of monkeys should be done jointly, with the subordinates leaving your office as they came in—with the monkeys on *their* backs!

Remember, to manage by doing less:

1. Delegate whenever possible.
2. Learn to say no.
3. Keep other people's monkeys off your back.

Working Faster

By working faster I do not imply that you should take vitamins, drink lots of coffee, and in general speed up the frantic pace at which you are already living. I am interested in helping you get more mileage from your existing time by using it wisely (see Figure 2-4).

Filtering out Interruptions

One of the most significant problems with which any manager must deal is interruptions. Every time you start a project, are interrupted, and return to the project, you lose valuable setup time.

The worst interrupter is the telephone. Individuals allow themselves to be interrupted in a group meeting by the phone, when they wouldn't dream of engaging in a digressing conversation with a personal visitor. When the phone rings, it might be the company president calling to congratulate you on a job well done. You can never be sure!

Because of its unknown and random nature, the telephone is extremely powerful; it can throw your management life into tremendous confusion. Thus you must establish a filter system. Establish guidelines with your secretary to protect you as much as possible from unwanted

Figure 2-4. How to manage by working faster.

1. Filter out interruptions.
2. Set priorities.
3. Develop a paper-flow system.
4. Use dictation equipment.
5. Keep a calendar.
6. Listen better.
7. Set aside time to reflect.

interruptions while leaving you accessible to those people who need to get in touch with you. Of course you don't want to be like the chief executive who will simply not talk on the telephone before noon so that he can use the morning for staff meetings, planning functions, and so on. After lunch he returns the telephone messages his secretary has collected. This technique works fine until he wants to talk to another chief executive, who will not accept telephone calls in the afternoon. The point is, make sure that *you* control the telephone and not vice versa.

A second major source of interruptions is people. Your subordinates, peers, superiors, and others wander through and engage in discussions on both work and nonwork matters. One company general manager had a partition installed to block the view of his desk through his opened office door. He had discovered that a number of interruptions were caused by his subordinates who, walking past and seeing him, felt compelled to bring him some good news about progress that they were making in various areas. By having the partition he hoped to save a few hours every week. Although he still maintained his open-door policy, the door was "open but tended."

Setting Priorities

Management is a job of priorities. No successful manager needs to be convinced of the necessity of setting priorities on how he spends his time. Many of the unsuccessful managers I have known have been hardworking and enthusiastic, but somehow they couldn't seem to set and maintain priorities. Regardless of any formal objectives-setting program that your firm may have (such as Management by Objectives), you should implement a plan with priorities for your personal use. Try this:

- *Annually*—Set global objectives; divide them into: (1) routine, (2) problem-solving, (3) innovative, (4) personal.
- *Monthly*—Evaluate your progress toward your global objectives; revise them as necessary.
- *Weekly*—Have a specific idea of what you want to accomplish this week.
- *Daily*—Set priorities on a "Do" list, preferably the night before.

Every action you take as a manager concerning the allocation of your time is at least implicitly evaluated against these priorities. Later in this book you will be asked to establish some priorities that may be quite different from those that you've had in the past. You are going to be asked to:

- Control your time
- Control your job
- Put a high priority on managing the stress you are under
- Manage smarter and more effectively
- Give your personal life the value it deserves

If you can accomplish this change in priorities, you will find yourself to be not only happier but also more effective as a manager.

Developing a Paper-Flow System

If there is anything that has had a more adverse effect on management time than the telephone, it is probably the high-speed reproduction machine. You can now get copies of everything, and probably do. You can now receive electronic mail, morning, noon, and night—even when away from the office. The average manager is confronted by an ever-increasing paper flow. When I asked a *Fortune* 500 CEO what his biggest "management" problem was, his answer was surprising. He had guided his company through a major crisis and was enjoying due regard. He responded, "Dealing with the paper flow across my desk." If even a chief executive officer, who is supposed to be buffered from day-to-day details, finds problems with paper flow, imagine the dilemma the average middle manager faces. You *can* develop an efficient and straightforward system for handling paper flow.

First, convince yourself that there are only three kinds of paper: (1) important, (2) worthwhile, and (3) junk. Important paper should be acted upon. Worthwhile paper should be read. Junk paper should be tossed. These categories can be broken down as follows:

1. *Important.* Take action.

   • Immediately: Take appropriate and complete action and dispense with the paper.
   • Pending: Initiate some action—only then put the paper in pending file (use this category only if you are unable to take immediate action).

2. *Worthwhile.* Read.

   • Distribute: Only if it is significant to others; be considerate—they get enough junk.
   • File: Only if you'll need to see it again.
   • Toss: When you have gained all the information it contains.

3. *Junk.* Toss.

Remember, handle each piece of paper only once. You are going to have to spend the same amount of time dealing with the piece of paper whether you've looked at it five times previously or not, so you might as well deal with it the first time you see it.

Have your assistant sort your incoming mail into categories 1, 2, and 3. Also, have that person act directly on as much mail as possible.

One high-ranking executive found that with appropriate screening his assistant could handle about 60 percent of his mail. He had no need to see it, and by having it directed immediately to others or tossed, he saved time and improved his performance.

Using Dictation Equipment

You can work faster by using dictation equipment. You can write at approximately 25 words per minute, but you can speak quite easily at 200 words per minute. For the bulk of your correspondence, it's faster and more efficient to use a dictating machine than to give dictation to your secretary. Why should the secretary sit silently while you are thinking, when there are other tasks that need to be done? Dictation skills take a small amount of training to develop, but once you have the knack, your handling of communications will be enhanced greatly.

Keeping a Calendar

On a daily, weekly, and monthly basis, know what is important and what you will be doing. Do you know what your schedule is for the rest of the week? Are you hitting the important tasks? The effective manager has a mental image of the total picture of his time and expectations, as well as a moment-by-moment awareness of what he should be doing.

Listening Better

Studies of general managers show that they spend a tremendous amount of time listening. It is not unusual for them to ask hundreds of questions in a meeting. They have learned that the ability to hear what others say can be invaluable. Getting the facts correct the first time can save you hours of time in the long run.

Setting Aside Time to Reflect

You are paid to think, not just to do. Schedule time every day, or at least three times a week, to sit down and reflect. Ask yourself, "Am I getting the important things done?" You have to continually refocus on high priorities. There is constant pressure to waste time on lower priority issues.

TIME-SAVING SUCCESS STORIES

Before you are asked to fill out your personal action plan for saving four hours a week, here are four examples (actual case studies) of practicing managers who used the techniques in this chapter to accomplish significant time savings.

Example 1: General Superintendent of Primary Operations

I used to spend too much time in the offices of subordinates. A typical day would involve one and a half to two hours in gathering data and directing subordinates. Therefore, I prepared data forms for each subordinate and required each department head to fill in the required data in duplicate. All data sheets are collected and brought to my office for review. Considerable time is saved in making my daily rounds by having a digest of performance and cost indicators given to me earlier. Also, these new reports have provided a broader common communications base between subordinates and myself.

Projected time savings: 5 hours per week[5]

---

[5]M. Kosanovich, personal communication, February 1977.

Example 2: Director, Energy and Materials Research

From a detailed two-day diary, I prepared a composite of my time utilization. The results were as follows:

1. Number of incidents per day—39

2. Average duration—13 minutes

3. Location
   My office—85 percent of incidents
   Superior's office—2 percent of incidents
   Subordinate's office—2 percent of incidents
   Other—10 percent of incidents

4. Allocation of time:

Superiors	12	Formal meeting	11
Peers	10	Informal meeting	40
Subordinates	26	Telephone	8
Other internal	11	Social	3
External	—	Reading	21
Personal	2	Writing	17
Alone	39	Reflecting	—
	100		100

I did not attempt to give a "functional" breakdown, as the categories had little meaning in the context of my work environment. I found somewhat surprising the amount of time I spent with subordinates. If I were to save 10 percent of this time, I would want it to be used for more thinking and reflective writing. I find analyses of this type quite helpful. One really does not recognize where time goes unless one takes the trouble to keep a log.

Projected time savings: 4 hours per week[6]

Example 3: Director of Marketing

I can identify three specific ways in which my productive time can be increased over current levels. The most important:

---

[6]B. A. King, personal communication, February 1977.

1. Increased delegation. An assistant marketing manager was hired at the beginning of the year. He can take over for me more frequently in the areas of initial client contact, routine client follow-up, planning of direct mailings, and some on-site marketing presentations.

Projected time savings: 4 hours per week

2. Minimized interruptions. I will attempt to reduce the number of unnecessary interruptions each day by working with my office door closed.

Projected time savings: 2 hours per week

3. Prioritized activities. A list of the day's priorities will be drawn up prior to the beginning of work (preferably the day before).

Projected time savings: ½ hour per week
Total projected time savings: 6½ hours per week[7]

Example 4: Senior Manager, Systems

My action plan for saving four hours per week is:

1. Have secretary open all mail (except what is classified as confidential), separating it into three categories: (a) immediate action, (b) information, (c) miscellaneous.

2. Schedule no meetings prior to 9:00 A.M. This allows 45 minutes (official start time is 8:15), at least, to be used to answer previous correspondence. This time is also used to read, plan, etc., which in essence is building a basic foundation/strategy for the rest of the day.

3. Increase my use of machine dictation, from just letter writing to notes and "things to do." I'll attempt to go from "draft" to final form on letters.

4. Use my secretary for writing letters of a low-priority, noncritical nature.

5. Establish a tickler, or follow-up, system.

Projected time savings: 4 hours per week[8]

[7]J. H. Dobbs, personal communication, February 1977.
[8]R. F. Zebroski, personal communication, February 1977.

YOUR TIME SAVINGS

In order to make your own personal improvement in time management, you will need to do the following:

1. Review data from your Time Management Daily Log (see Form 2-1).
2. Review your Management Activities Summary (see Form 2-2).
3. Complete the Time Management Action Plan shown in Form 2-3.
4. Implement your action plan.

CONCLUSION

The best managers are adept at managing time effectively. They are able to delegate properly, set priorities for their activities optimally, and decline responsibilities and tasks when necessary. Furthermore, they use their time more effectively by designing the proper working environment for themselves and their subordinates. Are you managing your time effectively? Can you save four hours per week and still accomplish your current level of performance? I believe you can. Consulting and training experience indicates that the methods presented here can both save you time and improve your performance. The monkey is now on your back to accomplish this positive change.

FORM 2-1.

TIME MANAGEMENT DAILY LOG

Complete the attached log for a "typical" day in your work. No day is truly typical, but do your best in selecting a day and sticking with it. Use the following steps in completing the log:

1. Select a typical day.
2. Record the start time for each activity.
3. Place a check mark (✔) in the "interruption" column if the activity was also an interruption.
4. Place a check mark (✔) in the "phone" column if the activity was an incoming or outgoing telephone call.

The following sample form shows how easy it is to have a large number of different activities in any typical management day. Don't be surprised by a large number of activities. Every time you change *what* you are doing, or with *whom* you are doing it, you have generated a new activity. Therefore, it is not unusual to find 20–200 activities per day.

Time Management Daily Log

	Start Time	Inter-ruption? (✔)	Phone? (✔)	Description
1.	7:55 A.M.			Start on mail
2.	8:03	✔	✔	Joe phones—needs production schedule
3.	8:05			Back to mail
4.	8:07	✔		Secretary arrives—give her tape
5.	8:11			Back to mail
6.	8:15		✔	Phone Harry about overtime
7.	8:20			Mail again
8.	8:25	✔		Charlie arrives—discuss staff meeting
9.	8:30			Staff meeting—my office
10.	9:05	✔	✔	Staff meeting interrupted by question from boss
11.	9:08			Return to staff meeting
12.	9:30			Meeting ends—coffee with Charlie

FORM 2-1.

	Start Time	Inter-ruption? (✔)	Phone? (✔)	Description
1.				
2.				
3.				
4.				
5.				
6.				
7.				
8.				
9.				
10.				
11.				
12.				
13.				
14.				
15.				
16.				
17.				
18.				
19.				
20.				
21.				
22.				
23.				
24.				
25.				

FORM 2-1.

	Start Time	Inter-ruption? (✔)	Phone? (✔)	Description
26.				
27.				
28.				
29.				
30.				
31.				
32.				
33.				
34.				
35.				
36.				
37.				
38.				
39.				
40.				
41.				
42.				
43.				
44.				
45.				
46.				
47.				
48.				
49.				
50.				

FORM 2-1.

	Start Time	Inter-ruption? (✔)	Phone? (✔)	Description
51.				
52.				
53.				
54.				
55.				
56.				
57.				
58.				
59.				
60.				
61.				
62.				
63.				
64.				
65.				
66.				
67.				
68.				
69.				
70.				
71.				
72.				
73.				
74.				
75.				

MANAGEMENT ACTIVITIES SUMMARY

Answer these questions based on the entries in your daily log:

1. Number of activities   _____

2. Average duration (minutes)   _____

3. Number of interruptions   _____

4. Location of activities

   My office   _____%

   Superior's office   _____%

   Subordinate's office   _____%

   Other   _____%

   Total   100%

5. Allocation of time

WHO?		HOW?		WHAT?		FUNCTION?	
Superiors	___%	Formal		Accounting/		Planning	___%
Peers	___%	meeting	___%	finance	___%	Organizing	___%
Subordi-		Informal		Mktg./sales	___%	Staffing	___%
nates	___%	meeting	___%	Production	___%	Directing	___%
Other		Telephone	___%	Personnel	___%	Coordinat-	
internal	___%	Social	___%	R & D	___%	ing	___%
External		Reading	___%	Public		Reporting	___%
contact	___%	Writing	___%	relations	___%	Budgeting	___%
Alone	___%	Reflecting	___%	General		Other	___%
Other	___%	Other	___%	Mgt.	___%		
				Other	___%		
Total	100%	Total	100%	Total	100%	Total	100%

6. Now answer these important questions:

	YES	NO
Do you have too many activities in a day to manage your job effectively?	☐	☐
Are the activities too short to be useful?	☐	☐
Do you have too many interruptions?	☐	☐

FORM 2-2.

	YES	NO
Do the same people keep coming back?	☐	☐
Are you spending your time in the wrong locations?	☐	☐
Would you like to change your time distribution in the following categories? (Question 5 previous page)		
• Who	☐	☐
• How	☐	☐
• What	☐	☐
• Function	☐	☐
Can you delegate more?	☐	☐
Do you need more time to think?	☐	☐
Do you need more support staff?	☐	☐
Would a personal computer or terminal help save time?	☐	☐
Do you talk too much on the phone?	☐	☐
Are you overwhelmed by paper?	☐	☐

Remember: Every YES requires action and represents an opportunity for time savings.

7. Effective activities

How would you characterize your most effective activities?
    Whom did you deal with?
    How did you perform the activity?
    What sort of business and functional areas were represented?
Effective activities lead to high-quality management performance.

List examples of your most effective activities below:

1. _____   5. _____

2. _____   6. _____

3. _____   7. _____

4. _____   8. _____

8. Ineffective activities

   How would you characterize your least effective activities?
      Whom did you deal with?
      How did you perform the activity?
      What sort of business and functional areas were represented?
   Ineffective activities lead to poor management performance.

   List examples of your most ineffective activities below:

   1. _____   5. _____

   2. _____   6. _____

   3. _____   7. _____

   4. _____   8. _____

TIME MANAGEMENT ACTION PLAN

Hrs. per Week Saved	Do Less	Person to Whom Delegated

_____ 1. DELEGATE

Task: _____   _____

Reporting policy (how and when?): _____
Decision authority: ☐ Act—notify routinely
                     ☐ Act—notify immediately
                     ☐ Recommend only

Task: _____   _____

Reporting policy (how and when?): _____
Decision authority: ☐ Act—notify routinely
                     ☐ Act—notify immediately
                     ☐ Recommend only

Task: _____   _____

Reporting policy (how and when?): _____
Decision authority: ☐ Act—notify routinely
                     ☐ Act—notify immediately
                     ☐ Recommend only

Task: _____   _____

Reporting policy (how and when?): _____
Decision authority: ☐ Act—notify routinely
                     ☐ Act—notify immediately
                     ☐ Recommend only

_____ 2. SAY NO

Task: _____

Consequences of saying no: _____

Task: _____

Consequences of saying no: _____

Task: _____

Consequences of saying no: _____

**Hrs. per
Week
Saved**

————— 3. KEEP OTHER PEOPLE'S MONKEYS OFF YOUR BACK

Monkey: ————— Person who should carry it: —————

How you will get it on his back: —————————

Monkey: ————— Person who should carry it: —————

How you will get it on his back: —————————

Monkey: ————— Person who should carry it: —————

How you will get it on his back: —————————

Work Faster

————— 4. FILTER PEOPLE

Filter managed by (e.g., secretary): —————————

Filter policy (describe): —————————

————— 5. FILTER PHONE

Filter managed by (e.g., secretary): —————————

Filter policy (describe): —————————

————— 6. SET PRIORITIES (Construct a "To Do" list the night before each working day)

————— 7. PAPER-FLOW SYSTEM (Remember, try to touch each piece of paper only once)

A1.	Action—immediate
A2.	Action—pending
B1, 2, and 3.	Read: distribute, file, or toss
C.	Toss

————— 8. DICTATION EQUIPMENT (Use on the following items)

—————————————————

—————————————————

FORM 2-3.

**Hrs. per
Week
Saved**

_____ 9. KEEP A CALENDAR
Do you do it now? Yes ☐ No ☐
Can you do it better? Yes ☐ No ☐

How? _____

_____ 10. LISTEN BETTER

_____

_____

_____ 11. SET ASIDE TIME TO REFLECT

Time: _____ Days of week: _____

_____ 12. OTHER TIME-SAVING ACTION STEPS

A. _____

B. _____

C. _____

_____ TOTAL TIME SAVED

Chapter 3

Intolerance as a Response to Noncompliance

12:42 P.M. Spencer Bernham, Harry Thorpe's finance and accounting manager, drops by. "Harry, I'm sorry, but we're not going to have those comparative lease versus purchase costs for you today."

"Why the hell not?" demands Harry.

"Well, we've just gotten backed up with quarterly report details," says Spencer. "We should have them for you by tomorrow, though."

"Dammit, Spencer!" shouts Harry. "How am I supposed to negotiate that truck leasing contract today without that information? I specifically told you we needed it today!"

"I know," responds Spencer, "but I thought the meeting was for Wednesday."

"We moved it up."

"Oh."

"Spencer, this is inexcusable!" Harry is about to totally lose his temper. "Either shape up that department or find somewhere else to work. Now get out of here and get me something to go on before three o'clock."

Why is Harry so angry? Should he be? How should he react? What is the appropriate response to noncompliance? This chapter answers

40

these questions for Harry and for you. It presents a framework that you can use to increase your conscious control and your management of what I call intolerance for noncompliance. What does this mean? It takes a while to develop the concept, but it is very powerful. Read on.

THE ULTIMATE REWARD: MODIFYING OTHERS' BEHAVIOR

I maintain that for many, the ultimate reinforcer—the ultimate satisfaction in human life—is the ability to modify other people's behavior. One of the greatest feelings of satisfaction occurs when we have effectively modified or changed the behavior of another person.

The ability to change behavior is the reason we want respect from others. It is the reason we want admiration. It is the reason we desire prestige in life. It is the reason we want to drive a big car, advance in the corporation, write a best-selling novel, become president, or win a Nobel Prize. If you have achieved a position of power and prestige, written a successful book, or acquired wealth, your ability to modify the behavior of others is enhanced. In fact, whenever we seek praise, our purpose is to enlarge our ability to modify the behavior of others.

THE ORIGINS OF POWER

Why do we achieve such satisfaction in modifying other people's behavior or, in a word, exercising power? The answer is probably rooted in a visceral level of human existence, planted there at a time when the ability to modify others' behavior was the key to survival. In prehistoric times, the individual who had power and could successfully modify the behavior of others was the one whose survival chances were highest. The person who could successfully modify the behavior of his tribe could enhance his own likelihood of survival and, if he was a good leader, could enhance the survival chances of the tribe as well.

The drive to modify behavior is no less strong today. Human beings are social animals; they spend much of their waking time in interaction. Consequently, existence even in the twentieth-century civilized United States is a constant exercise in power and conflict. We jockey for promotions, struggle for budget allocations, and constantly attempt to influence our supervisors, our peers, and those who work for us. We do all of these things to ensure that we will get enough resources to carry on and enhance our existence.

At the true gut level of performance, therefore, what you as a manager really do is constantly modify the behavior of other people to suit your needs. Accounting, finance, economics, and marketing are mere expedients to inform you of the correct direction in which to attempt to change behavior. The classic POSDCORB management functions are simply processes for accomplishing it. In the end, the true measure of managerial effectiveness is the degree to which you can successfully modify the behavior of those around you. If you never modify anyone's behavior, then you are unnecessary and your organization could do better without you. If you know the correct direction in which to modify behavior and are effective at this, then you are, by definition, an effective manager.

DETERMINING EFFECTIVE BEHAVIOR MODIFICATION: COMPLIANCE VS. NONCOMPLIANCE

Let's take a hypothetical case in your managerial life. You make a direct request to your subordinate, Charlie Mendes, to provide you with a report by Wednesday noon. You made the request last Monday, giving Charlie ample time to prepare the report. Suppose Charlie arrives in your office early Tuesday afternoon with a completed report that is much more thorough and better done than you had anticipated. Charlie has exceeded your expectations.

Charlie Mendes has achieved point A on the graph shown in Figure 3-1. He is above the 45-degree line. His degree of actual behavior modification is greater than the degree of behavior modification you desired. Therefore, he is in the "compliance" space. How do you feel? Charlie's performance leaves you feeling satisfied and rewarded. You feel good, Charlie feels good. You go home and tell your spouse it was a good day at the office. Charlie pleases you, and you are pleased that you have been able to modify his behavior so successfully. If you think about it, you'll find that most of your successes in management are not due to your solitary accomplishments but what you manage to get done through others.

Let's suppose that instead of being early and comprehensive, Charlie's report does not arrive on your desk by noon on Wednesday as scheduled. You walk by his office to ask him about it and find him in a confused state, attempting to complete his report. On your brief examination, you can see that not only will Charlie be late with the report but he also is not considering the certain pieces of information that a

Figure 3-1. Compliance and noncompliance space defined.

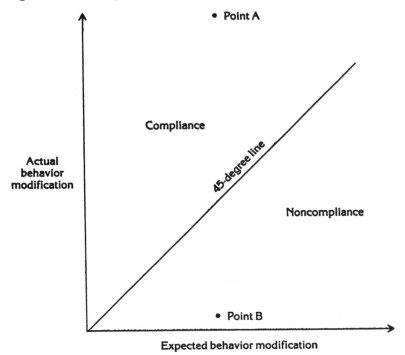

good manager would factor into the same situation. How do you feel? You leave his office with a feeling of frustration and dissatisfaction. You feel angry and let down. You may even want to punch him. Charlie's behavior puts him at position B in the "noncompliance" space in Figure 3-1. You are displeased not only with Charlie but with yourself as well. Your behavior-modification attempts were ineffective in producing the desired effect in your subordinate.

Of course, compliance creates little or no difficulty for you as a practicing manager, but noncompliance does. Compliance brings satisfaction and the feeling of accomplishment. Noncompliance brings frustration, dissatisfaction, and a feeling of failure. A key question any manager must ask is "What do I do about noncompliance?"

HOW INTOLERANT ARE YOU OF NONCOMPLIANCE?

Let's take the situation of an immediate subordinate who does not comply with your wishes. After you've managed your negative emotions, what course of action do you take? In order to answer that question, you must find out how intolerant you are of such noncompliance and how your intolerance varies with situational, personal, and organizational variables.

Intolerance for noncompliance may be defined as the amount of energy you would be willing to expend to achieve compliance in a given situation. Your level of intolerance for noncompliance should vary depending on the parameters of the particular situation in which you find yourself. Intolerance may be directed inward, as when you experience frustration or withdrawal, or outward, as when you express anger or make constructive attempts to solve the problem.

Now, let's see how you respond to noncompliance. Complete the following Intolerance Audit (Form 3-1) to see how you score. If you score above 55, you may be a Type A personality—an overly intolerant person, as we shall discover. Read on.

HOW IMPORTANT IS THE NONCOMPLIANCE?

The amount of intolerance for noncompliance should be in direct proportion to the importance of the situation. Effective, or "matched," managers follow the 45-degree line indicated in Figure 3-2. Their intolerance increases with the importance of the situation in which compliance is desired. They will not become extremely upset or intolerant over a minor typographical error by a secretary. But they will be extremely intolerant—and willing to expend a lot of energy to determine why— when a plant is having quality-control problems or when profits are down.

Managers should match their intolerance to the importance of the situation. You don't want to waste your energy on minor problems. You want to expend it in proportion to the importance of the problem under consideration. Since you have only a limited amount of energy you can devote to your job, it must be managed like any other variable; if you direct too much energy toward minor problems or not enough toward major problems, you will definitely be less effective.

THE TYPE A PERSONALITY: MISMANAGING INTOLERANCE

Not all of us perfectly match our intolerance for noncompliance with the importance of the desired behavior modifications. Many managers

Figure 3-2. Matching intolerance with importance of compliance.

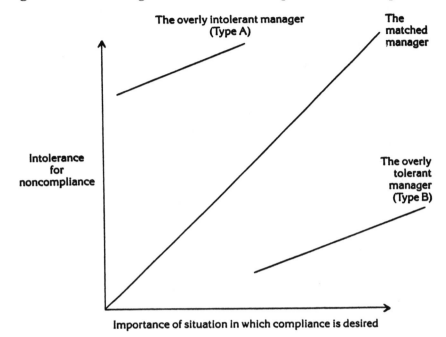

get very upset over minor noncompliances and maintain a relatively high level of general intolerance. They are represented as the Type A personality in Figure 3-2. Such individuals are highly intolerant of even minor noncompliances in their environment, and in general they stay at a highly "energized" state of intolerance.

I call such individuals Type A persons because they appear to be directly related to the Type A personality hypothesized by San Francisco cardiologists Meyer Friedman and Ray Rosenman.[1] They are described as follows:

Type A People

- Generally feel impatience with the rate at which most events take place
- Always move, walk, and eat rapidly
- Explosively accentuate words in ordinary speech, whether or not

---

[1] Adapted from M. Friedman and R. H. Rosenman, *Type A Behavior and Your Heart* (New York: Alfred A. Knopf, 1974), pp. 83–84.

there is a need for such accentuation, and rapidly utter the last few words in most sentences

- Indulge in polyphasic thought or performance; they strive to think or do two or more things at once
- Find it difficult to refrain from discussing in conversation subjects that interest them
- Almost always feel vaguely guilty when they relax
- Experience a chronic sense of time urgency, a sense of struggle that, according to Rosenman and Friedman, is the "kernel of the Type A behavior pattern"

Type A people like to do things their way and are willing to exert a lot of effort to ensure that even trivial tasks are performed in the manner they see fit. They often fail to distinguish between important and unimportant situations. For instance, they are upset when they have to wait 15 minutes to be seated in a restaurant, since this is not in compliance with their idea of responsive service. In short, the Type A person spends a lot of time directing energy toward the noncompliances in his environment. Still, Type As are "movers and shakers." They enjoy acting on their environment and like modifying the behavior of other people. They are primarily rewarded by compliance and punished by noncompliance.

Most successful managers are Type As. The secret to their success is that they are reinforced by compliance and expend substantial amounts of human energy in getting it. They "make things happen" in their organizations. At the same time, though, their generally high levels of intolerance for noncompliance may be dysfunctional for their subordinates (i.e., they may retard creativity and participation, and reinforce "yes sir!" behaviors) and may be associated with stress-related illnesses (see Chapter 4).

THE TYPE B PERSONALITY: MISMANAGING TOLERANCE

In contrast to the Type A personality, the Type B person may be represented by the lower line in Figure 3-2. This kind of individual is much more easygoing. Not many managers are this type, for Type Bs are overly tolerant of noncompliance from those around them, regardless of the importance of the situation in which the noncompliance is generated. Whereas Type As are reinforced by getting compliance, Type Bs do not actively seek compliance and are not highly punished by its lack.

In fact, the extreme Type B person is primarily reinforced by complying with others.

Type B People

- Generally are free of all the habits and traits characterizing the Type A person
- Do not suffer from a sense of time urgency
- Usually harbor little or no free-floating hostility, and feel little need to display or discuss their achievements
- Are patient, undemanding, and easygoing
- Tend to play for play's sake, to seek fun and relaxation rather than competition
- Can relax without guilt

Type Bs, then, in general are more tolerant. They do not easily become frustrated, angered, or expend a lot of energy in response to noncompliance. Type Bs may be excellent supervisors to work for—that is, until you need them to push upward in the organization on your behalf. They probably would permit you and other subordinates a lot of freedom, but might not provide the types of upward support necessary for effective leadership.

5.2 BILLION POTENTIAL PROBLEMS OR OPPORTUNITIES?

Currently, there are roughly 5.2 billion persons in the world. This means that if you are a Type A person, you have 5.2 billion potential problems. That is, your problems are, literally, limited only by the number of your interactions. If you could interact with everyone, everyone could be a problem, for each of these individuals might fail to comply at some point with your wishes. In contrast, if you are a Type B, you have 5.2 billion potential opportunities—in theory, the potential number of persons with whom you may comply. Roughly speaking, the Type A individual is a "pessimist," the Type B an "optimist."

The point is this: Truly effective managers need enough Type A traits to get the compliance they require from their environment, but not so many that they burn themselves out. You don't want to ineffectively or inefficiently expend energy seeking compliance in situations where the importance of the situation does not justify the effort. You need to learn to expend energy when and where appropriate.

HOW TO MANAGE INTOLERANCE FOR NONCOMPLIANCE

One important way to improve your personal managerial effectiveness is to consciously set your intolerance level for any noncompliance situation. When faced with noncompliance, we usually respond in an emotional manner characterized by anger and frustration. We have a natural urge to punish the noncompliant person, to respond to noncompliance with intolerance and attack. For instance, I visited a colleague in his office and found him handwriting a letter. Our conversation went something like this:

AUTHOR: Eric, how come you're handwriting a letter? Don't you always dictate them?

COLLEAGUE: [through clenched teeth] I want to make sure it is done right!

AUTHOR: What happened?

COLLEAGUE: Read this! [He hands me a long and highly biased, vituperative letter criticizing a paper he had published in a first-rate journal.]

AUTHOR: What are you going to do?

COLLEAGUE: [glaring] I'm going to set him straight, of course; what else?

AUTHOR: Do you really think that letter is going to do any good? You are not going to change his mind with a letter, are you?

COLLEAGUE: [thinking a moment] Probably not. But I can't just let it go. I mean, there is really no excuse for. . .

AUTHOR: What you really want to do is punish him, right?

COLLEAGUE: Damned right.

AUTHOR: Well, since you are not planning to change his mind and simply want to punish him, isn't there a way of doing that effectively without taking so much of your time?

COLLEAGUE: [toying with pencil] Got any ideas?

AUTHOR: Well, you could send him a short, cryptic note—something like "Thanks for your letter and valuable comments"—and have your secretary sign it. To let him know that you are taking his comments in such an offhand manner will be very punishing for him. And it will take very little of your time.

COLLEAGUE: Hmmm, that's not bad [putting pencil down]. I think I'll think a little more about this.

This vignette shows how you can consciously set intolerance levels for noncompliant behavior. If a high energy expenditure is going to result in zero behavior change, the energy spent is wasted. Why bother? Quite often, the first, gut-level reaction is to attempt to punish the noncompliant person. However, behavioral research indicates that punishment often just does not work. Thus, if you spend a lot of personal energy administering punishment to your subordinates in situations where you have little chance of modifying their behavior, you are wasting your time. You are also wasting your subordinates' time. All you are doing is alienating them.

Rather than simply reacting the next time you are faced with noncompliance in your managerial or personal life, ask yourself, "How intolerant should I be?" Consciously set your level of intolerance. You can do this by carefully following these six steps (also shown in Figure 3-3).

1. Estimate the degree of your intolerance to the situation on a scale of 0 to 10, from "none" to "total."
2. Estimate how important the noncompliance is, on a scale of 0 to 10, from "not at all" to "extremely."
3. Estimate your probability of success in changing the noncompliant situation through your expression of intolerance, on a scale of 0 to 10, from "low" to "high."
4. Decide, "Is it worth it?" (Is the situation important enough and your chances of changing it high enough to warrant expending your energy expressing your intolerance?)
5. Is the probability of success so low that you should not bother with the problem?
6. Weigh the degree of your intolerance (answer to question 1) against the importance of your situation (answer to question 2) to see whether your degree of intolerance is of the right proportion.

The grid in Figure 3-4 helps you match your degree of intolerance to the importance of the situation. If you rate your intolerance to an instance of noncompliance as a 5 but the importance of that instance as only a 2, then you would be at point X on the grid. In this case, your expression of intolerance is too high for what the situation warrants (a classic Type A response). On the other hand, if you consider the situation quite important, say 9, but you are only moderately intolerant of it, say 4, you would be at point Y—definitely not reacting strongly enough to the situation (a Type B response). Where you really want to be is somewhere close to the 45-degree line. That is the true measure of consciously regulating your intolerance so that it is proportional to the importance of the noncompliance situation.

Figure 3-3. How to consciously control intolerance for noncompliance.

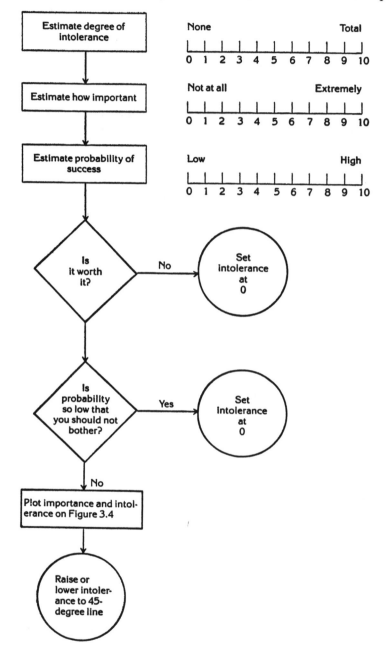

Figure 3-4. Grid for plotting intolerance for an instance of noncompliance in relation to its importance.

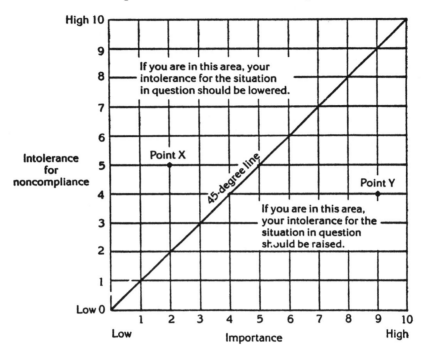

If this sounds a little complicated, try working through the six-step procedure in a specific noncompliance instance that you have experienced. Or the next time you suspect you may have over- or underreacted to a situation, turn back to these pages and work it out.

Following are some specific instances in which you would not be consciously regulating your intolerance to good effect.

Intolerance Too High

- You walk into your office Tuesday morning and blow up at your secretary because there is a dirty coffee cup and a full ashtray on your desk. The maintenance people missed it again. (Overreaction because importance is low.)

- Your son plays in a basketball game and is intimidated by an opposition guard. You've told him to be more aggressive in his play and call him "gutless" on the way home. (Overreaction because importance is low.)

- You dictate an important reply and find that the last half of the tape is unintelligible because the batteries in your portable unit are low. You angrily slam the machine into a drawer and break it. (Overreaction because probability of success is low.)

Intolerance Too Low

- Recently your boss has asked you to stay late several times to talk over routine matters that could be handled during the day. This is starting to have a bad effect on your family and interfere with your community commitments. You don't want to confront him. (Underreaction because importance is high.)

- Your 16-year-old daughter has come home after curfew three weekends in a row. You suspect that she and her boyfriend have been drinking and driving. You haven't said anything because you know your wife will. (Underreaction because importance is high and probability of success is high.)

- You find you've been putting on a couple of pounds per month for the last six months. You promise yourself that you'll start a diet sometime. (Underreaction because importance is high.)

CONCLUSION

If you can learn to bring your intolerance for noncompliance under conscious control, you can modify your own behavior. That is the first prerequisite of modifying the behavior of anyone else. Management is a job of self-discipline. Use self-discipline to control not only your behaviors but also your emotional responses. The better your self-control, the higher your managerial effectiveness.

INTOLERANCE AUDIT

How intolerant are you? Complete this form by circling the number that represents your amount of intolerance in each situation.

1. You had advised (not ordered) your purchasing manager to stock up on a particular item. He has not done it, and consequently your company is now faced with a shortage. The material is not readily available in the market.

0	1	2	3	4	5	6	7	8	9	10
(None)			(Slight)		(Moderate)			(High)		(Total)

2. You are standing in line at a bank. A stranger crashes the line ahead of you. You are in a hurry.

0	1	2	3	4	5	6	7	8	9	10
(None)			(Slight)		(Moderate)			(High)		(Total)

3. You are the new VP of purchasing for a company with widely dispersed plants. You want to centralize purchasing. You ask all buyers to clear all items above $10,000 through you, and they agree. In the next quarter you find no requests for clearance.

0	1	2	3	4	5	6	7	8	9	10
(None)			(Slight)		(Moderate)			(High)		(Total)

4. You ask your children not to watch certain TV programs. You find they are secretly watching them either at friends' places or when you are not at home.

0	1	2	3	4	5	6	7	8	9	10
(None)			(Slight)		(Moderate)			(High)		(Total)

5. You spend a lot of time and energy convincing your superior why the company should bid for a certain contract. Though he agrees with your arguments, he decides not to bid for some reason he is not prepared to explain.

0	1	2	3	4	5	6	7	8	9	10
(None)			(Slight)		(Moderate)			(High)		(Total)

6. You are driving on the highway. Suddenly a car cuts into your lane without signaling. As you move to pass him, he does it again.

0	1	2	3	4	5	6	7	8	9	10
(None)		(Slight)			(Moderate)			(High)		(Total)

7. You have a meeting with your subordinates at a fixed time and day each week. Some of your most important and busiest subordinates are constantly late and offer no apologies.

0	1	2	3	4	5	6	7	8	9	10
(None)		(Slight)			(Moderate)			(High)		(Total)

8. You have advised your administrative assistant to charge some of the expenses of your recent trip to your personal account. A month later you discover that all expenses have been charged to the company.

0	1	2	3	4	5	6	7	8	9	10
(None)		(Slight)			(Moderate)			(High)		(Total)

9. As sales manager you want the sales representatives to file periodic written reports. They call you frequently to keep you updated, but they do not file the written reports regularly. Some do not file at all.

0	1	2	3	4	5	6	7	8	9	10
(None)		(Slight)			(Moderate)			(High)		(Total)

10. Your company's last new product introduction failed because of a lack of coordination between advertising and sales. You issued a strong reprimand to the sales division. Now you find that while the ad agency is ready with the campaign, the sales division is not.

0	1	2	3	4	5	6	7	8	9	10
(None)		(Slight)			(Moderate)			(High)		(Total)

TOTAL YOUR SCORE _____

Chapter 4

Stress

12:50 P.M. Spencer Bernham has left with a stricken look on his face, feeling cowed by Harry's outburst. Harry sinks back into his chair. His respiration is twenty breaths per minute and his pulse rate is ninety-eight beats per minute; his muscles are tight, and his nerves are jumpy. He rubs his eyes. He wishes that he could just go out and get a drink somewhere. "I suppose I shouldn't have jumped on Spencer like that," he thinks, "but, my God, how am I going to make any kind of intelligent deal without those numbers? This damn job is getting to me!"

Quite obviously Harry is a suffering man. He is suffering from "executive stress," a life-shortening condition that afflicts and kills thousands of managers and administrators every year.

What about you? Are you continually under stress? What does it do to you, and what should you do about it?

THE GENETIC CONNECTION

Harry is both angry and anxious because of his genes; he has the same basic genetic structure that his ancestors had 10,000 years ago. In fact,

55

Figure 4-1. The caveman problem.

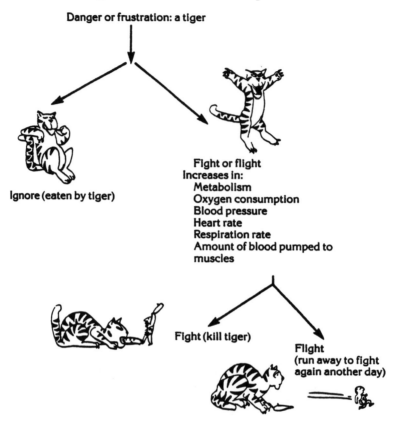

Danger or frustration: a tiger

Ignore (eaten by tiger)

Fight or flight
Increases in:
Metabolism
Oxygen consumption
Blood pressure
Heart rate
Respiration rate
Amount of blood pumped to
muscles

Fight (kill tiger)

Flight
(run away to fight
again another day)

the basic genetic structure of humans has changed very little in the last
10,000 or even 100,000 years. This genetic structure has been quite conducive to the survival of the species. Unfortunately for Harry, it has
recently become inappropriate for our "civilized" twentieth-century environment.

When faced with danger or frustration, the caveman of 10,000 years
ago had two choices (see Figure 4-1). Encountering a tiger at the mouth
of a cave, the caveman would choose either to ignore it or to evoke a
fight-or-flight response. This second choice represents the mobilization
of the entire being for either aggressive encounter (fight) or a high-speed
departure (flight). Whether the individual chooses to fight or flee, the
response of the autonomic nervous system is the same.

A fight-or-flight response results in the increase in various vital body
functions. This prepares caveman Thorpe either to fight the tiger or to

flee from it. As the figure shows, the survivability of those who chose to ignore the tiger was substantially less than the survivability of those who evoked the fight-or-flight response. This response has been conducive for human survival over the past several thousand years. Few cavemen who ignored threats lived to perpetuate the species.

In modern society, however, the fight-or-flight response has become dysfunctional. Our stresses are primarily psychological rather than physical. We have been an industrialized society characterized by large hierarchical organizations for only the last few hundred years—not long enough to result in any genetic change. Thus, when faced with the everyday stresses of his modern job, Harry Thorpe is likely to instinctively respond in a primitive fashion with a fight-or-flight response. Unless he can effectively alter his response to fit his environment, the fight-or-flight response may very well kill him, for reasons we shall document below.

If you really met a tiger, you would, of course, respond with your entire being. As you decided whether to fight or flee, every organ in your body would react. For example:[1]

- Your respiration rate would increase.
- Your heart would increase its output of blood.
- Your blood vessels would constrict in key muscle areas.
- Your kidneys would increase their activity.
- Your pituitary gland would secrete ACTH (stress hormone).
- Your adrenal glands would secrete adrenaline.
- Your liver would secrete cholesterol.
- Your brain would be increasingly alert.

In all of these ways your body is preparing for life-saving fight or flight.

Unfortunately, the "tigers" you face in your work are not the four-legged kind. Rather, they are daily frustrations, missed deadlines, conflicts, unachieved goals, rushed meetings, and noncompliant subordinates. Still, they provoke the same kind of response. The following are some reactions that deadlines and stress can have on cholesterol levels:[2]

---

[1] Adapted from H. Selye, *The Stress of Life* (New York: McGraw-Hill, 1956).

[2] S. M. Sales, "Organizational Role as a Risk Factor in Coronary Disease," *Administrative Science Quarterly*, Vol. 14 (1969), pp. 326–327. Reprinted by permission of the *Administrative Science Quarterly*.

- Cholesterol levels can be elevated in a laboratory in 60 minutes, merely by asking people to work faster than they can.
- Cholesterol levels of medical students have been observed to jump during final exams.
- Cholesterol levels of tax accountants have been found to reach a peak right around the April 15 tax-filing deadline.

As you no doubt know, a high cholesterol count can be associated with heart disease. The continual exercising of the fight-or-flight response as a result of excessive stress can have unfortunate physical consequences.

HOW STRESS KILLED THE EXECUTIVE MONKEY

One of the most graphic demonstrations of the effects of stress was conducted in the late 1950s. Scientists restrained a monkey in a chair and gave him a red button to push. Unless he pushed the button during the intervening period, the monkey received an electric shock every twenty seconds. After twenty-three days of being on the chair for six hours at a time, interspersed with six hours of rest, the monkey suddenly died. The cause, an autopsy revealed, was a perforated ulcer.

The same thing happened with a second monkey. Suspecting that the deaths were caused by the electric shock, the scientists placed a companion monkey next to the "executive" monkey. Every time the executive monkey received a shock, the companion monkey also received one, but his button had no effect on whether or not he received a shock. The companion monkey remained healthy and basically happy (although somewhat uncomfortable) throughout the experiment, but the executive monkey died, as before. In other words, the executive monkey's stressful job killed him.[3]

Harry Thorpe is an executive monkey, isn't he? Even though the situation is somewhat of his own making, his overload of deadlines means that he has a variety of red buttons to push, a fact that may be having some serious consequences on his physical well-being. The important thing to note, however, is that such harmful consequences are associated both with Harry's stressful environment and with his type of personality.

---

[3]Joseph V. Brady, "Ulcers in 'Executive Monkeys,' " *Scientific American*, October 1958.

STRESS DEFINED

The definition offered here for stress is overly simplistic. Stress is a complex phenomenon and each person responds differently to it. Nevertheless, I have found the following equation to be quite helpful in getting practicing managers to better understand and cope with their stress.

$$S = D - C$$

where:

S = Stress
D = Demands
C = Coping skills

By "demands," I mean any requirement for mental or physical action with some time constraint. Demands require you to do something. By "coping skills," I mean the psychological and physiological resources that you possess.

Two messages emerge very clearly when we look at the stress equation.

1. *No one is immune.* There is no one who is so "tough" that his coping skills cannot be exceeded. Every individual, no matter how resourceful, how physically and mentally strong, can have demands placed upon him that exceed his coping skills. Just like the executive monkey, every executive can be broken.

2. *Stress can be managed.* Since $S = D - C$, if we wish to reduce S, we can either reduce D or increase C. The objective of this chapter is to help you diagnose your stress situation and manage it effectively. Specific action plans are provided to help you reduce D and increase C. But first, let's take a look at Harry's life in terms of demands and coping skills.

Harry Thorpe: A Case in Stress

Harry Thorpe graduated with an undergraduate degree in civil engineering from a large state university. He immediately went to work for a nationally known engineering firm and made slow but steady progress until he was manager of a team of a dozen engineers. After six years, looking for additional opportunity, he made the job switch to his current employer, where he has been for the past fifteen years. He has been successful, but it hasn't been easy! He and his family are currently living in their fourth city, and he is getting tired of all the demands. He feels a constant overload from the requirements of continuously meeting new and different people, the large amounts of paper flowing across his desk, endless phone calls, and work-related travel. His subordinates seem to be claiming more and more of his time. He has a vague feeling that his job is "slipping away from him."

Recently, his health has begun to be affected. At age 43, he is not as young as he used to be and has suffered from sleepless nights and occasional "anxiety attacks" and fatigue. A recent visit to his general practitioner showed nothing overtly wrong with him physically.

His daughter has become a bit of a problem. Her grades in school are not good, and at age 15 she has recently announced that she really doesn't want to go to college. His son is the usual 12-year-old boy—beginning to feel his oats—and about to turn into the surly teenager. His wife has become less of a resource for him because of demands in her work. Three years ago she started her own company leasing decorative plants to commercial customers. She has worked the business well, now has five significant corporate clients and three full-time employees, and is breaking even. She's paid off the start-up loan, and feels that it is time to expand. However, the business has taken a personal toll. She has recently suffered a bout of migraine headaches and fatigue from the long hours. She has informed Harry that she is not willing to walk away from this investment if he decides to move in the near future.

Harry's job and career are currently on a positive trajectory—although it appears as though his next promotion will require a move to a larger plant or back to the corporate offices. He has always worked hard but somehow feels that his job is getting the best of him and his family.

Is Harry Thorpe under stress? You bet he is! The combination of increased demands and reduced coping skills have increased his stress level substantially. It is not very difficult to analyze Harry's case in terms of demands and coping skills.

Demands

- Moved three times and lived in four different cities
- Continuously meeting different people
- Travel
- Paper flow
- Telephone
- Subordinates' demands
- Daughter's grades
- Daughter's career aspirations
- About to have son become teenager
- Wife's business

And similarly, look at the reduction in coping skills.

Coping Skills

- Health—not as young as he used to be
- Fatigue
- Occasional anxiety attacks
- Family not as supportive
- Wife's own reduction in coping skills evidenced by migraines and fatigue
- Lack of management skills for higher level positions

As you can see, stress is defined in a dynamic way, and it can build with relatively small changes in demands accompanied by relatively small changes in coping skills. But it all accumulates, and it's the final S that determines stress level. Your job is to manage this S in such a way that it is suited for you.

Before we move to action steps, two familiar stress situations merit separate attention. Both frustration and significant life changes can easily exceed our coping skills and result in stress. However, they are manageable if you understand them.

FRUSTRATION DEFINED

Frustration occurs when you are striving for a goal and are blocked by some obstacle (see Figure 4-2). When faced with this situation, you can do three things:

Figure 4-2. Frustration defined.

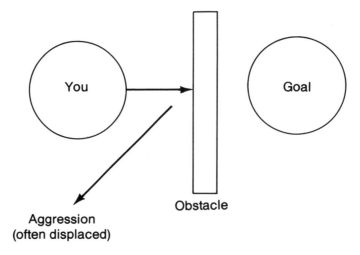

1. Go around the obstacle.
2. Remove the obstacle.
3. Change the goal.

Managers face numerous frustrations daily, so you must be able to handle them. Each of the three alternatives listed can be quite functional depending on the situation. For example:

• Howard Goldwyn could not get approval from the computer department to pay for the portable microcomputer he needed for the trade show. So he got his boss's approval, purchased it with his credit card, and submitted the bill on a travel expense report. Howard went around the obstacle.

• Adele Graziani had a salesman in a profitable region who was getting badly beaten by the competition. She sent the salesman to sales training courses and spent numerous hours coaching him, to no avail. Adele finally decided to give the salesman an inside customer-relations job and replaced him with a top performer. Adele removed the obstacle.

• James Holden set a goal of a 15 percent increase in sales to his industrial customers in region 3. But a long coal strike depressed industrial profits and firms delayed their capital-goods purchases. James decided a 5 percent increase was more reasonable, and with hard work made his target. James changed his goal.

The good news is that frustration can be managed functionally. The bad news is that it produces aggression. That's right. It is a widely accepted psychological fact that frustration produces aggression. This aggression can often be displaced against people or objects having nothing to do with the actual frustration. When you find yourself showing aggression to your wife or children because of on-the-job frustration, stand back and take notice. Say to yourself, "Uh oh, here I go again taking job frustrations out on the family." Ask yourself, "What is my goal? What is the obstacle? What functional position can I take?" Simply admitting your behavior will help you to control displaced aggression.

In Chapter 3, I talked a bit about Type A and Type B behaviors. Now let's examine them a little more closely. Assess yourself. Are you more a Type A or Type B? Answer the questions in the Behavior Activity Profile (Form 4-1), and refer to the following table.[4,5]

Type A Personality Traits

- Impatience
- Time urgency
- Abruptness of gesture
   and speech
- Intensive striving for
   achievement
- Ambition

- Competitiveness
- Excesses of drive
   and hostility
- Excess job responsibility
- Overcommitment to vocation
   or profession

Type B Personality Traits

- More easygoing
- Relaxed
- Not easily irritated
- Less ambitious

- Otherwise generally
   lacking the Type A
   attributes

(A caveat: As with all psychometric devices, the exercises in this book have significant limitations in precisely measuring individual personalities. So, if you have scored extremely high or low, don't panic. How-

---

[4]C. D. Jenkins, "Recent Evidence Supporting Psychological and Social Risk Factors for Coronary Disease," *New England Journal of Medicine*, Vol. 294 (1976), pp. 1033–1034. Reprinted by permission from the *New England Journal of Medicine*.
[5]C. D. Jenkins, R. H. Rosenman, and M. Friedman, "Development of an Objective Psychological Test for the Determination of the Coronary-Prone Behavior Pattern in Employed Men," *Journal of Chronic Diseases*, Vol. 20 (1969), pp. 371–379.

ever, with larger samples, these devices often have been shown to be statistically significant and predictive. In any case, the intention is simply to increase your level of awareness concerning your own personal style.)

It is estimated that over 40 percent of the American population are Type A; I would guess that almost 80 percent of practicing managers are Type A. The fact that you may be in good company is not cause for celebration. When Type As rush to meet a deadline, become irritable and aggressive, and so on, they may be elevating their blood pressure, raising their serum cholesterol level, and in other biochemical ways doing damage to themselves. In one study of men with coronary disease, it was found that the Type A score was more predictive of recurrent heart attack than was the number of cigarettes a person smoked or his or her cholesterol level. Indeed, Type As in some studies have been found to be two times as likely as Type Bs to suffer a coronary.[6]

The findings, however, are not all in the same direction and the final conclusions are not in concerning Type A behavior and health. Some later research has indicated that there are "hardy types" who appear to be unaffected by job demands.[7] They work long hours and keep to arduous schedules; yet they appear to flourish in terms of health. We have all met them, haven't we? Recent work has indicated that Type As may be more likely to survive a heart attack.[8] The key issue here is, how do you feel? Is your job getting you down or are you matched to it? The key philosophy is that you can attempt to consciously manage your stress level by controlling Ds and Cs (see equation, page 59) rather than being buffeted by your environment. Harry's environment is a problem for him, and his situation is looking more bleak every minute. He is a Type A personality operating in a Type A environment. His environment is interacting with his Type A personality. Let's take a look at the effect of life change on health.

LIFE CHANGE AND STRESS

Ever since Freud (and probably earlier), it has been suspected that emotions affect one's physical health; now it has become a well-established

---

[6]C. D. Jenkins, personal communication, 31 January 1978.

[7]J. H. Howard, D. A. Cunningham, and P. A. Rechnitzer, "Personality (Hardiness) as a Moderator of Job Stress and Coronary Risk in Type A Individuals: A Longitudinal Study," *Journal of Behavioral Medicine*, Vol. 9, no. 3 (June 1986), pp. 229–244.

[8]D. R. Ragland and R. J. Brand, "Type A Behavior and Mortality from Coronary Heart Disease," *New England Journal of Medicine*, Vol. 318, no. 2 (1988), pp. 65–69.

medical fact. But how can you figure out which emotions are the "good" ones and which are the "bad" ones? (Nothing is simple these days.)

Consider the case of a 39-year-old Boston educator who enjoyed excellent health. He suddenly "died" from cardiac arrest. His wife, an experienced nurse, gave him CPR (cardiopulmonary resuscitation). (Can you do it? Could you save someone's life? If you don't know CPR, you should take a short course.) He was revived, but surprisingly during the examination at the hospital, no evidence of heart damage was discovered. Later, however, interesting explanatory facts came to light. He had recently experienced a career setback. During that same time, his wife's father died. As a result, his wife had been unable to give him the emotional support he so badly needed. To add to his stress, while playing with his two daughters he experienced aggressive, erotic impulses that ran counter to his deeply religious, sexually repressed nature. The consequence of all these emotions was very nearly sudden death.[9]

This example shows the impact of life change on health. We are not just talking about work-related stress. Any life change—positive or negative—can increase stress; not only can it be trouble with your boss, or a move to a new city, or getting a speeding ticket, but also getting a promotion or a raise or taking a vacation.

How many recent life changes have you had? The Social Readjustment Rating Scale shown in Form 4-2 will enable you to estimate the amount of life-change stress you are under.

There seems to be a well-documented and clear relationship between life change and physical disease. Since most of these findings are statistical, it is impossible to make accurate predictions on an individual basis. However, you might be able to generally interpret your life change scores as follows:

Life-Change Score for Previous Year	Probability of Illness Within Next Two Years
Less than 150 (low)	Low
150–199 (mild stress)	30%
200–299 (moderate stress)	50%
300 or more (major stress)	80%

---

[9]"Emotions and Sudden Death," *Science News*, Vol. 109, No. 13 (27 March 1976): p. 199. Reprinted with permission from *Science News*, the weekly news magazine of science. Copyright 1976 by Science Service, Inc.

RESEARCH FINDINGS

Consider these findings:

1. In a study of eighty-eight resident physicians at the University of Washington, 93 percent of major health changes occurred within two years of life changes summing 150 points or more.

2. One hundred college football players were given the Holmes-Rahe Stress Test during the year prior to the football season, and were divided into groups with high, medium, and low life-change scores. During the season they experienced injury rates of 50, 25, and 9 percent, respectively. Seven out of ten players who had sustained multiple injuries were in the high-risk group.[10]

3. In Stockholm, sixty-seven persons experiencing sudden cardiac death were found to have an average of three times higher life-change scores in the last six months of life, as compared to earlier periods.

4. In a study at the University of Oklahoma, surviving coronary patients had steady levels of life-change scores over two years. Those who died of coronary diseases had peak rates of life changes seven to twelve months before death.

5. A study of 279 survivors of heart attack in Helsinki showed a rising rate of life change for the six months immediately before the attack.[11]

HOW COMPATIBLE ARE YOUR PERSONALITY AND YOUR ENVIRONMENT?

Air traffic controllers have a stressful job. If you have ever listened to their radio transmissions, you can understand why. They operate in a Type A environment, and the pressures and responsibilities are at times very high. Obviously, some people should not be air traffic controllers; they are just not cut out to handle that level of stress. Even if some people appear to be thriving in high-stress jobs, in reality they may be harming themselves. The same is true to a lesser extent of other jobs. Are you cut out to handle your job?

---

[10]T. H. Holmes and M. Masuda, "Life Change and Illness Susceptibility," in J. P. Scott and E. C. Senay, eds., *Separation and Depression: Clinical and Research Aspects*, a symposium at the Chicago meeting of the American Association for the Advancement of Science, December 1970 (Washington: AAAS, 1973).

[11]C. D. Jenkins, "Recent Evidence Supporting Psychological and Social Risk Factors for Coronary Disease," *New England Journal of Medicine*, Vol. 294 (1976), pp. 1033–1034.

The fundamental equation to consider is the following:

Type A personality + Type A environment = Trouble!

Maybe there isn't much you can do about some of the stressful life changes you've experienced. What's past is past. But if you have a Type A personality and are working in a Type A job, you may be asking for some stress-related illness.

You can get an estimate of your situation by completing the Personality-Environment Match shown in Form 4-3. Take your Type A score from Form 4-1 and indicate it on the left-hand scale. Now estimate your environment on the right. How hectic, aggressive, time pressured is it? Connect your two estimates with a straight line. If the straight line crosses the middle scale higher than at midway, you are asking for trouble. You should make a conscious effort to change your environment, yourself, or both.

CHANGING YOUR ENVIRONMENT AND YOURSELF

One of the most fundamental and important decisions you can make affecting your personal well-being is to say no to or get out of jobs that are not appropriate for you. Do you have responsibilities for areas in which you have little control? Are there certain elements of your job you would like to eliminate? Do you take on work-related responsibilities for which you do not have time? Are you involved in outside activities that you really don't like and consequently don't do well because of time pressures?

If you answer yes to any of these questions, then you obviously need to change your approach. You don't have to operate under chronic time pressures. In addition, you don't have to do everything you're asked to do. Successful managers have the ability to negotiate out of situations that have a high likelihood of failure.

The three keys to making even a high Type A manager's life a little more comfortable, as discussed in Chapter 2, are the following:

1. Set your priorities (job and personal). Distinguish carefully between what is important and what is not important to you. Follow these priorities religiously.
2. Delegate. Let someone else do it. Delegating that routine but nec-

essary report may mean you can set more realistic and leisurely deadlines on that new product introduction.

3. Say no. Don't do it. Refusing to serve on the school board may give you more time to go fishing with your kids.

LEARNING TO RELAX

There are things you can do to relieve life's pressures. One approach, introduced by Harvard physician Herbert Benson,[12] is the relaxation response. The relaxation response is an innate human response that is precisely the opposite of the fight-or-flight response. When you are practicing the relaxation response, you experience a decrease in oxygen consumption, respiration rate, blood pressure, and muscle tension—all the things that the fight-or-flight mechanism intensifies. It is well known that relaxation can be used to counteract the ravages of executive stress. Figure 4-3 shows how the process works.

YOUR DEMANDS AND COPING SKILLS

Now it is time to get a better idea of the specific demands placed upon you. Complete the Demand Audit in Form 4-4. It will give you a clearer idea of the stresses that exist in your environment.

Next, complete the Coping Skills Audit in Form 4-5. It will provide you with insight into the coping skills that work for you and how you might improve them.

Finally, complete your own personal action plan for stress management. This will help you improve the balance between the demands and coping skills in your life.

CONCLUSION

Now you've had an opportunity to diagnose your stress situation and to formulate action steps for managing stress. You are in a position to recognize, understand, and manage stress. What tigers are causing you stress right now? Your weight? Your lack of a clear career plan? That

---

[12] Herbert Benson, "Your Innate Asset for Combating Stress," *Harvard Business Review*, Vol. 52 (July-August 1974).

Figure 4-3. Relaxation exercise.

1. Find a quiet place, preferably a semidark room.

2. Think only about your eyes. Try to feel all of the muscles around your eyes and in your eyelids that are tense. Try to relax them. Take all of the time you need. When you have succeeded, you will feel like there is a very tense area above and below your eyes, but no tenseness in your eyes or eyelids themselves, since they are now totally relaxed.

3. Now focus on your toes. Your goal is to make the muscles in your toes feel like the muscles in your eyes—totally relaxed.

4. Move successively through the muscles of your feet, your calves, your thighs, your groin, your chest, and finally your neck and head.

5. Breathe through your nose. With each exhale, repeat the same sound or phrase to yourself.

6. Let your mind idle. Think of nothing special. If distractions keep interrupting your thoughts while you are trying to relax, concentrate on your breathing and let your mind float.

7. Practice this exercise for 20 minutes every day.

8. Do not worry about whether or not you are successful in totally relaxing. Just let relaxation occur at its own pace. What you need is quiet, a comfortable position, like lying or sitting, and willingness to try. As you get more and more practiced at using the relaxation response, you will be able to elicit it very quickly, even in noisy work environments.

negotiation for your department budget? Tools for fighting these and other tigers are presented in the other chapters, but the techniques you have learned in this chapter will help you to recognize and manage your response to the tigers in your jungle. There's one waiting outside your door right now.

BEHAVIOR ACTIVITY PROFILE

Each of us displays certain kinds of behaviors, thought patterns, and personal characteristics. For each of the twenty-one sets of descriptions below, circle the number which you feel best describes where you are between each pair. The best answer for each set of descriptions is the response that most nearly describes the way you feel, behave, or think. Answer these in terms of your regular or typical behavior, thoughts, or characteristics.

1. I'm always on time for appointments.   7 6 5 4 3 2 1   I'm never quite on time.

2. When someone is talking to me, chances are I'll:

   Anticipate what they are going to say by nodding, interrupting, or finishing sentences for them.   7 6 5 4 3 2 1   Listen quietly without showing any impatience.

3. I frequently:

   Try to do several things at once.   7 6 5 4 3 2 1   Tend to take things one at a time.

4. When it comes to waiting in line (at banks, theaters, etc.):

   I really get impatient and frustrated.   7 6 5 4 3 2 1   It simply doesn't bother me.

5. I always feel rushed.   7 6 5 4 3 2 1   I never feel rushed.

6. When it comes to my temper:

   I find it hard to control at times.   7 6 5 4 3 2 1   I just don't seem to have one.

7. I tend to do most things like eating, walking, and talking:

   Rapidly.   7 6 5 4 3 2 1   Slowly.

   TOTAL SCORE THIS PAGE _____ = S

8. Quite honestly, the things I enjoy most are:

Job-related activities.　　7　6　5　4　3　2　1　　Leisure-time activities.

9. At the end of a typical workday, I usually feel like:

I needed to get more done than I did.　　7　6　5　4　3　2　1　　I accomplished everything I needed to.

10. Someone who knows me very well would say that I would:

Rather work than play.　　7　6　5　4　3　2　1　　Rather play than work.

11. When it comes to getting ahead at work:

Nothing is more important.　　7　6　5　4　3　2　1　　Many things are more important.

12. My primary source of satisfaction comes from my job.　　7　6　5　4　3　2　1　　I regularly find satisfaction in non–job-related pursuits, such as hobbies, friends, and family.

13. Most of my friends and social acquaintances are people:

I know from work.　　7　6　5　4　3　2　1　　Not connected with my work.

14. I'd rather stay at work than take a vacation.　　7　6　5　4　3　2　1　　Nothing at work is important enough to interfere with my vacation.

TOTAL SCORE THIS PAGE _____ = J

15. People who know me well would describe me as:

Hard driving and   7 6 5 4 3 2 1   Relaxed and
competitive.   easygoing.

16. In general, my behavior is governed by:

A desire for   7 6 5 4 3 2 1   What I want to
recognition   do—not by
and achievement.   trying to
                                               satisfy others.

17. In trying to complete a project or solve a problem I tend to:

Wear myself out   7 6 5 4 3 2 1   Take a break or
before I'll give   quit if I'm
up on it.   feeling fatigued.

18. When I play a game (tennis, cards, etc.), my enjoyment comes from:

Winning.   7 6 5 4 3 2 1   The social
                                               interaction.

19. I like to associate with people who are:

Dedicated to   7 6 5 4 3 2 1   Easygoing and
getting ahead.   take life as it
                                               comes.

20. I'm not happy   7 6 5 4 3 2 1   Frequently,
unless I'm   "doing nothing"
always doing   can be quite
something.   enjoyable.

21. What I enjoy doing most are:

Competitive   7 6 5 4 3 2 1   Noncompetitive
activities.   pursuits.

TOTAL SCORE THIS PAGE _____ = H

Impatience (S)	Job Involvement (J)	Hard Driving and Competitive (H)	Total Score (A) = S + J + H

The Behavior Activity Profile attempts to assess the three Type A coronary-prone behavior patterns, as well as provide a total score. The three a priori types of Type A coronary-prone behavior patterns are shown below:

Items	Behavior Pattern		Characteristics
1–7	Impatience	(S)	Anxious to interrupt Fails to listen attentively Frustrated by waiting (e.g., in line, for others to complete a job)
8–14	Job involvement	(J)	Focal point of attention is the job Lives for the job Relishes being on the job Immersed in job activities
15–21	Hard driving and competitive	(H)	Hardworking, highly competitive Competitive in most aspects of life, sports, work, etc. Races against the clock
1–21	Total score	(A)	Total of S + J + H represents your global Type A behavior

Score ranges for total score are:

Score	Behavior Type
122 and above	hard-core Type A
99–121	moderate Type A
90–98	low Type A
80–89	Type X
70–79	low Type B
50–69	moderate Type B
49 and below	hard-core Type B

Percentile Scores

Now compare your score to a sample of over 1,200 respondents.

Percentile Score	Raw Score	
% of Individuals Scoring Lower	Males	Females
99	140	132
95	135	126
90	130	120
85	124	112
80	118	106
75	113	101
70	108	95
65	102	90
60	97	85
55	92	80
50	87	74
45	81	69
40	75	63
35	70	58
30	63	53
25	58	48
20	51	42
15	45	36
10	38	31
5	29	26
1	21	21

SOCIAL READJUSTMENT RATING SCALE

How many recent life changes have you had? Complete this instrument by checking off below each event you have experienced in the last twelve months.

Life Event	Mean Value	
1. Death of a spouse	100	___
2. Divorce	73	___
3. Marital separation from mate	65	___
4. Detention in jail or other institution	63	___
5. Death of a close family member	63	___
6. Major personal injury or illness	53	___
7. Marriage	50	___
8. Being fired at work	47	___
9. Marital reconciliation with mate	45	___
10. Retirement from work	45	___
11. Major change in health or behavior of a family member	44	___
12. Pregnancy	40	___
13. Sexual difficulties	39	___
14. Gaining a new family member (i.e., through birth, adoption, oldster moving in, etc.)	39	___
15. Major business readjustment (i.e., merger, reorganization, bankruptcy, etc.)	39	___
16. Major change in financial state (i.e., a lot worse off or a lot better off than usual)	38	___
17. Death of a close friend	37	___
18. Changing to a different line of work	36	___
19. Major change in the number of arguments with spouse (i.e., either a lot more or a lot less than usual regarding child rearing, personal habits, etc.)	35	___
20. Taking on a mortgage greater than $50,000 (i.e., purchasing a home, business, etc.)	31	___
21. Foreclosure on a mortgage or loan	30	___
22. Major change in responsibilities at work (i.e., promotion, demotion, lateral transfer)	29	___
23. Son or daughter leaving home (i.e., marriage, attending college, etc.)	29	___
24. In-law troubles	29	___
25. Outstanding personal achievement	28	___

Source: From T. H. Holmes and R. H. Rahe, ''The Social Readjustment Rating Scale,'' *Journal of Psychosomatic Research*, Vol. 11 (1967), 213–218. Copyright 1967 Pergamon Press, Ltd. Reprinted with permission.

Life Event	Mean Value
26. Wife beginning or ceasing work outside the home	26 ___
27. Beginning or ceasing formal schooling	26 ___
28. Major change in living conditions (i.e., building a new home, remodeling, deterioration of home or neighborhood)	25 ___
29. Revision of personal habits (dress, manners, associations, etc.)	24 ___
30. Troubles with the boss	23 ___
31. Major change in working hours or conditions	20 ___
32. Change in residence	20 ___
33. Changing to a new school	20 ___
34. Major change in usual type and/or amount of recreation	19 ___
35. Major change in church activities (i.e., a lot more or a lot less than usual)	19 ___
36. Major change in social activities (i.e., clubs, dancing, movies, visiting, etc.)	18 ___
37. Taking on a mortgage or loan less than $10,000 (i.e., purchasing a car, TV, freezer, etc.)	17 ___
38. Major change in sleeping habits (a lot more or a lot less sleep, or change in part of day when asleep)	16 ___
39. Major change in number of family get-togethers (i.e., a lot more or a lot less than usual)	15 ___
40. Major change in eating habits (a lot more or a lot less food intake, or very different meal hours or surroundings)	15 ___
41. Vacation	13 ___
42. Christmas	12 ___
43. Minor violations of the law (i.e., traffic tickets, jaywalking, disturbing the peace, etc.)	11 ___

Now add up the point values next to your check marks and record your total score below.

TOTAL LIFE-CHANGE SCORE _____

PERSONALITY-ENVIRONMENT MATCH

Does your personality match your environment? Take your Type A score from the Behavior Activity Profile (Form 4-1) and indicate it on Scale I. Then check your environment on Scale II. Draw a line connecting the points you have checked. The intersection on the line with Scale III tells you where you stand.

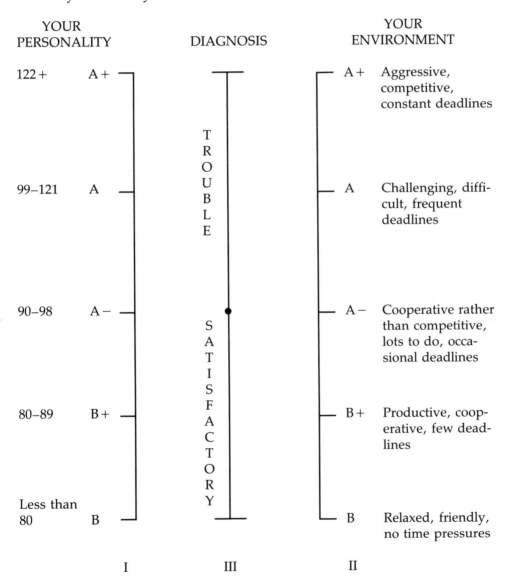

YOUR PERSONALITY	DIAGNOSIS	YOUR ENVIRONMENT

Personality		Diagnosis	Environment	
122+	A+		A+	Aggressive, competitive, constant deadlines
99–121	A	T R O U B L E	A	Challenging, difficult, frequent deadlines
90–98	A–	S A T I S F A C T O R Y	A–	Cooperative rather than competitive, lots to do, occasional deadlines
80–89	B+		B+	Productive, cooperative, few deadlines
Less than 80	B		B	Relaxed, friendly, no time pressures

I   III   II

DEMAND AUDIT

Diagnose the demands on you. Circle the number for each item below that represents your best estimate. Remember, D is a request for any mental or physical action with some time constraint. To what extent is each of the items below placing demands on you now?

	None	Slight		Moderate			High		Extreme	
			Level of Demand							
Ambiguity in my job responsibilities	0	1	2	3	4	5	6	7	8	9	10
Long workdays	0	1	2	3	4	5	6	7	8	9	10
Too much to do	0	1	2	3	4	5	6	7	8	9	10
Need for more resources	0	1	2	3	4	5	6	7	8	9	10
Need for more power	0	1	2	3	4	5	6	7	8	9	10
Dislike of work	0	1	2	3	4	5	6	7	8	9	10
Long commute	0	1	2	3	4	5	6	7	8	9	10
Travel	0	1	2	3	4	5	6	7	8	9	10
Type A personality	0	1	2	3	4	5	6	7	8	9	10
Type A environment	0	1	2	3	4	5	6	7	8	9	10
Difficult boss	0	1	2	3	4	5	6	7	8	9	10
Insufficient subordinates	0	1	2	3	4	5	6	7	8	9	10
Coordination with other departments	0	1	2	3	4	5	6	7	8	9	10
Conflict with others	0	1	2	3	4	5	6	7	8	9	10
Paperwork	0	1	2	3	4	5	6	7	8	9	10
Telephone interruptions	0	1	2	3	4	5	6	7	8	9	10
Meetings, meetings, meetings	0	1	2	3	4	5	6	7	8	9	10
Others (describe)											
_____	0	1	2	3	4	5	6	7	8	9	10
_____	0	1	2	3	4	5	6	7	8	9	10
_____	0	1	2	3	4	5	6	7	8	9	10

Now look at the data you have generated. Would you like to reduce any of the demands on you? If you would like to increase D, that is OK also.

List below any *demands* you would like to change.

1. _____   4. _____

2. _____   5. _____

3. _____   6. _____

D Reduction Steps

The D reduction checklist below may give you some additional ideas.

D Reduction Checklist

☐ Change job.   ☐ Reduce aspirations.
☐ Career plan.   ☐ Negotiate for more responsibility.
☐ Delegate.   ☐ Clarify job responsibility.
☐ Say no.   ☐ Travel less.
☐ Spend less.   ☐ Work shorter hours.

Summary Action Plan

List below any steps you would like to take to either reduce or increase your D.

_____

_____

_____

_____

_____

_____

The other approach to managing stress is to increase C. To help formulate an action plan on C, complete Form 4-5.

COPING SKILLS AUDIT

What coping skills do you possess? Circle the number for each item below that represents your best estimate. Remember, C represents your coping skills—any resource (psychological or physical) that helps you handle the demands placed on you. To what extent is each of the items below an effective coping skill for you?

	None	Slight			Moderate			High		Extreme	
Understanding my frustrations	0	1	2	3	4	5	6	7	8	9	10
Management skills	0	1	2	3	4	5	6	7	8	9	10
Organization of my job	0	1	2	3	4	5	6	7	8	9	10
Positive attitude	0	1	2	3	4	5	6	7	8	9	10
Discussing with others	0	1	2	3	4	5	6	7	8	9	10
Slowing down	0	1	2	3	4	5	6	7	8	9	10
Diet	0	1	2	3	4	5	6	7	8	9	10
Exercise	0	1	2	3	4	5	6	7	8	9	10
Reading	0	1	2	3	4	5	6	7	8	9	10
Humor	0	1	2	3	4	5	6	7	8	9	10
Shopping	0	1	2	3	4	5	6	7	8	9	10
Relaxation response	0	1	2	3	4	5	6	7	8	9	10
Physician	0	1	2	3	4	5	6	7	8	9	10
Clinician	0	1	2	3	4	5	6	7	8	9	10
Vacation	0	1	2	3	4	5	6	7	8	9	10
Hobbies	0	1	2	3	4	5	6	7	8	9	10
Music	0	1	2	3	4	5	6	7	8	9	10

Others (describe)

_____ 0 1 2 3 4 5 6 7 8 9 10

_____ 0 1 2 3 4 5 6 7 8 9 10

_____ 0 1 2 3 4 5 6 7 8 9 10

Now review the coping skills you have diagnosed. Would you like to increase the effectiveness of any of them?

List below the *coping skills* you would like to improve and how:

Coping Skill	How to Improve
1. _____	_____
2. _____	_____
3. _____	_____
4. _____	_____
5. _____	_____

Summary Action Plan

You have looked specifically at the demands and coping skills in your life. Summarize below any action steps you would take to better manage stress.

_____

_____

_____

_____

_____

_____

_____

_____

_____

_____

Chapter 5

Power

1:02 P.M. Harry phones George Lee, vice-president of purchasing at the corporate offices. "George," says Harry, "we've got to get this decentralized purchasing program going. We're losing production because of lack of parts. When can we get our teams together? I have my calendar right in front of me."

"Harry, I still don't think it is a good idea. Just last week your purchasing guy wanted to pay $110,000 for electrical components that we've got coming at $87,000."

"Yeah, but they are two weeks too late."

"If you'd just plan your manufacturing production to give us some decent lead times, that would not be a problem."

"Lead times," shouts Harry. "I'm up to my ears trying to meet marketing, customer, and now your lead times."

"I know," responds George, "but you've got to do some planning. Thirty days is not forever, you know."

"Well, if you are not going to cooperate with me informally on this thing," warns Harry, "I'll have to bring it up with Ron (the president) and see what I can get done formally."

"Fine, but I still think I am right on this one."

"We'll see."
"So long."
"Bye."

1:05 P.M.   Harry can be heard muttering to himself. . . . "Here we go again with the power politics. George is intransigent about decentralizing purchasing because it's his little kingdom. Decentralizing threatens him. I need it to shorten lead times. I know I don't plan very well but, for crying out loud, we're not building airplanes so that we can work with five-year lead times. What I need is more power! I wonder how I can get it. . . ."

Harry has a power problem, doesn't he? He lacks power. He doesn't know how to get it. But he also doesn't know what the consequences of having it might be.

In this chapter we will explore all of these issues so that you can play the power-politics game more effectively and with more insight. In this chapter you will learn how to:

- Define power
- Look at what power does to managers
- Diagnose your personal power situation
- Learn how to acquire and use power

POWER DEFINED

"Power" is a dirty word. We can talk comfortably and even positively about struggles for advancement, influencing someone for the better, competition, and success. We can even be at ease with our human needs for achievement, affiliation, inclusion, and self-actualization. But the need and desire for power is viewed with distrust and suspicion. The word alone triggers negative reactions.

Power-seeking persons make us uncomfortable. Imagine a presidential candidate announcing that the reason he was running for office was because he got a kick out of exercising power. He would definitely lose the election. He would also probably be called sick and unnatural.

We all have been frustrated by someone exercising power over us. History and literature are full of examples of powerful people who have hurt powerless persons. Remember Scrooge and Tiny Tim? And what about Idi Amin?

If A causes B to do something that B would otherwise not have done, A has exercised power over B. If you are instrumental in changing someone else's behavior, by definition you are exercising power over that person. A manager must be able to change the behavior of his subordinates. Therefore, he must have power and be able to exercise that power effectively. The more you understand this variable and its impact upon you, the more successful and satisfied you will be.

Potential Power vs. Actual Power

Potential power is simply power at rest. Actual power is power in use. Jeffrey Pfeffer calls power in action "politics," reserving the term "power" to apply to potential influence.[1] He claims that the exercise of power is unnecessary when there is no resistance or opposition. Therefore, if your subordinates, peers, and superiors never oppose your ideas, you will not need to use power. However, most organizations are composed of people with different opinions, values, and viewpoints. Managers need potential power and the skills to translate this into effective actual power.

Soft Power vs. Hard Power

Approaches to power have been described as hard or soft. A soft approach to the use of power is one that emphasizes collaboration and cooperation. It results in synergy and a win/win solution to a problem. Hard approaches to power, on the other hand, emphasize assertiveness and competition, resulting in a win/lose situation with one person controlling the other. Managers who only use hard power tend to see power as a limited commodity; they define it as a zero-sum variable. They believe that any power that another person has detracts from the power they are able to utilize.

THE GOOD, THE BAD, AND THE UGLY

Have you seen this film? Clint Eastwood is the good, Lee Van Cleef is the bad, and Eli Wallach is the ugly. It is a fascinating study of the implementation of power by means of guns and knives, and it serves as a useful model for us as we look at the three sides of power. Clint Eastwood does triumph over the bad and the ugly, but only after seri-

---

[1] Jeffrey Pfeffer, *Power in Organizations* (Boston: Pitman Publishing, 1981).

ous struggle. In order for you to triumph, to make good use of your power, you may also have to struggle with the forces of bad and ugly, which come tightly bound in the power equation. First, the good.

The Good

Rollo May says that "man's basic psychological reason for living is to affirm himself, to struggle for self-esteem, to say 'I am' in the face of nature's magnificent indifference."[2] We must struggle for power because power enables us to get things done. The president of a great nation is powerful. The president of a great corporation is powerful. The president of a great university is powerful. A successful manager is powerful within the sphere in which he operates. Power, even though it is a dirty word, must be exercised every day in the operation of any successful managerial post. David McClelland[3] has found that successful managers have a greater need for power than for affiliation; they need to exercise control more than they need to be liked.

Power gets things done. As in physics, it is the energy at work that enables you to move the organization toward its chosen goals. That's the good side.

Now the bad.

The Bad

Power has its price; it extracts substantial costs from the person who exercises it: the powerholder. The quest for power in organizations is itself emotionally and physically draining. Rollo May has argued for years that the greatest source of anxiety in our society is competition for success.[4]

Maslow's hierarchy (see Chapter 10) is turned upside down for the powerholder. Normally, as we mature we become progressively more self-sufficient. Self-actualization, the highest order need, is typically a solitary experience. You self-actualize when you read an excellent book, hear a great piece of music, learn a new skill, or see an exquisite sunset. Most of the time, you self-actualize alone. The manager is, however, dependent upon others. If the person on the shop floor produces a

[2] Rollo May, *Power and Innocence* (New York: Norton, 1972).
[3] David C. McClelland and David H. Burnham, "Good Guys Make Bum Bosses," *Psychology Today*, December 1975, pp. 69–70.
[4] Rollo May, *The Meaning of Anxiety* (New York: Pocket Books, 1977).

poor-quality part, Harry's needs are not met. If the secretary sends the report to the wrong address, Harry suffers. If the bookkeeper fouls up the budget, Harry loses self-esteem. Curiously, the higher managers move up the power ladder, the farther they move down the hierarchy of needs; the higher one's need for power, the greater one's dependence on others.[5]

Maslow's theory has further implications: "Since self-actualizing people depend less on other people, they are less ambivalent about them, less hostile, and less anxious."[6] It is not surprising, then, that managers who are dependent on others may experience hostility and anxiety, and have trouble with interpersonal relations. They say it is lonely at the top; colleagues are more rare, competition is more common. Acceptance and being one of the guys are absent. Suspicion and acquiescence take their place.

Power costs the powerholder. This is not a new discovery. Thomas Jefferson puzzled, "I have never been able to conceive how any rational being could propose happiness to himself from the exercise of power over others."

Now, even worse news.

The Ugly

Power changes the powerholder; it causes a metamorphosis in the manager. As the tadpole changes into a frog, he undergoes metamorphosis: a change in form, shape, structure, and behavior. The frightening thing about power is that it can trigger a metamorphosis in the manager that is no less dramatic than that of tadpole to frog. Power intoxicates just as do alcohol and mind-altering drugs. And insidiously, this mind-altered state can become permanent. Power changes the powerholder's concept of his self and his concept of others.

Four specific ways in which power can corrupt are:

1. Persons acquire a "taste for power" and restlessly pursue more power as an end in itself.
2. Access to power tempts the individual to illegally use institutional resources as a means of enriching himself.
3. With the control of power, persons are provided with false feedback

---

[5]David Kipnis, *The Powerholders* (Chicago: University of Chicago Press, 1976).
[6]Ibid., p. 18.

concerning their own worth and they develop new values designed to protect their power.

4. People with power devalue the worth of the less powerful and prefer to avoid close social contacts with them.[7]

This is not a new theme. According to Kipnis, even in the plays of Sophocles, great and peaceful rulers become transformed—metamorphosed so that they have an inflated view of their own worth and a reluctance to listen to others.

A friend of mine, a recently appointed general in the air force, says that now he must be careful about even his casual remarks. The importance of anything he says seems magnified and people jump to predict and fulfill his needs. Furthermore, they are generous with positive feedback and flattery. They agree with most everything he says. It is not surprising, then, that powerful people conclude, "I am effective, superior, and insightful." These behaviors on the part of both the superior and the subordinate are typical.

We have all seen examples of power metamorphosis, people in significant positions of power who have developed an attitude of arrogance and excessive self-importance. Too often, their life view becomes so distorted that they become tyrannical, insensitive, self-serving, and aloof.

Power corrupts. While we can predict the downfall of this self-inflated, egotistical person as inevitable, that does not tell a powerful manager how to behave in his day-to-day interactions. Subordinates do the manager's bidding, his opinions are listened to, his decisions have impact on the entire organization, and people admire and respect him. The role feels good! It is easy in this situation to miss, dismiss, or undervalue the contributions of others. And that is ugly.

Some Real-World Examples

The darker side of power can exact its toll in human suffering. A *Fortune* article on power reveals some fascinating insights into America's toughest bosses. Not all come out looking bad and ugly, but some of them do not fare very well:

Boss 1: "He often gets in an absolutely pissed-off-with-the-world mood," says a subordinate. "Then there's no way of dealing with him rationally." Another staffer adds, "One has to play a semi-

---

[7]Ibid., p. 178.

Machiavellian game just to function with him. We spend an unconscionable amount of time trying to find out when he'll be least obnoxious."

Boss 2:   Former employees said that his mercurial temperament made him brutally arbitrary. "One could be a member of his ruling clique and do no wrong," says a former high-ranking executive. "Then one day, for no apparent reason, he treated you as the dumbest guy in the world." Says another employee who moved on, "He has seldom admitted a mistake, and he has never hesitated to make subordinates pay for them. Many of his executives, once protégés, were put in the pincers and discarded."

Boss 3:   "X fires people arbitrarily and unpredictably. Under the former head of [the company's] international division, foreign sales and profits increased dramatically over four years. X dumped him nonetheless. Once he fired an employee with over fifteen years service and then refused to extend the man's medical insurance while he sought a job, even though he had a heart condition. After some wrangling, personnel executives got X to relent on the insurance and even allow the man to use a company office in his job search. Soon, though, X forced his personnel people to move the man's parking space. X didn't like running into him in the parking lot."[8]

Good, Bad, Ugly Power and You

Now see how power affects you. Complete the Good, Bad, Ugly Power Audit (Form 5-1). The percentile scores on the second page of the form will enable you to compare yourself with other practicing managers who have completed the instrument. The higher the score on each dimension, the more inclined you are to use your power in good, bad, or ugly ways. Typically, a good power user is surrounded by a healthy organization; a bad powerholder will suffer personally; and the ugly powerholder will cause harm to his subordinates, friends, and family.

A Word of Caution

There are brighter and darker sides to this complex human phenomenon called power. The good use of power facilitates organizational efficiency, effectiveness, coordination, goal achievement, smoothness of

---

[8]Steven Flax, "The Toughest Bosses in America," *Fortune*, 6 August 1984, pp. 18–23.

operation, staff development, and job satisfaction. The abuse of power results in inefficiency, turnover, reduced productivity, human suffering, and eventual disaster. Therefore, before you decide to increase your power, carefully assess your present power situation with an awareness of the bad and the ugly as well as the good. Powerful people must use their power with sensitivity, with an awareness of its impact.

POWER AND YOUR SUBORDINATES

Power can be used either positively or negatively. Negative use of power includes those behaviors that build upon feelings of powerlessness, self-degradation, dependence, hopelessness, ignorance, and insecurity. Positive use of power include behaviors that encourage feelings of efficiency, self-esteem, independence, aspiration, awareness, and a secure sense of identity.[9]

Let's take a look at how power affects your subordinates. Complete the Subordinate Power Audit (Form 5-2). The percentile scores on the second page of the form will enable you to compare yourself with other practicing managers who have completed the instrument. It might also be helpful to have your subordinates respond to the instruments and compare your scores. The higher the positive-use-of-power score, the more you empower your subordinates. The higher the negative-use-of-power score, the more you control and diminish your subordinates.

Do you need to move power from the negative side of the ledger to the positive side? If you make the transition, you'll have happier and more motivated subordinates. To help you make this qualitative change you need to understand where power comes from.

SOURCES OF POWER

Where does power come from? Power originates from different sources. Everyone has power, but the amount and kind vary based on the situation, relationship, background, and topic. Harry needed power to push through decentralized purchasing. Specifically, Harry needed legitimate power (authority).

There are two types of power: personal and positional. The manager has certain kinds of power because of who he is and his personality; he has certain other kinds of power owing to his position. These two types

---

[9]John E. McCluskey, "Beyond the Carrot and the Stick: Liberation and Power Without Control," in W. Bennis, K. D. Benne, R. Chin, and K. Carey, eds., *The Planning of Change*, 3rd edition (New York: Holt, Rinehart and Winston, 1976), pp. 382–403.

of power have been further broken down into six "bases" of power. Each base of power "provides a different possible reason for subordinates to comply with their manager's wishes . . . and a different way in which a manager can attempt to influence a subordinate."[10]

Personal Power

You must have personal as well as positional power to be a successful manager. Power of position is rarely enough. It is ineffective with peers and superiors, it is less acceptable to educated and sophisticated workers, and it reinforces the wall between manager and subordinate. For greater long-term effectiveness, the manager must have access to the personal power bases of information, expertise, and referent power. In Harry's situation, they would appear as follows:

- *Information power comes from facts, logic, data, and the ability to be convincing in the presentation of these facts.* Harry might use information power this way:

  "George, we've lost over $2 million by waiting for supplies and then by having to work overtime. We also could have secured that Ajax contract if we could have been more flexible in our production."

- *Expert power comes from the manager's knowledge, education, and superior judgment, along with the other person's belief that in this situation, he is the expert.* Employing expert power, Harry would say:

  "George, I'm telling you, I know what I'm talking about. Production people work better doing their own buying."

- *Referent power comes from the rapport, affection, and respect the manager develops with others. Feelings of liking and admiration make others want to cooperate.* Harry might use referent power in this way:

  "George, look, we've been friends a long time. Let's not screw up the relationship over something as small as this."

Positional Power

As a result of his position, a manager has access to the power bases of authority, reward, and coercion. Let's see how they would operate in Harry Thorpe's present situation.

---

[10]Kenneth W. Thomas, *Power Base Inventory* (Tuxedo, N.Y.: Xicom, 1985), p. 9.

- *Authority power comes from the manager's job description, from his delegated right to make decisions and the subordinate's acceptance of that right.* If Harry could use authority power, he would simply say:

  "George, I want decentralized purchasing operational by Monday."

- *Reward power comes from the manager's ability to provide the subordinate with something he wants and the subordinate's belief that this is so.* Utilizing reward power, Harry would say:

  "George, decentralize purchasing and I'll assign one of my staff to you to help with the transition."

- *Coercive power comes from the manager's ability to chastise the subordinate and the subordinate's desire to avoid such unpleasantness.* Harry tried this subtly in his reference to "taking this up with Ron." More straightforwardly, Harry might have said:

  "George, keep fighting me on this and you'll eventually pay the price."

Now examine your sources of power by completing the Sources of Power Audit (Form 5-3). The percentile scores will enable you to compare yourself with other practicing managers who have completed the instrument. Your scores demonstrate which of the power bases you most often use. The larger the score, the more frequently you use that power base. Use of a variety of power bases is the best approach. Therefore, if you score a zero or a very low score on the use of any one of the power bases, this represents an area in which you need practice. If you are unusually high on one power base utilization, it is possible that you overuse it.

Note: Because this instrument is brief, you may not agree that the results describe you. That's OK. The objective here is self-insight and self-examination. You may wish to place your marks in different places on the percentile chart, representing your best assessment of the bases of your power. Feel free to do so. The important thing is that you consciously think of where you get your power.

POWER USE

Power is a two-way street. In choosing a power base you must have the power, and the other person must accept your power. If you have expertise but no one is aware of it, you do not have expert power. If you can't enforce your decision, you don't have authority. If the employee does not value the reward, don't use that power base. If your expertise is not respected, present your knowledge as information. Choose your power base carefully. Take into account both your capabilities and the target person's acceptance.

Kenneth Thomas, in his diagnostic instrument, *Power Base Inventory*,[11] not only assesses one's use of power bases but also points out when to use which and the consequences of over- and underuse. The scheme presented next is based on his work.

Power Base	*When to Use*
Information	• When subordinate growth and development are desirable • When understanding and commitment are needed • When you have ample time
Expertise	• When you are much more capable than your subordinates • When you are sure of the decision • When data or rationale is complex or confidential
Referent	• When harmony is important • When friendships are valued • When subordinates trust you and share same values
Authority	• When the organization has clear procedures • When rapid compliance is needed • When you are willing to take total responsibility for the decision
Reward	• When you want to add incentives • When you want to recognize superior performance • When subordinates value rewards
Coercive	• When you need to reinforce rules • When discipline is needed • When basic ethics are violated

Substantial additional insight into the different types of power and its uses are available in Thomas's *Power Base Inventory*.[12]

Indicators that your power position is unsatisfactory come from many stimuli. These include:

---

[11] Ibid.
[12] Ibid.

- Your body (tension, headaches, hypertension, lethargy)
- Your habits (increased smoking, drinking)
- Your emotions (anger, anxiety)
- The organization's bottom line (lack of output, decreased profitability)
- Subordinate attitudes (surliness, carelessness, disrespect)
- The general climate of your work area (laissez-faire, tense)
- Your and subordinate's feelings of job dissatisfaction (absenteeism, lack of pride in work)

ORGANIZATIONAL POWER

Now, examine your organization and what power is doing to it by completing the Organizational Power Audit (Form 5-4). The percentile scores will enable you to compare yourself with other practicing managers who have completed the instrument.

Organizations can over- and underuse any of the power bases. When a power source is not adequately employed, signs and symptoms of this imbalance are apparent. What is happening in your organization? A lot has been written lately about corporate culture, the norms that shape employee behavior.[13] Do the norms in your organization support healthy power usage? A good manager tries to ensure that every member of the organization uses power in functional ways. Discuss with your peers the power culture norms that operate in your organization; decide if changes are needed.

POLITICS—THE IMPLEMENTATION OF POWER

"Organizational politics" has a negative connotation for most people. No one likes a corporate politician. Good managers are effective at what they do. They use careful decision-making and good managerial skills to be successful. Therefore, you should stay away from the political game, right? WRONG! Unfortunately, in order to be successful you must also be effective on the political side of the power equation. Let's try to define what this means and look at steps that you can take to improve your skills in this area.

Recently, theories of intelligence have suggested that individuals pos-

---

[13]Ralph H. Kilmann, *Beyond the Quick Fix: Managing Five Tracks to Organizational Success* (San Francisco: Jossey-Bass, 1984).

sess three basic sorts of intelligence. Suppose for a moment that you could have a high IQ in any of the three following areas:[14]

1. *Analytical capability*—the ability to solve problems, think in a careful decision-making way, remember numbers and events, set priorities, and all the other analytical aspects of human behavior.

2. *Creative capability*—the ability to come up with new and different ideas, new solutions, novel approaches, innovations, and fresh insights into problems.

3. *Practical capability*—the ability to handle the practical aspects of everyday life. This includes the "street smart" component: the ability to understand the culture in which you operate, to pick up on nonverbal communication, to interpret subtle signs in everyday dealings with people, and so forth.

These three types of intelligence may be independent of one another such that you might score very high on one and low on another. Good managers must be analytical. They must be able to remember details and solve problems. In fact, the informational component of the manager's job is very substantial, and as much as 75 percent of his time may be spent in the acquisition, dissemination, and analysis of information. We hope that good managers are also somewhat creative. While the term "manager" often has a negative connotation, implying a boring, dronelike existence, effective managers can and do come up with new and creative solutions to problems.

And finally, good managers are practical and can get things done in the organization in which they operate. The practical-capability aspect of intelligence might be viewed as analogous to political implementation skills. After all,

Politics = The implementation of power

It does you no good to have power if you don't have the practical political implementation skills to get things accomplished. "Politics" often implies going around the legitimate power system and getting things done using nontraditional, "off-line" power bases. In this sense, the term is neutral; it can be either good or bad. Any corporation is a human organization, and as a consequence, a manager must implement

---

[14]Robert J. Sternberg, *Beyond Intelligence* (New York: Cambridge University Press, 1985).

change through the humans involved. Therefore, political skills are often important. If you don't have good political skills, you may well end up being a staff advisor to a manager who does. Politics in the corporation becomes problematic, and can be termed bad when individuals behave in ways that are insincere and self-interested. Let's look at these concepts in a bit more detail.

The Machiavellian Factor

Since the publication of the *Prince* and the *Discourses* by Niccolò Machiavelli in the first half of the sixteenth century, the author's name has become synonymous with undesirable and exploitative political behavior. "Machiavellianism" has come to stand for the principles of insincerity, guile, duplicity, deceit, craftiness, and opportunism in dealing with people. This principle has been studied at great detail and carefully defined both conceptually and psychometrically.[15] Scales have been developed and a variety of research studies have been conducted. It is not our intent here to get into that level of detail. This is an oversimplification, but for the moment let us define a high Machiavellian individual as one who is insincere and brings a hidden agenda to the table. When dealing with a high Machiavellian person, you do not take what he or she says at face value; rather, you search for the hidden and underlying meaning.

The political tactics you use in your organization may be either "high Mach" or "low Mach." Playing tennis with the boss may be a low Mach, normal human interaction. Letting him win may be higher on the Machiavellian scale. Marrying his daughter, not because you love her but because you want to inherit the business, would be considered a high Mach intervention. Later in the chapter we attempt to sort specific political tactics on the dimension of Machiavellianism as defined here.

Goal Orientation

Another component of political activity in organizations has to do with the goal orientation of the manager. Are you primarily organizationally oriented in your goals, or are you primarily self-oriented? While it may be argued that altruism is dead and that everything we do stems

---

[15] Richard Christie and Florence L. Geis, *Studies in Machiavellianism* (New York: Academic Press, 1970).

from basic unbridled self-interest, for the moment let us suppose that you have observed behavior in organizations on various levels of self-interest versus organizational interest. Figure 5-1 splits these two dimensions so that we can look at them separately. (In some of the technical definitions of Machiavellian behavior the self-interest aspect is also included, but for the moment let us view this in terms of goals and sincerity in personal interaction.)

As the diagram in Figure 5-1 shows, four alternative strategies can be followed in political situations.

• Cell 1—*Team player.* This individual is low on the Machiavellian scale and his goals are organizationally oriented. You can take him at face value. He tends to be cooperative rather than competitive, and he has the long-term interests of the organization at heart. Cell 1 is the area in which you should try to spend most of your time.

• Cell 2—*Good but dangerous.* This individual is oriented toward the organization's goals, but he uses insincerity, guile, and deceit in their pursuit. This person worries us. We are constantly concerned about the political and corporate leader who feels that he can step out of normal channels "just to get things done."

• Cell 3—*Unsavory.* This individual is self-oriented and high Machiavellian at the same time. He really doesn't have much to offer unless your interest and his accidentally coincide. We've all known someone who falls into this cell. We don't enjoy interacting with this person,

Figure 5-1. The interaction of goals and Machiavellianism.

Organization orientation	Good but dangerous	Team player
GOALS	2	1
	3	4
Self-orientation	Unsavory	Narcissistic
	High	Low

MACHIAVELLIANISM

and he probably doesn't have a good, long-term future should the organizational power realities change.

- Cell 4—*Narcissistic.* This individual is self-oriented and often doesn't take the time and energy to be duplicitous in his pursuit of individual goals. However, if his self-interest coincides with the organization's, he may be a productive individual contributor.

The bottom line is that you should try to spend as much time in cell 1 as possible. The world is not all unselfish, open, trusting, and candid, but it never hurts to have a reputation as a good, solid performer and a team player.

Political Tactics

Power is implemented in an organization in a variety of fascinating ways. In your political behavior, you must have not only a good plan, but also good tactical implementation. Look at Figure 5-2. The list was generated when practicing managers were asked to list "any political tactics you have found effective in your personal experience or observation." The tactics have been sorted into high, moderate, and low Machiavellianism categories, based on the perceived level of insincerity or duplicity involved. Does this list stimulate any creative political approaches in your job situation? How Machiavellian do you want to be? What specific political tactics would you like to implement?

POWER PRESCRIPTION

There is no one best way to utilize power. It varies from situation to situation, from person to person, and from time to time. People are most often ineffective in their use of power because they get into a power rut; they do not use a variety of power bases. No one power base works in every situation. Managers should be at ease with all six power bases and habitually using at least four of them. In addition, the act of empowering others results in long-term, positive employee relations and enhances the manager's power and influence. Power is *not* a limited commodity.

Each power interaction is unique. To diagnose its effectiveness, you must take into account the personality and needs of both the power-holder and the other person. Therefore, in order to identify areas of

(text continued on p. 101)

Figure 5-2. Political tactics list.

High Machiavellianism

1. "Stepping over dollars while saving pennies, only because the boss is watching the penny and has not even noticed the dollar. Not pointing out the dollar to the boss because he will not admit the dollar is important."

2. "A boss of mine [general manager at the location] had a beautiful, expensively remodeled office. He actually had the floor slanted slightly so he was higher than you if you were in his office in front of the desk."

3. "Before my new boss [years ago] arrived from Erie, Pennsylvania, I looked up a couple of neighborhoods in Erie on the map so I could say, 'Gee, I have friends in Erie, they live in . . .' "

4. "Passing rumors."

5. "Marrying another powerful person."

6. "Seen in others: playing in all the camps, i.e., private meetings with the owner's representative, the owner's number-one client, and the architect-engineer prior to group meeting; discussing strategy and decisions to be made at the group meeting."

7. "Not inviting the 'enemy' group to any meetings."

8. "Doing a demo that shows your ideas will work [even though the demo has no substance]."

9. "My boss sharing a condo with the CEO while he is in town instead of having him stay at a hotel. This way, he can circumvent the president of the company."

10. "Fixing the door-prize drawings at company functions."

11. "Placing yourself [time and location] to meet third-level manager and planting seeds of ideas for program you are developing [info power]."

12. "I always form a close friendship with the boss's secretary—take her to lunch, buy birthday or Christmas presents; the payoff is extraordinary."

13. "I go around my boss if the situation allows it owing to time restraint, expertise, emergencies, after-hours information transfer knowing that the boss goes home early."

14. "Certain subordinates follow to the letter directives from top-position people and then disregard directives from immediate superiors—thus, they don't have to do much work, but to the people who control their rewards, they look like they are doing a great job. In addition, when an immediate superior complains to top-position people, they [immediate superiors] are not believed; their subordinate has exerted some power over them."

Source: Executive MBA Class of 1989, Katz Graduate School of Business, University of Pittsburgh.

15. "Holding pre-meetings to agree on 'scripts' for meetings so that a prede-termined result will be the outcome of the official meeting."

16. "Portraying a total cooperative approach and letting your peers-competi-tors 'hang' themselves."

17. "Playing tennis with the boss and letting him win."

18. "Getting on the boss's wife's side early, any way you can."

19. "Feeding upper management egos: flattery, compliments."

20. "Working behind the scenes to determine where the boss's mind is on certain topics; including that as a possible solution or scenario."

Moderate Machiavellianism

1. "Not criticizing programs developed by others—no matter how bad they are."

2. "Adopting an air of pomposity or arrogance; name-dropping; inflating your experience; inflating your involvement with entrepreneurial ventures."

3. "When trying to slam a point home, I sometimes throw a couple of low, decisive expletives around, which cause the squeamish to back down."

4. "Using nonverbal gestures showing agreement to points being made at a meeting."

5. "Talking to boss's spouse."

6. "Planting 'seeds' at casual gatherings."

7. "Going over a person's head to solicit boss's support before a meeting."

8. "Giving tickets or gifts to secretaries or department heads."

9. "Providing information and strategies to people in a power position to im-plement—allowing them a chance to discuss it on their own."

10. "Waiting until appropriate or strategic time [usually when project or issue is about to fail] and then become leader. Many times it is a win/win for the individual."

11. "Aligning oneself with the *known* leaders or winners of organization."

12. "I may even use client to make things happen internally."

13. "Personal entertaining of potential allies."

14. "Using information selectively with those who do not ordinarily have ac-cess to it."

15. "Going to parties or events you normally wouldn't."

16. "Developing a chain of communications and networking around subordi-nates and supervisors to always check information from two or three sources."

17. "Providing a technical-oriented super continually with graphics on both important and unimportant issues."

18. "Lending use of recreational townhouse to supervisor."
19. "Fighting superiors' politically sensitive battles, taking 'bad guy' position in meetings, vocally supporting superior who is 'good guy.' "
20. "Lobbying before a meeting where important decision will be made."
21. "Involving others within a meeting, such as 'As Bill previously pointed out.' "
22. "When attending presentations, always asking questions of the presenter, especially if upper management is involved."
23. "I go to the annual company Christmas party and mingle with the big guys and dance with the right people, etc."
24. "Using company meetings to make yourself visible to senior management. Examples—gain control over A/US they need, or groups which provide the handouts, rooms, etc. Also asking good questions (safe ones!)."
25. "Name-dropping."
26. "Selectively releasing information to drive or motivate a decision—to lead the decision."
27. "A particular person has used his knowledge of wine to gain high position: the 'if he is knowledgeable about wine, he must be knowledgeable' syndrome."
28. "Keeping up on events that are of interest to those in power."
29. "Buying Girl Scout cookies from the boss's daughter."

Low Machiavellianism

1. "Generating leads to new clients, even though you may not be a marketing person."
2. "Networking—above and below."
3. "Running with the boss."
4. "Going to happy hour with the boss."
5. "Presenting and analyzing alternatives to a potential problem [to your boss] before it becomes an actual decision-making situation."
6. "Copying your boss on correspondence that you feel may generate a departmental issue."
7. "Offering to 'chair' the United Way Campaign."
8. "Taking a social-oriented supervisor golfing."
9. "Warning a superior of upcoming trouble owing to superior's poor decision when discovered."
10. "Remembering secretaries at Christmas and Secretary's Week to maintain a positive relationship—and expressing thanks for the 'extras.' "
11. "Involving as many people in discussion at a meeting as possible, to be sure issues don't surface after a meeting."

12. "Ending a meeting restating issues and conclusions to be sure of agreement or record."

13. "Always looking attentive when others are speaking."

14. "Volunteering for in-house charity drives, company picnic, quality circles, etc., that lead to direct meetings, reports, dialogue with senior managers at a personal level."

15. "MBWA on the executive level—delivering things yourself, not via your secretary or through the mail. Opportunity exists for personal communication if you go yourself."

16. "Attending various Sunday key events to keep myself visible, which is important to the political circuit."

---

your power behavior that need to be changed, answer the following specific questions:

- What power bases do I presently use? With whom?
- Whom do I empower? Whom do I seek to control?
- Which power situations make me feel good, bad, ugly?
- What power options do I most often overlook?

Figure 5-3. Sample Form 5-5.

POWER ASSESSMENT LOG

Complete this log by recording the type of power that you use when you interact with others.

Remember, there are six power bases: information, expertise, referent, authority, reward, and coercive.

Time	Target Person	Power Base	Feeling	Effectiveness	Other Option
9:10	Jeff	info.	good	OK	referent/expertise
10:00	Mary	referent	good	+	information
11:00	Dan	coercive	fair	+	?
11:20	Ralph	authority	OK	OK?	expertise

The Power Assessment Log (Form 5-5) is designed to help you answer these questions. Figure 5-3 shows how you might use it.

Keep a running record of how and why you use power. Record all your power interactions for a typical day. This log will be quite subjective, but it will raise your sensitivity to your daily use of power.

POWER ACTION PLAN

You've done the diagnosis. Now it's time for action! The Power Action Plan (Form 5-6) is included to help you start. After you become aware of your faulty power patterns, the key to behavior change is practice and risk taking. Since power behavior is an integral part of your whole leadership style, change your behavior in handleable amounts. You'll be asked to back up your requests (demands), to follow through on your threats, and to prove your expertise. But, go ahead. Try a new approach! Make the changes you want.

GOOD, BAD, UGLY POWER AUDIT

What is power doing to you? Circle the number for each item below that represents your best estimate.

The role of the powerholder has pluses and minuses. In the aftermath of a power confrontation, whether I "won" or "lost,"

	Never	Sometimes	Always
1. I feel I was firm and fair.	0 1 2	3 4 5 6 7	8 9 10
2. I believe I behaved with strength and integrity.	0 1 2	3 4 5 6 7	8 9 10
3. I feel I asserted myself.	0 1 2	3 4 5 6 7	8 9 10
4. I feel I both listened and was heard.	0 1 2	3 4 5 6 7	8 9 10

TOTAL _____ = G

5. I feel anxious and nervous.	0 1 2	3 4 5 6 7	8 9 10
6. I feel lonely and angry.	0 1 2	3 4 5 6 7	8 9 10
7. I feel unable to do my job well.	0 1 2	3 4 5 6 7	8 9 10
8. I am distressed by my lack of interpersonal skills.	0 1 2	3 4 5 6 7	8 9 10

TOTAL _____ = B

9. I feel righteous.	0 1 2	3 4 5 6 7	8 9 10
10. I feel sure of myself and my opinion.	0 1 2	3 4 5 6 7	8 9 10
11. I wonder about the incompetence of others.	0 1 2	3 4 5 6 7	8 9 10
12. I am sure there is more than one standard of measuring right and wrong. Sometimes, the end justifies the means.	0 1 2	3 4 5 6 7	8 9 10

TOTAL _____ = U

GOOD Effects	BAD Effects	UGLY Effects

Percentile Scores

Now compare your scores to a sample of 163 managers.

Percentile Score		Raw Score	
% of Individuals Scoring Lower	Good Effects	Bad Effects	Ugly Effects
100	42	30	38
90	35	21	30
80	33	18	27
70	31	15	25
60	31	13	24
50	29	11	22
40	28	10	21
30	27	9	20
20	26	7	19
10	24	5	16
0	16	1	5

SUBORDINATE POWER AUDIT

What is power doing to your subordinates? Circle the number for each item below that represents your best estimate.

When I talk with employees about unsatisfactory work behavior, it is most important to me that:

	Never			Sometimes				Always			
1. They know how to become more efficient.	0	1	2	3	4	5	6	7	8	9	10
2. They believe they can do better.	0	1	2	3	4	5	6	7	8	9	10
3. They know that trial and error are part of the job.	0	1	2	3	4	5	6	7	8	9	10
4. They think they can do more.	0	1	2	3	4	5	6	7	8	9	10
5. They have learned something new about the business.	0	1	2	3	4	5	6	7	8	9	10
6. They understand their value to the organization.	0	1	2	3	4	5	6	7	8	9	10

TOTAL _____ = Positive use

	Never			Sometimes				Always			
7. They realize that I am in charge.	0	1	2	3	4	5	6	7	8	9	10
8. They know what they did wrong.	0	1	2	3	4	5	6	7	8	9	10
9. They know to ask before making any errors.	0	1	2	3	4	5	6	7	8	9	10
10. They know the limits.	0	1	2	3	4	5	6	7	8	9	10
11. They realize they don't know everything.	0	1	2	3	4	5	6	7	8	9	10
12. They realize their job is on the line.	0	1	2	3	4	5	6	7	8	9	10

TOTAL _____ = Negative use

Percentile Scores

Now compare your scores to a sample of 163 managers.

Percentile Score	Raw Score	
% of Individuals Scoring Lower	Positive Use of Power (Empowerment of Subordinates)	Negative Use of Power (Subjugation of Subordinates)
100	61	59
90	52	42
80	49	38
70	48	35
60	47	32
50	45	30
40	43	28
30	41	26
20	39	23
10	36	18
0	24	17

SOURCES OF POWER AUDIT

Where do you get your power? Circle the number for each item below that represents your best estimate.

My role, experience, education, and personality are a part of how I do my job. When I attempt to influence others, they usually comply:

	Never	Sometimes	Always
1. Because they are convinced of the facts I present.	0 1 2	3 4 5 6 7	8 9 10
2. Because of my logical presentation.	0 1 2	3 4 5 6 7	8 9 10

TOTAL _____ = Information

3. Because of my experience.	0 1 2	3 4 5 6 7	8 9 10
4. Because of my education, my knowledge.	0 1 2	3 4 5 6 7	8 9 10

TOTAL _____ = Expertise

5. Because they like me.	0 1 2	3 4 5 6 7	8 9 10
6. Because they want to be cooperative.	0 1 2	3 4 5 6 7	8 9 10

TOTAL _____ = Referent

7. Because they respect my position, rank.	0 1 2	3 4 5 6 7	8 9 10
8. Because that is part of their job.	0 1 2	3 4 5 6 7	8 9 10

TOTAL _____ = Authority

9. Because they know they will be rewarded.	0 1 2	3 4 5 6 7	8 9 10
10. Because they know I recognize cooperation.	0 1 2	3 4 5 6 7	8 9 10

TOTAL _____ = Reward

11. Because they know I can punish them.	0 1 2	3 4 5 6 7	8 9 10
12. Because they know I will enforce my decisions.	0 1 2	3 4 5 6 7	8 9 10

TOTAL _____ = Coercive

FORM 5-3.

Percentile Scores
Now compare your score to a sample of 163 managers.

Percentile Score		Raw Score	
% of Individuals Scoring Lower	Information	Expertise	
100	18	18	
90	16	17	
80	15	16	
70	15	15	
60	15	15	
50	14	14	
40	14	13	
30	13	12	
20	13	11	
10	12	10	
0	10	5	

FORM 5-3.

Raw Score

Referent	Authority	Reward	Coercive
19	20	19	18
15	16	16	14
14	15	14	13
13	14	13	11
12	13	12	10
12	13	11	9
11	12	10	8
10	11	9	6
9	10	8	5
8	8	6	3
2	2	2	0

ORGANIZATIONAL POWER AUDIT

What is power doing to your organization? Circle the number for each item below that represents your best estimate.

Organizational characteristics paint a picture of power usage. In describing your organization to a colleague, what would you say about each of the following?

	Never		Sometimes			Always	

1. There is a lot of teamwork.   0 1 2 3 4 5 6 7 8 9 10
2. People share information.   0 1 2 3 4 5 6 7 8 9 10
3. Meetings are used efficiently.   0 1 2 3 4 5 6 7 8 9 10
4. People consult with others.   0 1 2 3 4 5 6 7 8 9 10

INFORMATION USAGE TOTAL = _____

5. There is someone able to "step into"
   every job.   0 1 2 3 4 5 6 7 8 9 10
6. Employees feel confident.   0 1 2 3 4 5 6 7 8 9 10
7. Employees use good judgment.   0 1 2 3 4 5 6 7 8 9 10
8. Employees respect their bosses' abili-
   ties.   0 1 2 3 4 5 6 7 8 9 10

EXPERTISE USAGE TOTAL = _____

9. Employees trust their bosses.   0 1 2 3 4 5 6 7 8 9 10
10. Harmony is evident in work groups.   0 1 2 3 4 5 6 7 8 9 10
11. Employees like their bosses.   0 1 2 3 4 5 6 7 8 9 10
12. Employees try to behave like their
    bosses.   0 1 2 3 4 5 6 7 8 9 10

REFERENT USAGE TOTAL = _____

13. Company policies are obeyed.   0 1 2 3 4 5 6 7 8 9 10
14. Lines of authority are clear.   0 1 2 3 4 5 6 7 8 9 10
15. Bosses use lots of authority.   0 1 2 3 4 5 6 7 8 9 10
16. Bosses are respected for their posi-
    tions.   0 1 2 3 4 5 6 7 8 9 10

AUTHORITY USAGE TOTAL = _____

	Never				Sometimes				Always		
17. People feel adequately appreciated.	0	1	2	3	4	5	6	7	8	9	10
18. Employees know that extra effort will be rewarded.	0	1	2	3	4	5	6	7	8	9	10
19. Pay is fair.	0	1	2	3	4	5	6	7	8	9	10
20. Outstanding performance is recognized.	0	1	2	3	4	5	6	7	8	9	10

REWARD USAGE TOTAL = _____

21. Discipline is strong.	0	1	2	3	4	5	6	7	8	9	10
22. Rules are strictly enforced.	0	1	2	3	4	5	6	7	8	9	10
23. Bosses are tough.	0	1	2	3	4	5	6	7	8	9	10
24. Substandard performance is punished.	0	1	2	3	4	5	6	7	8	9	10

COERCIVE USAGE TOTAL = _____

FORM 5-4.

Percentile Scores

Now compare your score to a sample of 163 managers.

Percentile Score		*Raw Score*	
% of Individuals Scoring Lower	**Information**	**Expertise**	
100	40	40	
90	32	31	
80	30	30	
70	28	28	
60	27	27	
50	26	26	
40	23	23	
30	20	22	
20	18	20	
10	16	17	
0	7	7	

Raw Score

Referent	Authority	Reward	Coercive
40	37	39	38
29	32	32	27
27	31	28	23
26	29	24	21
25	28	23	20
23	26	21	19
22	25	19	17
19	24	15	15
17	22	12	13
14	19	9	11
7	12	4	5

FORM 5-5.

POWER ASSESSMENT LOG

Time	Target Person	Power Base	Feeling	Effectiveness	Other Option

POWER ACTION PLAN

1. What are your power strengths?

_____

_____

_____

_____

_____

2. What are your power weaknesses?

_____

_____

_____

_____

_____

3. How could you make changes?

_____

_____

_____

_____

_____

4. Write down your specific action plan.

_____

_____

_____

_____

_____

Chapter 6

Behavior Modification

1:12 P.M. Harry takes another bite of the ham sandwich that has been lying on his desk. It tastes like cardboard. He hasn't been eating right, he reflects. There are quick breakfasts and hurried or high-calorie business lunches. Plus, he eats and drinks too much in the evening, all of which may be why he is 20 pounds overweight.

Harry remembers the form for a weight reduction plan handed out last week by a psychologist during a Rotary Club lecture on behavior modification. He finds the form in his desk and begins filling it out. The form tells him that he needs to eat only 15 calories per pound of his weight each day in order to survive. Thus, after some computations and reflection, Harry fills out the form as follows:

Weight Reduction Plan

Current behavior: 192 pounds.
Target behavior: 172 pounds in twenty weeks. Lose 1 pound per week. Eat 2,100 calories per day for twenty weeks, maintain at 2,500 per day thereafter.

Feedback system: Weigh self each morning. Calorie chart on bedroom wall. Carry pocket calorie counter.

Consequences or rewards: Reward = dinner out; punishment = no martinis.

Timing: If I hit target when weighed every Friday morning, dinner out that weekend; if not, no martinis for the weekend.

What is Harry doing? He is experimenting with a behavior change technique called behavior modification. This chapter shows you what it is and how you can use it to change yourself and others.

Do you have behaviors you would like to change? Eating? Drinking? Exercising? Arriving on time for meetings? Are there behaviors in others you would like to change? Do subordinates not complete call reports on time? Is absenteeism or quality control a problem in your organization? Do your kids have trouble keeping their rooms neat? These and many other problems are appropriate for using behavior-modification techniques.

THE LESSONS OF EMERY AIR FREIGHT

Emery Air Freight is a worldwide freight forwarder. It picks up your freight in its trucks, then delivers it to one of the airlines for transportation to another city. There, Emery picks it up again and delivers it to the final destination. To minimize expenses, company policy is to place small packages in large air-freight containers, which are then used by the airlines.

In 1971, Emery asked its managers what percentage of the time they were using containers in relation to the number of times they should be using containers. Their response: 95 percent.

Upper management then actually measured the percentage and discovered that the true answer was 45 percent! Using the standard managerial problem-solving approach, they then asked their managers to suggest ways to correct this performance deficiency. The suggestions ranged from "Give us more help" and "Pay a higher wage" to "Implement a supervisor's training program" and "Construct a new terminal."[1] Instead of following this expensive advice, Emery implemented a behavior-modification program. It asked each worker to complete a

---

[1] E. J. Feeney, "Practical Applications of Behavior Modification," in W. C. Byham and D. Bobin, eds., *Changing Employee Behavior*, proceedings of a November 1972 conference sponsored by the Graduate School of Business, University of Pittsburgh, November 1973.

simple checklist indicating each time a container was used and each time it could be used.

The result:

1. Container use rose from 45 percent to 90 percent.
2. The company saved $650,000 annually.
3. The program cost only $5,500.

Behavior modification works. Although it has been applied in industry in a major way only since the late 1970s, behavior modification has improved performance dramatically in a number of different situations. Some examples are:[2]

• A large manufacturing and distribution center wanted to reduce absenteeism. A lottery system was devised in which the employee was allowed to pick a card from a deck of playing cards each day he came to work on time. At the end of the five-day week, the employee in the group of twenty-five with the winning poker hand won $20. As a result, absenteeism dropped from 3.01 to 2.46 percent. When the procedure was stopped, absenteeism went back to its old level. When the procedure was reinstituted, absenteeism immediately dropped again to 2.46 percent.

• The Illinois State Employment Service in Jackson County started offering a reward for information on job openings that led to employment of one of the service's applicants. A $100 reward was offered to the provider of the information ($25 at hiring and $25 at the end of each week for three weeks). Ten times as many job leads were generated and eight times as many placements were accomplished. The average cost per placement was $130 using the reward procedure, as compared to $470 for the no-reward condition.

• An electronics company in Oceanside, California, implemented behavior-modification programs with the following results:
    Attendance: 3.1 percent improvement
    Engineering drawings completed correctly: 49 percent improvement
    Savings in purchasing: 11.5 percent improvement
    Profits: 25 percent over forecast

Though recent to industry, behavior modification is based on fifty years of behavioral research. Indeed, scientists have been studying its

[2]P. L. Brown and R. J. Presbie, *Behavior Modification in Business, Industry, and Government* (New Paltz, N.Y.: Behavior Improvements Associates, Inc., 1977).

underlying principles, the principles of operant conditioning, since the 1930s.

HOW BEHAVIOR MODIFICATION STARTED

The story that follows is apocryphal, but it points out two key developments in operant conditioning that are central to behavior modification.

In 1931, in a Harvard University laboratory, psychologist B. F. Skinner and his associates placed a hungry pigeon into a "Skinner box," a cage with a magazine controlled by the experimenters that could deliver food pellets into a feeding tray. The pigeon pecked around exploring its environment and finally pecked a circular white target on the side of the cage. At this point the experimenter delivered a food pellet into the feeding tray. The pigeon pecked some more and finally hit the target again, and again a food pellet was delivered. The puzzled pigeon looked around, then consumed the pellet and resumed its activity. In a very short time, the pigeon was regularly pecking at the target and eating the pellets.

To see what would happen, the researchers turned off the pellet magazine. As you would think, the pigeon kept pecking at the target for a day or two, but slowly stopped as it realized that the rewards—that is, the reinforcement—had been discontinued.

The researchers had thus discovered the first basic principle of motivation: Behaviors that are rewarded (reinforced) are repeated; behaviors that are not rewarded are not repeated.

PARTIAL REINFORCEMENT

One night the automatic magazine went haywire, and instead of receiving a pellet for each peck of the target, the poor pigeon received a pellet for only about 10 pecks plus or minus 5 on a random basis. The experimenters returned to the lab the next morning, and to their horror discovered what had happened. They decided that the pigeon had been ruined for their research and would have to unlearn this behavior. They put it in a cage where no pellet would be administered for pecking the target. To their surprise, the pigeon pecked the target 20,000 times before extinguishing its behavior.

The researchers had discovered the second basic principle of motivation: Behavior that is reinforced intermittently is more persistent than behavior that is reinforced continually.

Partial reinforcement occurs any time an organism is intermittently rewarded for a behavior. It produces tremendous strength of learning. In fact, pigeons can be trained using partial-reinforcement techniques to expend more calories in getting a reward pellet than are contained in the pellet itself. Thus, they would slowly disappear (starve) as the result of this behavior but nevertheless still persist in it.

Partial reinforcement explains many aspects of behavior characterized by tremendous persistence and repetition. For example:

- *Answering the telephone:* You're never sure who is on the other end. After all, it might be a reward.
- *Opening the mail:* You're not always sure what's in a letter. It might be good news.
- *Gambling:* Sure, the odds are against you. But you might get the big payoff.
- *Management:* Sometimes you get a pellet; sometimes you don't.

SHAPING

Researchers also discovered that they could train pigeons to perform very complicated tasks. A pigeon in the cage might move a few degrees to the right, and when the researcher administered a pellet, the pigeon would then engage in additional exploratory behavior and eventually move even farther in a circle to its right. As the researcher continued to administer pellets, in a short time the pigeon would be spinning in a complete circle. The concept of shaping of behavior was discovered.

The researchers found that by insisting on successive approximations to the desired behavior, they could teach pigeons to do amazing things: play Ping-Pong, play the national anthem on a xylophone, guide bombs to their targets, and perform a variety of other complex behaviors. In the acquisition of any new skill, a substantial amount of shaping must occur. We must link together a sequence of independent and rather simple behaviors.

The same holds true for people learning management skills. In order to learn the extremely complex set of behaviors that can be called good management, we must train ourselves or our subordinates to do little, simple pieces of the behavior that can be reinforced. Then we can put them together to make the fascinating and very complex whole.

The third basic motivational principle researchers discovered was: Extremely complex behaviors are made up of simple bits. Complexity can be achieved by reinforcing those simpler pieces and linking them together.

WE REPEAT REWARDED BEHAVIORS

A reward can be an extremely powerful change device. Witness the following:

During the year 1984, Wendy Penning, age 9, and Jerry Penning, age 10, watched absolutely no television. Their motivation to forgo an obvious pleasure of twentieth-century life was originally fueled by a monetary reward. This was later replaced by the desire to achieve an ambitious goal.

In December of 1983, my wife, Peggy, and I felt that our two children were watching too much television at the expense of their outside interests and school grades. With the input of Wendy and Jerry, Peggy, and me, it was decided that if both children would forgo the watching of any television during the calendar year 1984, they would each receive $200 in cash to be spent as they desired. The following rules were established:

1. The time period would run from January 1, 1984, through December 31, 1984.
2. This would be on a voluntary basis. Neither Wendy nor Jerry would be denied television viewing if they desired.
3. Each child was independent of the other. (If Jerry resumed watching, Wendy could continue not watching to earn her $200 on January 1, 1985.)
4. No television watching was allowed at friends' homes, stores, or school. If a school assignment required the watching of a program, alternate arrangements would be made with the teacher by one of the parents.
5. If television watching was resumed, the wager would become void and would not be offered again.
6. Both parents could continue watching television.[3]

The above shows that rewards, in the proper context, can be a very powerful behavior-modification device. If rewards are so powerful, it is even more important that they be administered appropriately. Often managers, when looking for one sort of behavior, reward inappropriate behaviors. For example, how unlikely are the following stories?

---

[3]Bruce E. Penning, personal communication, April 1988.

- *Vinegar pellet tastes good:* Jack Kulik is insubordinate to his boss. He is given a three-day suspension. He goes home, smiling to himself, thinking that he'll spend three days on the lake fishing.

- *Sirloin tastes bad:* Marty Grossman is rewarded for twenty years' outstanding performance as a star salesman. He is promoted to sales manager. He hates the new job and performs below par.

- *Misbehavior is encouraged:* "How can I get anything done if you keep changing your mind?" Albert Castiglione explains to the boss. "I've had it!" His boss is surprised and hurt. He immediately has a long talk with Albert and sets weekly meetings to clear the air. Albert smiles.

Perhaps these stories ring true for you. How often do we do this in management? For instance, how often do we provide reinforcement through time and energy to chronically complaining employees? How often do we truly reinforce productive behavior when we should?

As a manager, you must: (1) reward, (2) punish, or (3) ignore each behavior of your subordinates. If you punish Jack Kulik, make sure the punishment is not really a reward. If you reward Marty Grossman, make sure it's a reward to him. And, if Albert Castiglione is neurotic, make sure you don't encourage him.

Are you controlling behavior correctly? If you're having behavior problems in your organization, don't ask, "What causes it?" Ask, "What follows it?"

A psychologist friend of mine did not want his son to suffer the traditional traumas of toilet training, so when the child wet his bed during the night, his parents would change him and then give him a lollipop to show him that they were not angry or unhappy with him. This worked quite effectively until he was taken to the barber shop for his first haircut, and the barber gave him a lollipop! The moral here is that the consequences of a behavior are terribly important in predicting whether that behavior will occur again. If you reinforce a behavior, it is likely to reoccur. If you ignore it or punish it, it is less likely to reoccur.

ELEMENTS OF BEHAVIOR MODIFICATION

For behavior modification to work, there are five basic elements that must be managed successfully. They are described here, and then you will be given the opportunity to use them in an exercise at the end of the chapter.

Current Behavior

Current behavior is the existing behavior you are going to try to change. In describing it, you should be as specific and nonevaluative as possible. Suppose, for example, you have a subordinate who is causing problems. You might describe his behavior in incorrect or correct ways.

Incorrect

- Bad attitude
- Aggressive
- Disruptive

Correct

- Failed to complete a maintenance report on time
- Asks, "Why should I?" in a humorous but aggressive way when given an assignment
- Distracts other workers from their jobs by arguing politics

Current behavior should be described in a quantifiable and specific fashion. Most often this behavior is measured in terms of frequency of responses (e.g., number of sales calls per day; number of units per week of good-quality parts produced; number of orders booked per month). If you want to lose weight, for example, describe your current behavior in terms of your present weight and present calorie consumption.

Target Behavior

Target behavior is the behavior you would like to achieve. It should also be expressed in specific and quantifiable terms. Do you want to lose ten pounds? Reduce absenteeism by 20 percent? Improve profits by 10 percent? Run eight miles per week? How much exactly will you call successful?

Feedback System

The feedback system is the most essential element of the behavior-modification approach because it tells you when to administer rewards.

A simple, self-administered feedback system must be developed. It must indicate progress from the current behavior toward the target behavior. If the feedback system is too complex or too time-consuming, it probably will not be maintained.

Consequences and Rewards

The consequences or rewards are what happens if the target is met or not met. You should spell out explicitly—including quantity, type, and timing—what the "pellets" are and how they will be given. For example, if absenteeism is reduced by 20 percent, will a 5 percent raise be given? How will it be administered? What will happen if absentee levels start to creep up again?

Most of us find rewards in a variety of elements in our environment. When practicing managers are asked to brainstorm a list of potential rewards, they can usually come up with 50 to 100 different rewards without much difficulty. Elements such as praise, recognition, advancement, modified work schedules, and rescheduled breaks are only a few.

Timing

The final step is to tie the reward to the performance in a timely manner, to decide when the reward is to be given. Since much of behavior modification is based on immediate reward, timing the reward may require special effort. A delayed reward is an ineffective reward. In his weight loss program, Harry is going to reward himself by dining out once a week if he has achieved his target for that week.

THE MANAGER AS THE GREAT REINFORCER

Over the years, managers have become stereotyped as "The Great Punishers." This is not surprising. In the Pittsburgh steel industry at the turn of the century, the blue-collar worker labored twelve hours a day, six days a week in return for a wage of two dollars or less a day. It's no wonder that managers were characterized as tough and coercive. They could easily punish the workers at a time when the loss of a job resulted in great suffering for the worker and his family. In today's world, things have changed dramatically. The manager no longer has the same capability to punish; he must rely on reinforcers. These reinforcers are different, as well. Most workers are substantially above subsistence level, and the traditional rewards that managers used in the past, such as praise and perks, may not be as effective. Your job is to seek out those reinforcers that work and apply them on a regular daily, or even hourly basis. This takes work! It requires sensitivity and energy.

It is hard work to praise and reinforce desired behavior. It is hard work to be constantly aware of which behaviors should be reinforced and which behaviors should not, but this is the essence of the management task from the perspective of behavior modification. You are a combination of cheerleader and football coach. It is your job to make sure the employees are enthusiastic about their work, feel a sense of fairness, and know they will be rewarded when they do well. There are no simple solutions to this problem. However, understanding the issues and making reinforcement a high managerial priority is the essential first step.

BEHAVIOR MODIFICATION AND JOB ENRICHMENT

Job enrichment has been a powerful device for improving performance for the past dozen-plus years. Why? Because job enrichment links reinforcers to specific behaviors. By redesigning a job to include more responsibility, achievement, recognition, and meaningful work, the manager automatically ties these rewards to performance of the job. In other words, the key task in job enrichment is to tell the manager what "pellets" are tasty for the employee and what techniques will automatically tie them to the job itself. In cases where job enrichment does not work, where behavior modification fails, the pellet usually is just not tasty enough; the reinforcer is inappropriate. For example, sometimes employees don't want increased responsibility, recognition, or whatever.

THE TROUBLE WITH PERFORMANCE APPRAISAL AS A BEHAVIOR MODIFIER

The most commonly used pellet system in management is performance appraisal, but it is also one of the most ineffective systems in the managerial behavior-modification kit. Performance-appraisal systems can be compared to the problem of getting a rat to walk from one corner of a room to another on a relatively narrow and well-defined path. Two approaches are possible. The operant-conditioning approach uses a handful of small pellets and a small stick. When the rat moves in the right direction, the researcher administers reinforcers (pellets) to the rat. When the rat deviates from the path, he is punished slightly with a light tap of the stick. The performance-appraisal approach in management uses a giant pellet placed at the end of the room and a baseball bat. The "rat" gets his pellet only after he has accomplished the entire task. If he deviates a large amount from the path, he is clobbered with the bat! This is why performance appraisal does not work for behavior change and day-to-day coaching does. This is detailed further in Chapter 7.

APPLYING BEHAVIOR MODIFICATION

Behavior modification works! It is an excellent managerial as well as personal-development tool. It can help you be more effective both as a manager and as a person. The first step in using behavior modification is to select areas in which you want improvement. Consider the following possibilities:

Personal Goals

☐ Lose weight

☐ Initiate exercise program

☐ Stop smoking

☐ Better schedule leisure time

☐ Arrive on time for commitments

☐ Spend more time planning on the job

☐ Other _____

Family Goals

☐ Have fewer arguments

☐ Spend less money

☐ Improve neatness

☐ Develop better study habits

☐ Eat better diet

☐ Get more exercise

☐ Other _____

Goals for Subordinates

· ☐ Reduce absenteeism

☐ Reduce turnover

☐ Improve product quality

☐ Reduce costs

☐ Submit reports on time

☐ Reach performance goals

☐ Accept more delegated matters

☐ Take more initiative

☐ Develop telephone manners

☐ Other _____

When implementing your behavior-modification program, keep the following three principles in mind:

1. *Quantify behavior.* Even if you have to estimate some items, you are better off using quantified numerical judgments than qualitative ones. You can do this in a number of areas that don't appear to be easy to measure. For example, if one of your goals is to "feel better about my job," stop and analyze more specifically what you mean by that. Do you mean you want to make more money? How much? Do you need more vacation time? How much time? Do you need to improve your performance? In precisely what way? What is it you need to "feel better?"

2. *Use self-feedback.* Most successful behavior-modification applications have the target employees themselves completing the feedback forms.

This is because of the powerful effect that information has on people. Most of us don't know what it is we do, therefore we don't know how to change it.

3. *Keep feedback simple*. The simpler the feedback system, the easier it is to understand and the more likely it is to be completed.

Now take one or more of the goals you've selected and specify your Behavior Modification Action Plan (Form 6-1).

BEHAVIOR MODIFICATION ACTION PLAN

Select some area of your behavior that you would like to modify and specify the details of your behavior-modification plan.

Definitions

1. *Current behavior* is the existing level of behavior being experienced. This should be quantitatively measurable.
2. *Target behavior* is the new level of behavior you would like to reach. This also should be quantitatively measurable.
3. *Feedback system* is the precise way in which you will provide feedback concerning performance.
4. *Consequences or rewards* are the positive reinforcements you will use when achieving progress toward the target.
5. *Timing* indicates when rewards will be given.

Action Plan

Indicate in as specific a manner as possible the details of the five elements of your action plan and any additional information.

1. Current behavior: _____

   _____

   _____

2. Target behavior: _____

   _____

   _____ By (date): _____

3. Feedback system: _____

   _____

   _____

4. Consequences or rewards: _____

   _____

   _____

5. Timing: _____

Chapter 7

Management by Objectives

1:32 P.M. Harry meets with Henry Carothers to go over the performance appraisal shown in Figure 7-1. "Henry," begins Harry, "as you know, we are already late with this and I need your signature to send it on to personnel. We really don't have time to do it justice today. However, you are generally doing well; there are only a couple of areas where I would like to see you show some improvement." Harry straightens papers on his already neat desk and looks anywhere but at Henry.

"I see," reacts Carothers, "you don't think much of my leadership style." The performance-appraisal form is getting wrinkled by Henry's tight grasp.

"Well, delegation is a bit of a problem for you, I think," Harry continues. "You seem to get too wrapped up in the day-to-day details. I've been noticing your assistant, Don. He seems to be coming along very well. Why don't you use him more?"

"Actually, I had been doing that, Harry, but just last Monday you accused me of overdelegating and made me pull the Fleming project away from Don."

Figure 7-1. Example of an annual performance appraisal.

For _H. Carothers_ Completed by _H. Thorpe_

Position _Sales Manager_ Date _3-31-92_

	Unsatisfactory	Should Improve	Adequate	Very Good	Outstanding
Cooperativeness	1	2	3	(4)	5
Integrity	1	2	3	4	(5)
Leadership	1	(2)	3	4	5
Planning	1	2	(3)	4	5
Dependability	1	2	3	(4)	5
Initiative	1	2	3	(4)	5
Assertiveness	1	(2)	3	4	5
Delegation	1	(2)	3	4	5
Time management	1	2	3	4	(5)

Signature _Henry J. Carothers_ Signature _Harry M. Thorpe_

"I believe that you abdicated more than delegated [see Chapter 9] on that one, and I think I said so at the time," says Harry, "but I guess I can see how you might claim mixed messages. Also, you're not asser-tive enough. Sometimes, in meetings, you don't take the ball and run with it, especially if someone is strongly opposing you."

"Yeah, I've been thinking about enrolling in a karate class. Do you think that will help?" says Henry sarcastically.

"Look, Carothers, we're spending this time for your own good. If you don't want to improve, just say so." By now Harry is sitting up very straight in his chair and his head is pounding.

"All right, what about my leadership style? What's wrong with that?"

"Henry, sometimes I feel that you just let things happen to you rather than plan for them," indicates Harry.

"Can you be specific?" asks Henry.

"Well, that national sales meeting comes to mind. Some decisions did not get made on time for that; do you remember?"

"Yes," growls Carothers, "I did get a bit overwhelmed by that one, but it was nine months ago. I think I've improved a lot since then. . . ."

And on they go, not hearing one another, getting more and more angry, defensive, and hostile. Harry wants to get through this annual requirement and Henry doesn't want these ratings to be put into his permanent record.

Carothers is upset, defensive, and threatened. Harry Thorpe is ill at ease and uncomfortable. Jointly, they are discovering what most of you probably already know.

Performance appraisal does not work as a behavior change device.

Traditionally, performance appraisal has a variety of purposes; it is used by managers to make several decisions. It works reasonably well in some areas but is a colossal failure in others. A "report card" for performance appraisal, in general, is shown in Table 7-1.

Performance appraisal may work well for record keeping, but it is ineffective as a behavior change mechanism. Performance appraisal is fraught with problems such as the following, identified by twenty-five personnel executives:[1]

- Conflicting multiple uses
- Ratings biased by pay considerations
- Unclear goals of the system
- No conceptual justification for the system
- Lack of clear performance criteria
- No validation of appraisal system
- Absolute versus relative standards of performance
- Personality versus performance ratings

Table 7-1. *Performance-appraisal use and effectiveness.*

Use	Effectiveness
Promotion	Fair
Salary decision	High
Diagnosing developmental needs	Fair
Manpower planning	Fair
Performance improvement	Poor
Motivation	Poor
Goal setting	Poor

[1]Robert I. Lazer and Walter S. Wickstrom, *Appraising Managerial Performance: Current Practices and Future Directions,* a research report from the Conference Board's Discussions of Management Research, © 1977. Used with permission.

- Separation of potential from performance on the appraisal
- "Halo" persistence in ratings
- Managers' dislike of giving feedback
- One-way communication between superior and subordinate
- Rater biases
- Nonfunctional forms—that is, forms designed for one purpose and used for another
- No developmental or performance follow-up
- Susceptibility to manipulation by managers
- No built-in reinforcement for doing the appraisal
- Use by managers not trained to administer
- Conflicting coach and evaluator roles
- Punishment process for all concerned
- Not used for top management
- No credibility in the organization
- An administrative chore not related to business goals
- No impact on performance

PERFORMANCE APPRAISAL: WHY DOESN'T IT ACHIEVE ALL ITS OBJECTIVES?

When managers talk about performance appraisal, they always seem to focus on the performance feedback and performance improvements aspects of the process. One study found that performance improvement was a third-ranking objective and performance feedback was the number-one-ranking use of the appraisal information. However, the traditional performance appraisal is particularly ineffective at changing employee behavior for a variety of reasons.

It Comes Too Late

What happens if you wait five seconds between the moment when the pigeon in the Skinner box pecks the target and the moment when the reward is administered? That's right! Absolutely no learning for the pigeon. While humans, obviously, are not pigeons, we learn more easily and more thoroughly when reinforcers or punishers follow closely the behavior that triggers them. People can understand the relationship between past behavior and current rewards or punishments, but it is very difficult to get an employee excited about changing an action that may have occurred up to twelve months earlier. One secret to promoting learning is to immediately administer the reinforcers and punishers.

Some years ago, when times were quite different, I visited Haiti. Purchasing a four-dollar mahogany piece of artwork in the marketplace necessitated my using a ten-dollar bill. "I'll get change," quipped a young man and disappeared into the crowd. I wrote off the six dollars change, since it represented about a week's wages at that time. I was surprised when, after 5 minutes, the young fellow returned and counted out six wrinkled dollar bills. I commented on the lack of fighting and stealing in Port-au-Prince.

"Oh, no," he said, "there is no fighting or stealing here." In response to my "why?" he very seriously replied, "If you steal, the police take you to the police station and kill you." The consequences of this undesirable behavior were immediate and decisive. And not very appealing.

One of the criticisms of the criminal justice system in this country is the terrible time lag between crime and punishment. Applications of learning theory are absent in our penal system. Your performance appraisal may be having the same effect. If you want someone to be more assertive, tell him in day-to-day coaching. "Henry, if you had been more assertive, stood up to Tom during the planning meeting, this whole project could have been handled there and we would not be redoing this report. You had all the data at your fingertips. All you had to do was cite it." Henry can understand what happened and how to prevent it in the future, and he won't be so defensive about feedback. This brings us to the second reason performance appraisals don't work for behavior change.

People Get Defensive

When you criticize people about some basic aspect of their personality or denigrate a fundamental work behavior, they become defensive. In a classic study at General Electric, observers sat in on performance appraisals and noted reactions. The majority of criticisms were met with defensive reactions; less than 10 percent of the critical statements were met with constructive responses. When people are told that they are not good enough, their first reaction is to protect themselves. Feedback, although necessary for survival, must be given in ways that receivers can assimilate. If you are told that you have a problem with planning, leadership, assertiveness, or any other general trait, you will become defensive. Your basic self-concept, your sense of self-worth, is threatened. And you defend yourself. It is difficult to see yourself as a 3 (or even a 6) on a 10-point scale. When accused of being inferior, you seek to describe your intent, to justify your existence, to demonstrate that you are a good person.

A record of all the things we are not, a listing of all the ways we do not measure up (and often, much of this is new information, virgin territory), is not conducive to an open, receptive response. Rarely is the performance appraisal the snapshot it is supposed to be. Too often it is instead used as a recital of all the "bad" things the employee has done in the past year that the manager did not mention at the time. This style of recital makes the employee feel naked, unprotected, afraid, and consequently, defensive.

You must accept the fact that if you conduct the usual performance appraisal, if you provide criticism in the traditional appraisal format, you are virtually guaranteed a defensive subordinate.

It Is Not Specific

Most traditional performance-appraisal forms focus on the "global aspects" of human behavior. Typical terms include dependability, assertiveness, leadership, intelligence, cooperation, initiative, and friendliness. These concepts can correspond to any of a variety of behaviors. Assessing these qualities is usually done in terms that are much too vague to be of any help to an individual attempting to change.

"You're not assertive" is very little help to a subordinate. "You did not stick up for one position in the ten o'clock meeting" has more impact. A good football coach doesn't stop with "You played a lousy game at right tackle." He goes on to say, "Every time we did a sweep to the right, you blocked your man to the outside. You know very well the purpose of the sweep is to allow the runner free running space and you are supposed to block to the inside. Work on it."

When feedback is directed toward specific behaviors, it becomes useful. When behaviors are described rather than given an evaluative label, corrective action can be taken. If you are in the habit of giving performance appraisals that emphasize global dimensions, your subordinate is not likely to change.

TWO POSSIBLE SOLUTIONS

Now that the traditional appraisal process has been soundly criticized as a means of changing behavior, what does work? It's very simple: Use day-to-day coaching, and modify the traditional appraisal into Management by Objectives.

Coaching

Much has been written about this issue and most managers have a good idea of what this concept entails. We each have experienced good coaches and bad coaches, either in our career or in some sports activity. Even so, coaching is one of the least used management tools. Managers seem to be afraid of criticizing the work of their subordinates and are hesitant to comment on good performance. Effective coaching is somewhat informal and is constantly practiced. It results in better relations between worker and supervisor, and increases the likelihood of satisfactory job performance. Effective coaching begins with the belief that subordinates want to do the job correctly, and when they do things wrong, it is usually due to a lack of knowledge or understanding. The goal of coaching, then, is to inform the employee of the most effective way of doing the job. Here is a list of effective coaching rules that a manager should follow on a daily basis:

1. *Observe* employee behavior. This takes energy and insight. What is going on around you?
2. *Evaluate* employee behavior. Is it good or bad? How good? How bad? Management is a job of evaluation.
3. *Analyze* employee behavior. Why did he do it this way? Could he do it right if his life depended on it? "Yes" indicates a motivational problem. "No" indicates a training or ability problem.
4. *Feed back* useful information to the employee. Be specific. Explain carefully in what ways he is doing the wrong thing. Carefully show the desired behavior, step by step. Give both positive and negative feedback—negative in private, positive in public.

Remember, a good coach has energy, compassion, intelligence, and warmth. It's a lot of work, but the payoff is more effective long-run employee performance.

Management by Objectives

This term—Management by Objectives (MBO)—was coined by Peter Drucker in 1957, and in the past thirty years it has been tried in virtually

Figure 7-2. The steps of MBO.

1. Objectives setting: annually
2. Progress review: quarterly
3. Accomplishment report: annually

every major corporation in this country. It has probably failed many more times than it has succeeded, but I feel that most of those failures can be accounted for by the lack of commitment and implementation energy on the part of organizations. It is a behaviorally sound system because it does not have the same deficiencies that have been listed concerning traditional performance appraisal. MBO works because:

- *It is not too late.* Progress reviews are held quarterly or more often if necessary.
- *It does not create defensiveness.* MBO is future oriented and participative, and less likely to create defensiveness.
- *It is not nonspecific.* Good objectives are specific and to the point.

MBO is useful because its steps (see Figure 7-2) provide a map to help navigate the confusing waters of any organization. It also provides motivation. How many times have you felt good when you set a specific goal and met it?

OBJECTIVES SETTING

The success of the MBO program rests upon appropriate objectives setting. Since the objectives serve as the foundation for all following steps, they are crucial. If the program is to be successful, three factors are essential in establishing the objectives: (1) participation, (2) good objectives, and (3) organizational commitment.

Participation

The most successful MBO systems are characterized by participation between the subordinate and the manager. A typical sequence that might be followed in the objectives-setting stage is as follows:

1. *General target meeting—one hour.* Supervisor meets with all his subordinates, either individually or in a group. The group process is usually preferred as the mechanism to discuss general goals of the subunit. Key performance areas are highlighted, but specific objectives are not yet formulated.

2. *Subordinates formulate objectives—two hours.* Subordinates identify their individual objectives, write them down, and submit them to the supervisor. These twelve-month goals should be as specific as possible.

3. *Supervisor reviews objectives—one hour.* Supervisor reviews all individual objectives, making sure they are in line with his own objectives and those of the organization. Adjustments may be necessary to coordinate all subordinates' objectives.

4. *Joint objective setting—one hour.* The supervisor and each subordinate decide together on the individual's objectives for the coming year. The choice of objectives is supplemented by specifics of how the supervisor and subordinate can work together to achieve them.

Good Objectives

As you formulate your objectives, keep the traits of good objectives in mind.

1. *They are on target.* The objective should be in tune with the organization as a whole and the subunit in particular. Examples for a manufacturing organization that is phasing out a product follow:
   • On target—Learn technology for new product X38.
   • Off target—Take college course on technological diffusion.

2. *They are clear.* The objective must be easily understood, be unambiguous, and be concise. It is not stated in jargon and does not use ''in'' expressions. Examples follow:
   • Clear—Be able to produce up to standard on new machine within two months.
   • Unclear—Determine and specify the maximal approach to adaptation to the new technology.

3. *They are measurable.* Objectives should be quantifiable—they should contain numbers. They should clearly indicate how to determine if they have been reached. Examples might include:

- Measurable—To reduce absenteeism by 15 percent over the next twelve months.
- Unmeasurable—To defuse the hostility of the work force.

4. *They are time bound.* Objectives have specific dates for completion; they specify time parameters. Examples are numerous:
   - Timed—To increase sales by 20 percent during twelve months ending August 1.
   - Untimed—To increase sales by 20 percent.

5. *They are challenging.* Objectives should make the employee stretch and grow. They should not be either too easy to achieve or so difficult there is little chance of success. Again, examples are everywhere:
   - Challenging—To reduce scrap by 40 percent.
   - Not challenging—To reduce scrap by 4 percent.
   - Too challenging—To reduce scrap by 94 percent.

Commitment

The organization must be committed to the goals of Management by Objectives. It is true that MBO has failed. It gets lost in massive paper shuffling, in canceled meetings, and in poor objectives setting. But the primary reason it does not work is lack of commitment. Managers are often unwilling to invest the necessary time. They are often more interested in short-term results. MBO takes time, energy, thought, reasoning, teaching, revamping, and perseverance. It is a system that has a fair amount of up-front cost (time and effort), but one that emphasizes staff development and has long-term payoffs. Each organization must modify the "pure" MBO model to fit its unique characteristics and employees.

Managers are easily impatient for this "panacea" to do its thing and cure all the organization's ills. Consequently, inappropriate objectives are established, fantastic numbers of goals are set for the subunit, and little time is given to learning the system. Research has demonstrated that people have the perceptual ability to hold seven (plus or minus two) items in short-term memory. If you have a list of eighteen objectives you are planning to accomplish, it is unlikely that you will use the system to its best advantage. Whether or not your total organization uses MBO, you can use it for yourself and your subordinates. But first, you must learn the system.

LEARNING THE SYSTEM

To use MBO effectively, a manager must understand the basic system. During this section, refer frequently to the Management by Objectives System (Form 7-1). To get you started, look at the flowchart shown in Figure 7-3.[2]

Objectives Setting

Objectives are set in the following four categories:

1. *Routine:* Repetitive tasks
2. *Problem solving:* Definitions and solutions to major problems
3. *Innovative:* Creative and unusual solutions
4. *Personal:* Self-development goals

During the joint objectives-setting meeting, it is important for the manager to realize that his role is one of expert and advisor as well as boss. As you make sure the objectives are on target, also be aware of the coaching or developmental needs of your subordinate. You know the ropes. You can help him to learn them, too. If you set good objectives, you'll have a motivated subordinate and be moving toward personal and organizational effectiveness.

Progress Review

The progress review is held to:

1. Measure progress
2. Modify objectives
3. Add new objectives

The quarterly progress review is just what it says. It is held quarterly. It is not to be dreaded. It is to be conducted as a more formal coaching session. Use the agreed-upon objectives as the guide and examine the progress made toward each goal. This is the time to adjust goals up-

---

[2]Dennis P. Slevin and William T. Wolz, "Breakthrough in MBO: Computer Augmentation," unpublished working paper #47, Graduate School of Business, University of Pittsburgh, May 1973.

Figure 7-3. Management by Objectives system.

Objectives Setting	Progress Review	Accomplishment Report
1. Routine 2. Problem solving 3. Innovative 4. Personal	1. Measure progress 2. Modify objectives 3. Add new objectives	1. Evaluate accomplishments 2. Establish basis for new objectives
Annually	Quarterly	Annually

1. OBJECTIVES SETTING (Annually)

   a. Subordinate completes Objectives-Setting Form and Action Plans (Form 7-1) for each objective.

   b. Supervisor and subordinate review objectives, negotiate; both agree on final objectives and sign the first page of the Objectives-Setting Form.

2. PROGRESS REVIEW (Quarterly)

   a. Subordinate and supervisor complete the Progress Review Form for each objective (100% = on target for that quarter).

   b. Subordinate and supervisor review progress, determine overall percentage of accomplishment, and sign last page of the Progress Review Form.

3. ACCOMPLISHMENT REPORT (Annually)

   a. Subordinate and supervisor evaluate percentage of accomplishment for each objective on Accomplishment Report Form.

   b. They discuss success or failure.

   c. They determine overall percentage of accomplishment for the year.

   d. Subordinate and supervisor establish basis for new objectives.

ward or downward. Circumstances often change during the course of a year; it is disheartening to come to the end of the year and find that you haven't met any of your goals. Change the objectives so they stay within reach. It is also important at this meeting for the manager to ask whether he is doing all he can to help each employee meet his goals. The setting of these objectives was a joint endeavor; the meeting of them should mean as much to both parties, too.

Accomplishment Report

The accomplishment report is intended to:

1. Evaluate accomplishments
2. Establish the basis for new objectives

This replaces the traditional performance appraisal. In the accomplishment interview, employees meet individually with the boss, do an analysis of their accomplishments, and use their progress to set the basis for the objectives for the next year.

The annual accomplishment report looks at and records accomplishment. Obviously, if the goal was 50 percent met, it was also 50 percent unmet, but the emphasis is on what was completed! A percentage of accomplishment is an appropriate measure given our earlier discussion on measurability, specificity, and the like. The reasons for success and failure should be examined along with their implications. A formal report should be prepared and kept in the employee's file. The annual report is also the time for establishing the basis for the objectives for the coming year.

In many ways, MBO is a "formal" way of doing what you already do. It forces you and your subordinates to be specific, to write down goals, to modify those goals, and to track accomplishments. Most importantly, MBO is a communications device. The communications you thought were so clear are even clearer with MBO.

The Management by Objectives System (Form 7-1) is suggested as an effective method of recording the various steps in the process. It is designed to be used as a work sheet, not as a piece of artwork. Experiment, work with it!

MBO AND COMPENSATION

We pay people based on performance. Right?
    Right!

Therefore, we should discuss pay raises in the accomplishment-report session. Right?

Wrong!

MBO should be tied to pay and promotions but not during the accomplishment report. If you bring up pay at this point, you dramatically up the stakes. Emotions run high. Defensiveness increases.

Objective evaluation and goal setting happen best in a climate of openness, trust, and mutual problem solving. Therefore, while the accomplishment report is the input to the compensation-promotion decision, the two issues are dealt with in separate meetings. A meeting to discuss compensation is most productive six to eight weeks after the accomplishment-report session.

A PERSONAL NOTE FOR YOU

There they were—bright-eyed, bushy-tailed recruits ready for the new job. They had been selected, all 274 of them, by the Bell System of A.T.& T. They had been through an assessment center (see assessment-center description, page 145), the results of which had been kept totally confidential.

Here they are again, eight years later. They have gone from an average age of 22 to one of 30 years. They have worked for eight years in a managerial position. How have these leaders of industry changed? You guess.

Did they go up, down, or stay the same on the measured dimensions of intellectual ability, administrative skills, interpersonal skills, and overall management ability? After these years of leadership experience, retesting showed the following results. Intellectual skills were up, administrative skills stayed the same, interpersonal skills went down, and overall managerial skills remained the same.

How did you do? Very few people respond correctly on all four issues. Are you surprised?

We could talk at length about the causes of this phenomenon, but for our purposes the significance is, gratefully, that we do seem to get brighter! Sadly, we lose some of our relationship skills! And importantly for the manager, we don't get better at the job with just experience.

MBO provides a usable method for coordinating subordinate growth and development. What about yourself? Are you learning? How? As you move through your career, are you improving your technical and managerial skills? Are you attending seminars, workshops, executive training? Have you set personal objectives for improvement? One of the serious handicaps of the managerial role is a lack of feedback, of collegial stimulation, of someone's expecting you to continue to grow. Your growth and development are left up to you. But setting personal objectives for both self-actualization and skill enhancement is essential to your effectiveness and to your mental health. You also need a plan for growth—an Agenda for Learning (Form 7-2).

THE ASSESSMENT CENTER

As a practicing manager, you may encounter an assessment center (see Figure 7-4), either directly or indirectly, over the next several years. Hence you should know something about it. First, the assessment center is misnamed. It is not a place; it is a process. The assessment center is a process whereby participants engage in simulated managerial behaviors while being watched by trained observers. Second, a fundamental assumption of this technique is that the best predictor of future human behavior is past human behavior. Thus, if we can observe managers in simulated situations, perhaps we can judge how they will behave in real situations. We do it with airline pilots, why not with managers? Third, the assessment center has been shown through careful research to be a good device for evaluating managerial potential. Like all behavioral devices, it has its inaccuracies, but it gives the user insight into the candidate's overall potential and specific capabilities, or typically ten to fifteen behavioral dimensions. (These dimensions are listed in detail in Chapter 13, Staffing.) Fourth, you should know something about the assessment center because you may need to use its results in your staffing decisions. Figure 7-4 provides you with quick insight into a typical assessment center.

CONCLUSION

We have discussed a number of issues in this chapter; certain strong principles emerge:

- Traditional performance-appraisal systems do not change behavior.
- Day-to-day coaching is essential for good managerial performance.
- Management by Objectives (MBO) is a workable approach to both subordinate and self-growth.
- An Agenda for Learning is necessary for continuous improvement in management skills.

Figure 7-4. A typical assessment center.

PLACE: Hotel or conference center

LENGTH: 2½ days for participants
            5 days for observers

PEOPLE INVOLVED: 1 administrator
                        12 participants
                        6 observers

ACTIVITIES: Small-group simulations
                Background interviews
                In-basket activities
                Leaderless group discussions
                Oral presentations

INTENT: To identify management potential

PROCESS: Participants engage in management simulations; observers
             record behavior and make evaluations

OUTCOME: Comprehensive report on each candidate, giving
             quantitative scores on about 12 typical dimensions of
             managerial behavior—e.g., leadership, planning,
             organizing, and communication skills

COSTS: Variable

BOTTOM LINE: Probably the *best* device available for assessing
                 managerial potential

MBO has been given an aura of mysticism. It seems to have definite rules; if you violate them, you cause the whole system to self-destruct. Such is not the case. MBO is just good, logical, sound managerial thinking. Try it. Modify it. Make it work for you!

MANAGEMENT BY OBJECTIVES SYSTEM

Objectives-Setting Form (Annually)

Subordinate _____   Date _____

Supervisor _____   Date _____

ROUTINE Objectives (Repetitive tasks)   DATE

    R1 _____   _____

    R2 _____   _____

    R3 _____   _____

    R4 _____   _____

    R5 _____   _____

PROBLEM-SOLVING Objectives (Definitions of and solutions to major problems)

    PS1 _____   _____

    PS2 _____   _____

    PS3 _____   _____

    PS4 _____   _____

    PS5 _____   _____

INNOVATIVE Objectives (Creative and unusual solutions)

    I1 _____   _____

    I2 _____   _____

    I3 _____   _____

    I4 _____   _____

    I5 _____   _____

FORM 7-1.

PERSONAL Objectives (Self-development goals)

P1 ————————————————————————— ————

P2 ————————————————————————— ————

P3 ————————————————————————— ————

P4 ————————————————————————— ————

P5 ————————————————————————— ————

Action Plans
(Specific Action Steps for Each Objective)

For ROUTINE Objectives	Action Plans	Date
	1. _____	_____
R1	2. _____	_____
	3. _____	_____
	1. _____	_____
R2	2. _____	_____
	3. _____	_____
	1. _____	_____
R3	2. _____	_____
	3. _____	_____
	1. _____	_____
R4	2. _____	_____
	3. _____	_____
	1. _____	_____
R5	2. _____	_____
	3. _____	_____

FORM 7-1.

For PROBLEM-SOLVING Objectives	Action Plans	Date
PS1	1. _____ 2. _____ 3. _____	_____ _____ _____
PS2	1. _____ 2. _____ 3. _____	_____ _____ _____
PS3	1. _____ 2. _____ 3. _____	_____ _____ _____
PS4	1. _____ 2. _____ 3. _____	_____ _____ _____
PS5	1. _____ 2. _____ 3. _____	_____ _____ _____

FORM 7-1.

For INNOVATIVE Objectives	Action Plans	Date
I1	1. _____	_____
	2. _____	_____
	3. _____	_____
I2	1. _____	_____
	2. _____	_____
	3. _____	_____
I3	1. _____	_____
	2. _____	_____
	3. _____	_____
I4	1. _____	_____
	2. _____	_____
	3. _____	_____
I5	1. _____	_____
	2. _____	_____
	3. _____	_____

FORM 7-1.

For PERSONAL Objectives	Action Plans	Date
	1. _____	_____
P1	2. _____	_____
	3. _____	_____
	1. _____	_____
P2	2. _____	_____
	3. _____	_____
	1. _____	_____
P3	2. _____	_____
	3. _____	_____
	1. _____	_____
P4	2. _____	_____
	3. _____	_____
	1. _____	_____
P5	2. _____	_____
	3. _____	_____

FORM 7-1.

Progress Review Form (Quarterly)

ROUTINE Objectives	Quarter	Date	% Accom-plishment	Comments
R1	1			
	2			
	3			
	4			
R2	1			
	2			
	3			
	4			
R3	1			
	2			
	3			
	4			
R4	1			
	2			
	3			
	4			
R5	1			
	2			
	3			
	4			

FORM 7-1.

PROBLEM-SOLVING Objectives	Quarter	Date	% Accomplishment	Comments
PS1	1			
	2			
	3			
	4			
PS2	1			
	2			
	3			
	4			
PS3	1			
	2			
	3			
	4			
PS4	1			
	2			
	3			
	4			
PS5	1			
	2			
	3			
	4			

FORM 7-1.

INNOVATIVE Objectives	Quarter	Date	% Accom-plishment	Comments
I1	1			
	2			
	3			
	4			
I2	1			
	2			
	3			
	4			
I3	1			
	2			
	3			
	4			
I4	1			
	2			
	3			
	4			
I5	1			
	2			
	3			
	4			

FORM 7-1.

PERSONAL Objectives	Quarter	Date	% Accom- plishment	Comments
P1	1			
	2			
	3			
	4			
P2	1			
	2			
	3			
	4			
P3	1			
	2			
	3			
	4			
P4	1			
	2			
	3			
	4			
P5	1			
	2			
	3			
	4			

FORM 7-1.

Quarter	Overall % Accomplishment	
1		Subordinate comments: _____ _____ Signature: _____ Date: _____ Supervisor comments: _____ _____ Signature: _____ Date: _____

Quarter	Overall % Accomplishment	
2		Subordinate comments: _____ _____ Signature: _____ Date: _____ Supervisor comments: _____ _____ Signature: _____ Date: _____

Quarter	Overall % Accomplishment	
3		Subordinate comments: _____ _____ Signature: _____ Date: _____ Supervisor comments: _____ _____ Signature: _____ Date: _____

Quarter	Overall % Accomplishment	
4		Subordinate comments: _____ _____ Signature: _____ Date: _____ Supervisor comments: _____ _____ Signature: _____ Date: _____

FORM 7-1.

Accomplishment Report Form (Annually)

12-Month Period Ending _____ (Date)

Subordinate _____ Date _____

Supervisor _____ Date _____

ROUTINE Objectives (Repetitive tasks)

	Description	% Accom-plishment	Comments
R1			
R2			
R3			
R4			
R5			

PROBLEM-SOLVING Objectives (Definitions of and solutions to major problems)

	Description	% Accom-plishment	Comments
PS1			
PS2			
PS3			
PS4			
PS5			

FORM 7-1.

INNOVATIVE Objectives (Creative and unusual solutions)

Description	% Accom-plishment	Comments
I1		
I2		
I3		
I4		
I5		

PERSONAL Objectives (Self-development goals)

Description	% Accom-plishment	Comments
P1		
P2		
P3		
P4		
P5		

Date _____

AGENDA FOR LEARNING

During the next twelve months, I plan to expand my management skills by:

Subscribing to (journals/magazines/newsletters/newspapers):

1. _____   7. _____

2. _____   8. _____

3. _____   9. _____

4. _____   10. _____

5. _____   11. _____

6. _____   12. _____

Reading the following books on management:

1. *The Whole Manager* _____   4. _____

2. _____   5. _____

3. _____   6. _____

Attending the following short seminars (one week or less):

1. _____   4. _____

2. _____   5. _____

3. _____   6. _____

Attending the following intensive formal or informal courses (executive-development programs, MBA programs, etc.):

1. _____   2. _____

FORM 7-2.

Practicing the skills learned in the following chapters of *The Whole Manager:*

_____   _____   _____   _____

Other activities (describe):

_____

_____

Chapter 8
Effective Communications

1:55 P.M.   Harry gets a call from Sam Dettner, director of safety.

"Harry, this is Sam. I'm at the loading dock and we've had a little accident."

"What happened?" Harry's voice is tense. He sits forward and grabs a pencil.

"Nothing to be alarmed about; I just thought you should know. One of the guys was hurt and there was a spill. Carl called in a new company to haul out our stock of waste solvent and they weren't very experienced. They rolled a drum off the truck; it struck one of the workers and sprung a leak."

"Any fire danger?" asks Harry.

"No, I think we have everything pretty much under control. We've cleaned things up, we're flushing the drains right now, and the fire chief is on his way to make an inspection," says Sam.

"How bad was the fellow hurt?" Harry wants to know.

"He will need to have stitches in his leg and he breathed some of the fumes, but really, I think he is going to be fine," Sam assures him.

"Why in the world did we use another hauler?" demands Harry. "Our regular people are so careful."

"Well, Carl said you wanted this material moved as soon as possible. Something about the neighbors complaining about toxic waste. He couldn't schedule our regular guy 'til next week so he brought in this alternate instead," explained Sam.

"Well, yes, I did say as soon as possible, but I didn't expect him to panic," says Harry in a tone of exasperation.

"Whatever the reason, Carl got the idea that it was pretty important. In any case, it's water over the dam now and things are under control. I just thought you would want to know."

"Thanks, Sam. Keep me posted and let me know if there is any deterioration in the situation," responds Harry.

"Will do. So long."

Harry rocks back in his chair, throws his pencil on the pad of paper, and wonders in frustration, "What did I say to panic Carl? I wanted him to know that rapid disposal is important. After all, I just had that meeting with the neighborhood groups, but I never meant to stampede him into taking risks. Communicating with precision is really a problem."

Harry is right. It is an important problem. The practicing manager spends as much as 90 percent of his day in the company of other people or talking on the telephone. He may spend as much as 40 percent of his time exclusively on transmitting information. Communication skills are absolutely essential for effective management behavior.

Communication is a combination of stimuli (inputs), perception, and behavior (outputs). It is operationalized in a variety of forms: verbal, written, nonverbal, formal, informal, in small and large groups. The purpose of this chapter is to:

- Sensitize you to perception
- Outline communication principles
- Help you with oral communication
- Provide tips on written communication skills
- Suggest public speaking aids
- Structure a communication effectiveness audit

PERCEPTION

Note the following conversation between a 4-year-old girl and her aunt.[1]

AUNT: What a beautiful new shirt you have.

[The niece smiles happily.]

---

[1]J. L. Briggs, "Morality Play: The Creation and Maintenance of Interpersonal Values in Inuit Society," progress report to Canadian Ethnology Services, 1976.

AUNT: Why don't you die so I can have it?

    [Niece looks at aunt.]

AUNT: Don't you want to die?

    [Niece raises eyebrows, signifying that she does not want to die.]

AUNT: Don't you want to die? Do die, then I can have the shirt.

    [Aunt reaches out to shirt with a clutching gesture.]

AUNT: [changing the subject] Did you see your new baby brother?

    [Niece beams happily.]

AUNT: Do you love him?

    [Niece indicates yes.]

AUNT: Did you carry him on your back?

    [Niece smiles.]

AUNT: You love him? I don't love him. You love him? Why don't you tip him out of your parka and kill him?

Call the child welfare worker? The police? The social worker? Definitely! If the preceding conversation were heard in the United States, the aunt would be seen as cold and potentially abusive. But this conversation occurred on Baffin Island, between members of the Inuit tribe, and such talk is a common form of teasing. No one there would see anything amiss in the interchange. In this case, what is bizarre to our culture is normal conversation in another.

The difference is caused by perception, frame of reference, the special way each individual notices and interprets what he sees. It can be a major stumbling block to communication.

Robert Burns, the famous Scottish poet, said, "Oh wad some Power the giftie gie us/To see oursels as ithers see us!" For the practicing manager, we could rewrite that more appropriately, "To see the *world* as others see it."

WHY DO WE SEE THINGS DIFFERENTLY?

Input Greatly Exceeds Our Capacity to Process

We have a tremendous central processing unit. The number of neurons in the human brain is estimated to be about 50 billion or more. Thus, we each possess an extremely powerful, portable, energy-efficient, low-maintenance computer. As a central processing unit, the brain is fantastic. In contrast, we have a very limited capacity to input and output data. Specifically, people generally are able to read 500 words per minute, to speak 200 words per minute, and to write 25 words per minute.

I observed a computer at a major military base that was capable of printing 1,100 pages per minute. In contrast, the human "computer" is extraordinarily slow at input and output.

We Filter Input

A person is bombarded by literally millions of bits of data per second. All five senses are involved in taking in the data. Therefore, we must filter the data and thus have developed a marvelous filtering system. Try this: Select a noise from your environment right now and listen to it. Are you reading this sentence as intently as you did the previous ones?

We have a dramatic ability to focus on priority information. Have you ever attended a cocktail party and selectively listened to a conversation going on across the room while successfully tuning out all the intervening conversations?

Our Filter Is Affected by Many Variables

An individual's perceptual filter is affected by a number of variables (see Figure 8-1). We are often unaware that these variables are operating. A knowledge of perception principles will help you understand the nature of perception and thereby communicate better.

PERCEPTION PRINCIPLES

What affects what you see? Here we will be using the word "see" in its broadest sense: how you perceive the world.

How You Feel Physically

Have you ever hallucinated while driving for long hours late at night on a deserted road? It is as though the fatigued mind and body were attempting to call a halt to the trip and enable you to get some sleep. A racing bicyclist who crossed the United States said the orange dog running next to his bike helped him through the last two days.

How often, when fatigued or recovering from a common cold, have you missed a nuance of conversation, forgotten your wife's birthday, made a mistake in your checkbook, or misinterpreted your subordi-

Figure 8-1. The perception process.

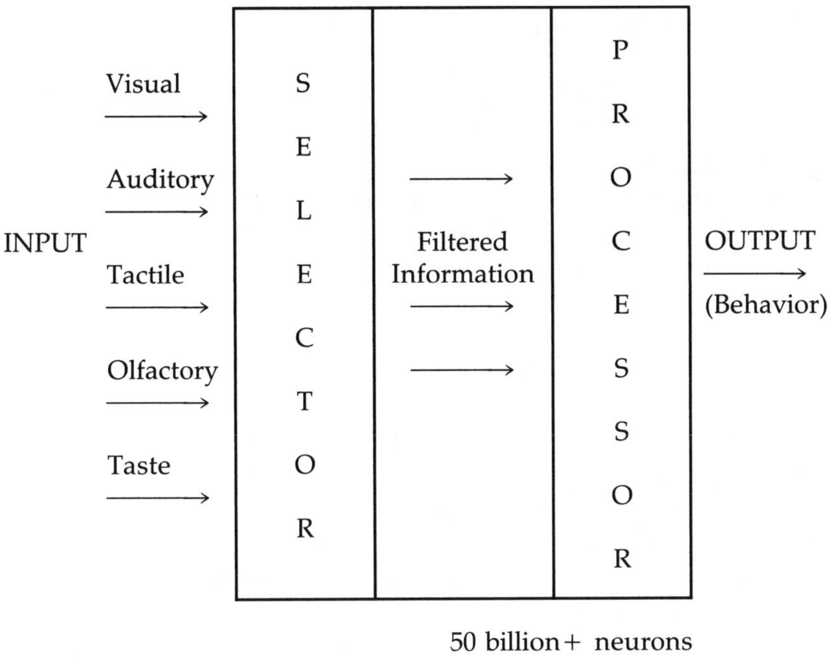

| INPUT | | SELECTOR | Filtered Information | PROCESSOR | OUTPUT (Behavior) |

Visual →

Auditory →

Tactile →

Olfactory →

Taste →

S
E
L
E
C
T
O
R

Filtered
Information →
→
→

P
R
O
C
E
S
S
O
R

50 billion+ neurons

Very limited input/output:
  Read 500 words/min.
  Speak 200 words/min.
  Write 25 words/min.

Input	=	Data collected by the five senses
Selector	=	Filtering device that selectively filters out input
Processor	=	The internal information-processing mechanism that enables us to think, act, etc.
Output	=	Human behavior: the results of the input, filtering, and processing

nate's request? The bottom line is that your basic physical state may affect what you see in various situations.

How You Feel Emotionally

A phenomenon called perceptual readiness makes us more attuned to see certain things. Have you ever been frightened on a hike by coming upon a poisonous snake? During the rest of the hike, you probably saw many more "snakes," only to find that they were sticks or similar items. Your fear made you emotionally ready to see things you would otherwise not see.

During times of family discord, events can take on unusual meaning; reactions may be magnified or suppressed. An argument with your spouse can sometimes turn the morning staff meeting into a disaster. Feelings of optimism make an accounting error seem less significant than do feelings of depression. In short, your underlying emotional state may affect what you see in various situations.

Your Values

When words are displayed on a screen for a time interval just below visual threshold (approximately one tenth of a second), individuals see the words that correspond to their strongly held values more quickly than other words. For example, deeply religious persons will be more likely to see the words God, faith, prayer, and the like than will people without strong religious values.

Conversely, valued behavior can be taken for granted, not seen. How often has a subordinate complained (or you've heard him mumble behind your back), "All I ever hear is what I've done wrong"? Values play a large and often unconscious part in what you see.

First Impressions

Salesmen in a men's clothing store in Montgomery, Alabama, dramatically improved their sales by changing the way they dressed. Wearing suits increased their sales by 43 percent compared to when they wore just shirtsleeves and ties and by 60 percent compared to when they wore opened-collar shirts. The customer believed the salesmen to be more competent when dressed in suits.

I vividly recall an early consulting experience. After I had spent the afternoon with my client, he invited me to have dinner with him at his exclusive club. I arrived with fresh ideas and a fresh Ph.D., and I was wearing a very loud sports jacket. I thought my client would have a coronary on the spot. Sports jackets are not the expected attire at this club. Since then, I have had many enjoyable meals and delightful interactions there, but always in a pin-striped suit.

Helping people match the presentation of their self with other people's expectations has become big business. Books and workshops are devoted to instructing people on dressing right and acting properly. Principles such as the following are extolled:[2]

1. Walk slowly and purposefully. Plant some pauses along the way.
2. When talking to Mr. Big, try to copy whatever he does.
3. When walking downstairs, look not down but straight ahead to project the image of being level headed.
4. When sitting in a chair, move it one inch to establish territory.

All this may seem a bit too much emphasis on form rather than substance. After all, we are supposed to be judged on what we think and say, rather than on how we say it. But in the complex human arena of management, form and substance begin to merge. And we expect them to be consistent, congruent, the same. Years ago, a successful business executive advised me to "always dress prosperously." I believe it is safe to pass that advice on to you.

First impressions can become self-fulfilling prophecies. Some years ago, a guest lecturer addressed two sections of an MIT physics class. He gave the identical lecture, but the introduction given to one class described him as a "rather warm" person and the one given to the other class described him as a "rather cool" person. Which class gave the lecturer the highest teaching rating? Which interacted more warmly with him? Right! The class that expected him to be warm.

Stereotypes

Walter Lippmann first called it stereotyping in 1911, describing the phenomenon as "pictures in people's heads." Because of information overload, we sort people and objects into categories. It simplifies decision making; one word can be used to consolidate a myriad of qualities and characteristics.

Parents try to imprint stereotypes on their children in order to control them: "Drugs are bad," "Teachers are wise," or "Strangers are suspect." Managers use their stereotypes to make decisions: "Buying is better than leasing," "Supporting local industry is best," or "The customer is always right."

---

[2] "Body Language: Teaching the Right Strut," *Time*, 30 April 1984, p. 54.

However, often stereotypes are not correct. We can easily misclassify persons and things into the wrong categories. For example: "Women make poor managers," "Accountants lack imagination," "Blondes are dumb," or "Engineers are unemotional."

But the most deleterious effect of stereotypes is that they do not permit you to see alternatives. They imprison you in the past; they paralyze your creative responses. For the manager, the consequences are serious. Sometimes leasing is the best decision; the best supplier is in the next city; customers are wrong; women make good managers.

Stereotypes are very strong, long lasting, and both useful and injurious. For years, I ran a company in the coalfields. The company held a negative stereotype regarding long-term debt. Working in such an uncertain industry, I did not feel prepared to assume long-term debt responsibilities. The stereotype enabled me to quickly eliminate such debt-related strategic plans. The stereotype served me well for over a decade.

On the other hand, the stereotypically ideal ballerina in the United States is 5'7" tall and weighs ninety-five pounds. While this seems almost impossible to attain, the stereotype is so powerful that it is reported that 50 percent of the young women studying ballet suffer from eating disorders and 10 percent are true anorexics. Interestingly, this stereotype does not hold true in Europe. The ideal ballerina there is permitted to have a more normal body structure.

Stereotyping greatly affects what you see. *Be aware* of your stereotypes, biases, and prejudices. When situations arise in which you know you may not be open to all the alternatives, draw on other people as resources.

The Halo Effect

The Halo Effect is a peculiar type of stereotyping. It occurs when an individual who is excellent in one dimension is automatically accorded excellence in other areas as well. The Halo Effect is used to good advantage. Movie stars and sports heroes advertise beer, shampoo, shaving supplies, makeup, and the like. It is used to disadvantage by managers when they assume that Carol, the excellent accountant, will make an equally excellent director of accounting; or that because Bob is well liked, he is the optimal choice for project manager. A negative halo is also possible, like a black cloud, and it can make a manager believe that because Chris is physically handicapped, he is unqualified for employment.

Subliminal Issues

During the 1950s, a researcher flashed "eat popcorn" on a movie screen at a duration much below the perceptual threshold. That is, the message was flashed for such a short time that the patrons were not conscious of it. The researcher claimed that subsequently there was a 50 percent increase in popcorn sales. Consequently, a tremendous interest surged across the research industry and in the advertising world with regard to subliminal perception. Would it be possible to control people's minds by using subliminal messages on television and motion picture screens? The technique was laid to rest in the seventies as essentially ineffective in influencing individuals' behavior. It seems to be having a resurgence now, as evidenced by recent full-page ads touting the benefits of "subliminal stimulation." Additional research is being conducted in the area of subliminal perception of magazine and billboard ads.

In my judgment, the bottom line is that subliminal perception does not work and has never been demonstrated to work in a replicable fashion. If it did work, there would be an ethical issue: Is it right to manipulate people without their knowing about it? But, perhaps fortunately, it does not work and therefore this is not an issue.

Selective Perception

Doctors see physical characteristics and symptoms, decorators note color, dentists are aware of jawlines, mothers notice children, teachers watch grammar.

Selective perception is important for the manager. Individuals tend to see solutions to problems based on their backgrounds. If the company has a problem, salesmen see the solution in increased sales, accountants in rationalized cash flows, production managers in stabilized production, and so on. It is essential that you know how you and others selectively perceive in order to manage effectively.

PERCEPTION: THE BOTTOM LINE

Your perception is affected by many variables. This is not an attempt to make you doubt your decision-making ability, but rather, to alert you to potential errors in your perceptual filter. Managers need to be extremely sensitive to perception distortions. The consequences of inaccurate perception can have long-term impacts on the organization. The message for the manager is clear:

1. Know yourself: your biases, values, prejudices, stereotypes, and physical and emotional states.
2. Know others: their biases, values, prejudices, stereotypes, and physical and emotional states.
3. Manage your image: recognize at times that how you dress, walk, and talk may have an impact on your effectiveness.

THE SELECTION INTERVIEW

What does the previous material on perception tell you about the traditional, casually conducted interview? That's right, it implies that the selection interview does not work when conducted in the traditional fashion. Interviewers tend to focus on irrelevant cues: style of dress, verbal fluency, firmness of handshake, and so on. They tend to shape the behavior of the candidate by their verbal and nonverbal encouragements and discouragements. Interviewers often make quick judgments, sometimes in as little as 4 or 5 minutes, concerning the evaluation of a candidate. In general, what we know about perception tells us that it is very easy to be misguided in a selection interview. It is worth remembering this now, while the perception research is fresh in your mind. We will discuss this in more detail and provide techniques for effective interviewing in Chapter 13.

COMMUNICATION PRINCIPLES

Managers spend an extraordinary amount of their day in communication activities. Why? Do they have a high need for affiliation? Probably not! Do they just love to talk? Doubtful! Do they need to communicate in order to get other people to do what they want? Yes!

The simple truth is that communication has as its goal behavior change, either physical or intellectual, in a targeted person. The purpose of communicating with another is to get that person to do something you want done or to think in a way that is similar with your way of thinking. Management is the practice of getting others to do what you want done; communication is the method of accomplishing this.

Activity by both sender and receiver is necessary for adequate communication. The sender actively relays a message. The receiver must acknowledge this message by means of some overt behavior if communication is to take place.

Communication skills are essential for managerial success. The average general manager can ask literally hundreds of questions in a typical meeting. Perhaps he's learned the costs of "communication break-downs" between himself and someone else in the organization. At times these communication breakdowns can be quite costly. Witness the following true story:[3]

> The director of a nonprofit agency approached an architectural firm and commissioned it to design a new headquarters building. The contract was signed, but the budget for the total project was only discussed cursorily. Months into the design phase, the client decided to add additional conference rooms, an indoor running track, additional locker rooms, and two racquetball courts. Other add-ons substantially enlarged the project's scope as well. The architectural firm complied, and after several revisions and additions, the design development drawings were complete and a preliminary cost estimate was made. It turned out to be $2 million over budget! The client accused the architectural firm of failure to notify concerning potential cost increases and refused to pay the invoice for work done.

This story shows the importance of clear and frequent communications between the client and the consultant. In many aspects of management, individuals are placed in a consultation mode. Even when you assume the directorship of a major project, you often are trying to anticipate top management's objectives to ensure that the project stays on track. Use Figure 8-2 to help enhance your client-consultant relationship.

CLIENT-CONSULTANT PROBLEM-SOLVING PROCESS

The flowchart shown in Figure 8-2 can perhaps help you avoid unnecessary communication problems if you are called into a consulting situ-

---

[3]Deepak Wadhwani, personal communication, April 1988.

Figure 8-2. Client-consultant problem-solving process.

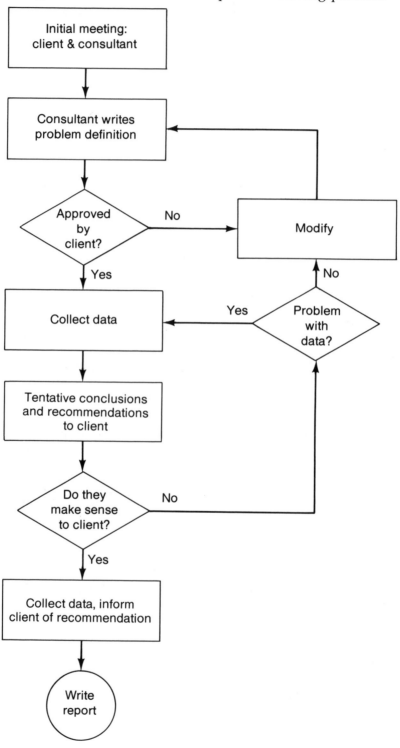

ation. Initially meet with the client and make sure you understand his or her objectives or needs. Make sure that the person you are talking to is in fact the client! I have had numerous occasions when subordinates or subordinates of subordinates have contacted me concerning a consulting project. I insist on talking to the top manager to ensure that his objectives are clearly communicated at the outset.

How many times have you seen expensive consulting studies that are quite well done, rigorously analyzed, and yet off target because no one really communicated the client's basic objectives? The flowchart suggests that the consultant put the problem definition in writing and have it approved by the client. You'd be amazed at how often the written word assumes a different significance from mere verbal exchanges in meetings. After this, approval data are collected and the consultant goes through a tentative conclusion and recommendation process. At this point numerous iterations can take place between the client and the consultant. Communicate frequently. I strongly recommend writing weekly reports to the file, with copies to your client and his key subordinates. This permits everybody to know where you are going and what's happening. In the vignette just noted, don't you think that the architectural firm would have been much better off sending out a number of memos on a weekly basis, alerting the client to the fact that changes might be costly?

Finally, the consultant informs the client of the set of recommendations that have been developed and writes the report. If the consulting process has been conducted properly, this should be almost anticlimactic. You have had the client involved and on board throughout the entire study, and the written report should be a mere documentation of where things stand at this point. Remember, as a consultant you have a responsibility to accomplish *behavior change*. If nothing happens as the result of your involvement with the client, then he doesn't need your consulting expertise. Make sure you manage the process as well as the substance of the client-consultant problem-solving effort.

THE FIVE Rs OF TRANSMISSION

In the class assessment-center studies at A.T.&T., oral communication skills were the best predictor of future managerial success. You can improve your communication skills by thinking in terms of the Five Rs of transmission and reception as shown in Figure 8-3. Whenever you communicate as a manager, it is essential that the communication process be optimal. As sender in this process, you can use the Five Rs to maximize your effectiveness.

Figure 8-3. Communication principles.

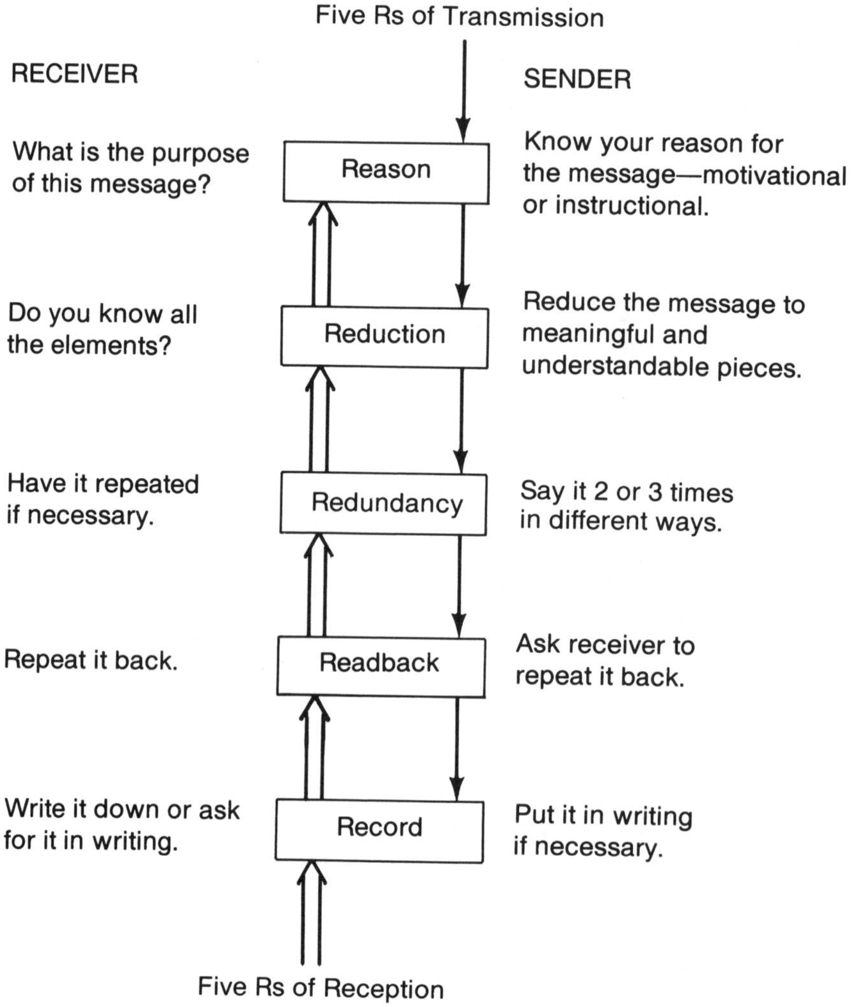

Five Rs of Transmission

RECEIVER		SENDER
What is the purpose of this message?	**Reason**	Know your reason for the message—motivational or instructional.
Do you know all the elements?	**Reduction**	Reduce the message to meaningful and understandable pieces.
Have it repeated if necessary.	**Redundancy**	Say it 2 or 3 times in different ways.
Repeat it back.	**Readback**	Ask receiver to repeat it back.
Write it down or ask for it in writing.	**Record**	Put it in writing if necessary.

Five Rs of Reception

Reason

Know the reason for the communication. Are you seeking to motivate, convince, instruct, inspire, or simply gain compliance? Make the message, the tone of voice, the words chosen, and the facial expression consistent with the reason. For example, "Charley, I wonder if you're going to be around later on today. I thought we could grab a cup of coffee and visit" is indicative of a very different "reason" for getting together than "Charley, my office at two o'clock. Be there!"

Reduction

Reduce the message to its meaningful and understandable pieces. B. F. Skinner was able to teach pigeons to play the national anthem, to play Ping-Pong, and even to guide bombs to targets by reducing these complex tasks to a sequence of simple steps. Reduction in communication is equally necessary in transmitting a complex message. For instance, "Write that up" is not as helpful as "Write up what you heard in the meeting as a report, make duplicate copies, and present it to me for signature. Use the same format as the one we use for the monthly staff meetings."

Redundancy

Say the same thing in more than one way. The positive outcome of this behavior is especially obvious in cross-cultural exchanges. If you keep repeating yourself in different ways, eventually the listener will say, "Oh, you want . . ." It also helps in routine interoffice communications. For example, "Drive safely. Wear your seat belt. Go slower than you think is safe, it's been raining. Check the wiper solution, visibility may be a problem. And call me when you get there." I guess it sounds like a worried parent, but the message is very clear. Drive safely!

Readback

Ask the receiver to read back what he heard you say. It sounds like an assignment in an interpersonal communication lab, doesn't it? Nevertheless, it is a good habit to get into, just to make sure you are being heard accurately. We are familiar with repeating messages when we are not in visual contact with the other person. How often have you had your credit card number repeated back to you when you placed a telephone order? It is also a good habit to use in face-to-face communication.

Professional commercial pilots use readback as a matter of routine. Consider the safety ensured in the complete message that follows:

TOWER: United 259, turn left 330 degrees, intercept the localizer, cross Wyler at 4,000 feet or above. Cleared for the approach, runway 32.
UNITED 259: Left 330 degrees, intercept the localizer, cross Wyler at 4,000 feet or above. We're cleared for approach, runway 32, United 259.

Contrast this with the scenario that follows of an overworked and perhaps frightened private pilot with less experience:

TOWER: 34 Quebec, turn left 330 degrees, intercept localizer, cross Wyler at 4,000 feet or above. Cleared for approach, runway 32.
34 QUEBEC: Cleared for approach.

The pilot of 34 Quebec may think incorrectly that he has been cleared for a runway other than runway 32, but he did not read back the complete message, so the tower might not realize his mistake until it is too late. Readback reduces many errors.

Record

Writing encourages a great deal of clarity that may not seem necessary when you have the other person's reactions for feedback on your message. Not only is the message clear, it is also recorded in corporate memory for future reference and for legal record. In my experience, effective managers have made it a habit to dictate memos to the file as a routine documentation procedure.

THE FIVE Rs OF RECEPTION

For the receiver of communications, the process works in the opposite direction. The Five Rs of reception provide suggestions and help for the receiver. They represent the transmitter rules backwards.

1. *Record.* Write it down or ask to have it in written form.
2. *Readback.* Repeat what you understand to be the message.
3. *Redundancy.* Get the sender to say it again or say it another way.
4. *Reduction.* Identify or get the speaker to identify all the specific elements or steps to the message.
5. *Reason.* Be sure you know the purpose of the message. If you have any doubt, ask.

THE MESSAGE ITSELF

Communication can be inaccurate because of distorted perception or because of errors in the process of sending and receiving the message. But it can also be handicapped by the message itself. Clarity of expression is based in part on the vocabulary of the sender; it is modified by the vocabulary of the receiver. It is dependent on the voice quality of the speaker and on the hearing ability of the listener. It is influenced by the relationship between the two parties.

The English language is perhaps the most ambiguous of all spoken languages. Many words have more than one meaning. In addition, words have connotative meanings that are often more important than their denotative meanings. The denotative meaning is the primary meaning—if you will, the dictionary definition. The connotative meaning is the bundle of secondary meanings based on people's values, experiences, and so forth. Do the following words have positive or negative connotations for you? Gay, marijuana, marriage, sex, living together, abortion, nuclear, deficit? The speaker can very easily give an unintended message by forgetting the connotation of the words he chooses.

The message contained in the communication process can easily be distorted. This distortion is most often accomplished by "double messages," or "mixed messages." In both instances, the verbal message is contradicted by the nonverbal behavior. The message "Yes, I have time to talk with you" is belied by paper shuffling, taking phone calls, and skim reading the report on your desk. Likewise, "I have every confidence in you" is not believable when the assignments given to the employee are routine and unchallenging.

The following tips are useful for the management communicator. They are explicit and usable, and will enhance the effectiveness of your communication.

Written Communication

1. Use the Five Rs of transmission:
   • Reason
   • Reduction
   • Redundancy
   • Readback
   • Record
2. Provide the reader with a road map: where you are taking him,

in what order, for what purpose. An outline that has worked in hundreds of reports is:
- Executive summary
- Introduction
- Problem statement
- Conclusions
- Recommendations
- Analysis
- Summary or closing
- Appendices

3. Keep sentences simple.
4. Use correct grammar.
5. Avoid jargon.
6. Write at the level of sophistication of the reader.
7. State assumptions clearly and early in the report.
8. Make recommendations specific and operational.
9. Use headings, subheadings, and bullets (as in this book).

Public Speaking

1. Use the Five Rs of transmission:
   - Reason
   - Reduction
   - Redundancy
   - Readback
   - Record
2. Provide the listener with a road map. It sounds simplistic, but some public speakers recommend the following outline:
   - Introduction: This is what I'm going to say.
   - Middle: Now I'm saying it.
   - Closing: This is what I said.
3. Establish contact with the audience.
4. Use language at the level of the audience.
5. Avoid unnecessary jargon.
6. Make use of your body.
7. Speak with expression.
8. Maintain meaningful eye contact.
9. Speak loud enough to be heard.
10. Use pauses effectively.
11. Use audiovisual aids; adults use multiple senses in learning.
12. Speak slowly.

13. Keep it simple; it is easier to drive home three points than ten.
14. Know your audience; recognize their perceptual biases.
15. Use examples; they are very powerful.
16. Use humor if possible.
17. Lead the audience; outline where you are going.

Interpersonal Communication

1. Use the Five Rs of communication:
   • Reason
   • Reduction
   • Redundancy
   • Readback
   • Record
2. Establish a comfortable situation.
3. Establish contact.
4. React to the listener.
5. Be attuned to nonverbal cues.
6. Listen actively.
7. Make the communication interactive.
8. Match the tone of voice with the message.
9. Know when to stop.

COMMUNICATION EFFECTIVENESS AUDIT

Now it's time to diagnose how you rate in the various areas of communication. Take the Communication Effectiveness Audit (Form 8-1). Be as honest as possible. Break out of your old perceptual sets and attempt to get a clear diagnosis. Perhaps your spouse or a coworker can respond to the audit for you as well.

Then use this diagnostic information to formulate your Communication Action Plan (Form 8-2). It's only a start, but it is fundamental for progress on the road to executive survival.

COMMUNICATION EFFECTIVENESS AUDIT

How effective a communicator are you? Circle the number of each item below that represents your best estimate.

How effective are you in each of the following areas?

	Never	Sometimes	Always

1. REASON:
   I know my reasons for communica-
   tion.   0 1 2 3 4 5 6 7 8 9 10
2. REDUCTION:
   I reduce my messages to meaningful
   pieces.   0 1 2 3 4 5 6 7 8 9 10
3. REDUNDANCY:
   I phrase my messages two or three
   different ways.   0 1 2 3 4 5 6 7 8 9 10
4. READBACK:
   I ask my receiver to repeat it back.   0 1 2 3 4 5 6 7 8 9 10
5. RECORD:
   I put messages into writing whenever
   possible.   0 1 2 3 4 5 6 7 8 9 10

TOTAL _____ = Communication process

6. I am effective at oral communication
   with:
   Supervisors   0 1 2 3 4 5 6 7 8 9 10
   Subordinates   0 1 2 3 4 5 6 7 8 9 10
   Peers   0 1 2 3 4 5 6 7 8 9 10
   Outsiders   0 1 2 3 4 5 6 7 8 9 10
   Family   0 1 2 3 4 5 6 7 8 9 10

TOTAL _____ = Oral communication

7. I am effective at written communica-
   tion with:
   Supervisors   0 1 2 3 4 5 6 7 8 9 10
   Subordinates   0 1 2 3 4 5 6 7 8 9 10
   Peers   0 1 2 3 4 5 6 7 8 9 10
   Outsiders   0 1 2 3 4 5 6 7 8 9 10
   Others (name)   0 1 2 3 4 5 6 7 8 9 10

TOTAL _____ = Written communication

	Never	Sometimes	Always

8. I am effective at public speaking before:

Small groups	0 1 2 3 4 5 6 7 8 9 10
Large groups	0 1 2 3 4 5 6 7 8 9 10
Formal affairs	0 1 2 3 4 5 6 7 8 9 10
Informal extemporaneous meetings	0 1 2 3 4 5 6 7 8 9 10
Strangers	0 1 2 3 4 5 6 7 8 9 10

TOTAL _____ = Public speaking

9. I am effective at nonverbal communication using:

Eye contact	0 1 2 3 4 5 6 7 8 9 10
Facial expression	0 1 2 3 4 5 6 7 8 9 10
Hand movements, etc.	0 1 2 3 4 5 6 7 8 9 10
Physical proximity	0 1 2 3 4 5 6 7 8 9 10
Posture	0 1 2 3 4 5 6 7 8 9 10

TOTAL _____ = Nonverbal communication

Percentile Scores

Now compare your scores to those of a sample of 135 managers.

Percentile Score		Raw Score			
% of Individuals Scoring Lower	Communication Process	Oral Communication	Written Communication	Public Speaking	Nonverbal Communication
100	48	50	50	50	50
90	37	44	43	42	42
80	36	42	39	40	40
70	34	40	36	38	38
60	33	39	35	36	35
50	31	37	33	33	33
40	30	36	31	30	31
30	28	34	30	28	29
20	26	32	28	26	25
10	23	29	25	23	23
0	20	15	8	1	13

COMMUNICATION ACTION PLAN

1. What are your communication strengths?

_____

_____

_____

_____

2. What are your communication weaknesses?

_____

_____

_____

_____

3. How could you make changes?

_____

_____

_____

_____

4. Write your specific action plan.

_____

_____

_____

_____

Chapter 9

Leadership

2:02 P.M. Harry meets with John Decker, a computer specialist from corporate staff. "John," says Harry, "before we finalize this deal this afternoon with Edgerton Systems, we have to decide where to put the remote terminals. What's your recommendation?"

"Well, my advice is to place one in Kingsley's office, one in Walters' office, and one in the warehouse."

"What about Freeman?"

"I don't think she needs one," Decker replies.

"She says she does."

"I know, but she can get her information from Kingsley."

"OK, thanks," Harry says.

After Decker leaves, Harry worries about not having enough information and time with which to make an intelligent decision. He would like to get additional input from the staff and talk confidentially with Walters and Kingsley; and he frets over the fact that status-sensitive Freeman might get upset because she won't have a terminal and Kingsley will.

"If this new production control system is going to work smoothly," he thinks, "I'm going to need the staff's support. Sure would be nice if they could participate in making this decision—then they'd be apt to give their support willingly. But, darn it, there just isn't the time on this one. Guess I'll have to do what I usually do: get the job done first and then satisfy the people variables later.''

Harry is faced with a leadership decision-making situation common to managers of every rank and station in corporate life. His task is not so much deciding how to be a leader or how to resolve the particular management dilemma at hand. Rather, the kernel of the management task, when the nonessentials are stripped away, is to decide how to decide. This decision involves two dimensions.

TWO DIMENSIONS OF A LEADERSHIP DECISION

When you make a leadership decision, you must answer two basic questions:

1. Where will you get your information input? (Whom do you ask?)
2. Where should you place the decision authority for this problem? (Who makes the decision?)

The first question involves which members of your group will furnish information about a particular decision. The second is to what extent you maintain all the decision-making authority and how much you "share" with members of your group in more or less democratic fashion. The first dimension is one of information, the second of authority. These two critical dimensions are essential for effective leadership.

Before we bias you one way or the other with the theory, let's get a diagnostic on the way you lead. Answer the questions on the Jerrell/Slevin Management Instrument (Form 9-1). This will give you some useful feedback and set the stage for the discussion of the theory.

FOUR LEADERSHIP STYLES

You now have feedback on your leadership style in terms of percentiles. Your score on each decision can range from 1 to 100 percent in comparison with other managers. You should have already plotted your score on the graph. For convenience, we refer to the horizontal axis (Decision Authority) first and the vertical axis (Information Input) second when discussing scores.

This plotting system can be used to describe almost any leadership

Figure 9-1. Bonoma-Slevin leadership model.

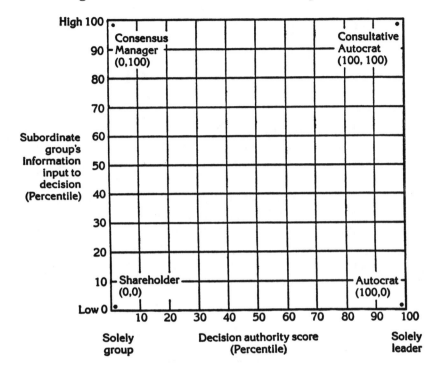

style (see Figure 9-1). The four extremes of leaders (depicted in the four corners of the grid) are the following:

1. *Autocrat* (100, 0). Such managers solicit little or no input from their groups and make the managerial decisions solely by themselves.
2. *Consultative autocrat* (100, 100). In this managerial style intensive input is elicited from the members, but these formal leaders keep all substantive decision-making authority to themselves.
3. *Consensus manager* (0, 100). Purely consensual managers throw open the problem to the group for discussion (input) and simultaneously allow or encourage the entire group to make the relevant decision.
4. *Shareholder manager* (0, 0). This position is literally poor management. Little or no information input and exchange take place within the group, while the group itself has ultimate authority for the final decision.

The advantages of the leadership model, apart from its practical simplicity, become apparent when we consider three traditional areas of leadership and managerial decision style: (1) participative management, (2) delegation, and (3) personal and organizational pressures affecting leadership. Let's consider each area.

PARTICIPATIVE MANAGEMENT

Behavioral researchers traditionally have represented the participative manager as being at one end—the consensus end—of a continuum going from consensus to autocratic leadership styles. Participative managers ordinarily involve their subordinates in one or more steps of the decision-making process.

When participative management is expressed as shown in Figure 9-2, this simple view of participation is not so simple after all. Does "participative management" mean increases in just the information input-exchange process (A to B) between leaders and subordinates? This seems reasonable, because contributing input into a decision, or even having knowledge of which decisions are being made, is certainly a way

Figure 9-2. Whither participation?

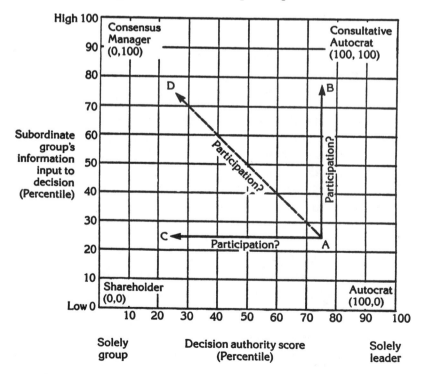

of satisfying subordinates' participation needs. I asked managers, "What does it mean to be participative?" Most responded, "Well, I ask my subordinates for their input before I decide."

To practicing managers, "participation" is an informational concept.

But what about increasing subordinate "control" over the decision itself? Surely this movement on the model from points A to C is also a satisfactory way of getting participation, of giving employees a "hand in their own fate." I asked my academic colleagues, "What is participative management?" A typical response was "Participation means sharing the power, letting each person vote on the outcome."

To academics and scholars, "participation" is often a decision-making authority concept.

Which is right? The concept of participation is two dimensional (A to D). The three very different notions of participation implied by Figure 9-2 represent equally legitimate, but radically different managerial styles.

First, the traditional perception of participation, in which subordinates give increased input but gain little increase in control over the making of decisions, is a valid way to speak about increased participation in management. Second, equating participative management with shifting decision-making authority from the formal leader to the group, but with no necessary mention of an increase in information sharing among superiors and group members, is also a valid path to participation. Third, the "compromise path," in which group input and exchange and decision-making authority are increased simultaneously, is probably the most appropriate way to define participative management.

The point is that it is possible to be talking about at least three different concepts of "participation." As a manager, it is critically important that:

1. You decide which kind of participation you will seek with your subordinates.
2. You communicate your meaning of participation to them.
3. You act in a manner consistent with your own and your subordinates' understanding of the term.

Here is what happens when a manager hasn't clarified his thinking on participation:

Your boss calls you Friday A.M. and requests that you give him some preliminary figures for next quarter's equipment budget.

You've done some advance thinking about your needs and are able to give him some ballpark figures. You tell him you'll get to him first thing Monday with a firm estimate, and he says that will be fine.

You work ten hours over the weekend and find that your preliminary figures were quite close to your detailed analysis. On Monday morning you call your boss to tell him the final equipment figures are ready. His secretary says, "Oh, we don't need them anymore. The budget went out Friday afternoon."

You set up a meeting with your boss, and then angrily confront him about why he didn't wait for your final figures. He says, "What are you complaining about? You're getting everything you asked for, aren't you?" You feel like you've been had.

Why do you feel bad? You got what you wanted, didn't you? You feel bad not because of the outcome but rather because of the process. You felt that your boss had agreed to consult you more fully before making a final decision. Instead, he made a basically autocratic decision after minimal consultation. Even though the outcome was OK, the process led to conflict and reduced morale. Don't do the same thing with your subordinates. As the example shows, the decision-making process can be as important as the decision itself.

DELEGATION

Delegating authority means transferring some of your decision-making rights to your subordinates. But, of course, you retain evaluative and veto rights over their decisions.

Think about delegation for a minute. There are two requirements for good managerial delegation:

1. You must give up some, but not all, of your decision authority.
2. You must make sure enough exchange of information takes place within your subordinate group, and between the group and you, so that the subordinates can successfully solve their problems.

To understand the first point, look at points B and C on Figure 9-3. Leaders who are at point B, who give too much authority to the group, are not good delegators; they are giving up their job as manager, which is to control the activities of others even when they are doing the job.

Figure 9-3. Leadership model showing amounts of delegation.

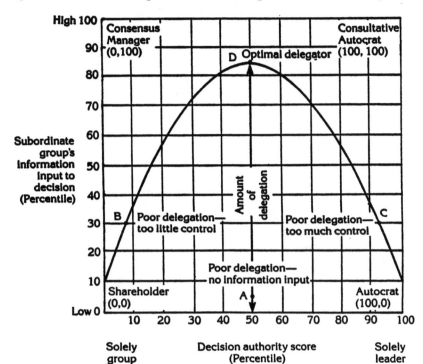

On the other hand, leaders who give no authority to their subordinates (point C) cannot be good delegators either, for they simply don't understand what delegation means. The managers who give up some but not all of their authority are the best delegators; they are the managers near the midpoint on the "delegation curve" in the model.

Now look at points A and D in Figure 9-3. Just because you give up some but not all of your authority to your subordinates does not necessarily mean you're a good delegator. Harry Thorpe might be at point A on the model. He gives his subordinates a job to do and also tells them to go ahead and make the decisions. Unfortunately, he doesn't take any steps to ensure that they are getting the information they need to make effective decisions. He doesn't share what he knows about the problem with them, either. He is a poor delegator. But if Harry were to give up some of his authority *and* ensure high information exchange between himself and his subordinates, he would be an optimal delegator, point D on the model.

PERSONAL AND ORGANIZATIONAL PRESSURES AFFECTING LEADERSHIP

As a manager, you may act differently as a leader under different conditions, depending on three kinds of pressure: (1) problem attributes pressures, (2) leader personality pressures, and (3) organizational and group pressures. Think of the leadership model in terms of a map, with north at the top. Table 9-1 summarizes these pressures on leadership style in terms of geographical direction (for example, a movement "north" is upward on the vertical axis of the leadership model, and so on). Now let's view the leadership model in terms of these types of pressures.

Problem Attributes

Problem attributes generate eastward pressures on the leader. This is especially true when problems are characterized as any of the following:

- Time bound
- Important
- Personal "pet" decisions
- Structured and routine tasks

In such cases, it is very tempting to take personal "control" over the decision making and "get the job done."

However, northward pressures can occur too, given the following situations:

- When the decisions are important
- When you as the leader lack the resources to make the decision yourself
- When subordinate implementation is critical to success

In these cases, input and exchange of information should be maximized. Harry has to decide today on the location of the remote terminals in the plant. The time pressure pushes him toward the east. He also has to worry about the possible conflict between Freeman and Kingsley, because Freeman might not get a terminal and Kingsley will. The fact that Harry needs the support of both to implement his decision will push him toward the northwest. It's a well-known behavioral finding that people cooperate more in implementing decisions they have helped make.

Table 9-1. *Three leadership style pressures.*

Type of Pressure	Direction of Pressure on Leadership Grid
PROBLEM ATTRIBUTES PRESSURES	
Leader lacks relevant information; problem is ambiguous.	North: more information needed.
Leader lacks enough time to make decision adequately.	South and east: consensus and information collection take time.
Decision is important or critical to organization.	North: information search maximized.
Decision is personally important to leader.	North and east: personal control and information maximized.
Problem is structured or routine.	South and east: little time as possible spent on decision.
Decision implementation by subordinates is critical to success.	West and north: input and consensus required.
LEADER PERSONALITY PRESSURES	
Leader has high need for power.	East: personal control maximized.
Leader is high in need for affiliation, is "people oriented."	North and west: contact with people maximized.
Leader is highly intelligent.	East: personal competence demonstrated.
Leader has high need for achievement.	East: personal contribution maximized.
ORGANIZATIONAL AND GROUP PRESSURES	
Conflict is likely to result from the decision.	North and west: participative aspects of decision making maximized.
Good leader-group relations exist.	North and west: group contact maximized.
Centrality: formalization of organization is high.	South and east: organization style matched.

Leader Personality

Some managers tend to be inflexible in their leadership style because of who they are and how they like to manage. For example, such managers have a high need for power, are task oriented, or are highly intelligent. They make many decisions themselves that might otherwise be left to subordinates, and they also may make decisions without acquiring information from the group.

People-oriented leaders, on the other hand, act to maximize input from their subordinates and share their authority as well. Both activities are people processes.

Organizational and Group Pressures

If conflict is likely to result from a decision, effective managers are most likely to want their subordinates as involved as possible in both the input (northward) and authority (westward) dimensions, so as to help manage the potential conflict. Should good leader-group relations exist, northward (but *not* necessarily westward) pressure will be felt. The leader will also feel great pressures to fit into the "culture" of the organization. The R & D lab expects a consensual approach; most business groups expect a consultative autocrat approach; the factory floor may expect an autocratic approach. It is important that a manager match his style to the norms, needs, and expectations of his subordinates.

FINDINGS FROM THE FIELD

Based on the presentation to and discussion of this model with thousands of practicing managers, I share with you my conclusions concerning important principles.

1. *You're more autocratic than you think.* In the eyes of your subordinates you are probably closer to the autocrat on the graph than you are in your own eyes. Why? Because you're the boss and they are the subordinates. No matter how easygoing, friendly, participative, and supportive you are, you are still the boss. There is almost always a perceptual difference in leadership style between supervisor and subordinate.

2. *But it's OK.* Often, when you ask subordinates where they would like their boss to move, they respond, "Things are OK as they are."

Even though there are perceptual discrepancies concerning leadership style, there may not necessarily be a felt need or pressure for change. The status quo may be OK.

3. *It's easy to move north and south.* It's easy to move vertically on the graph. Why? Because management is a job of communication. It's easy to collect more or less information before you make the decision. The information dimension is the least resistant to change.

4. *It's hard to move west.* Most managers find it quite threatening to move westward too quickly. Why? Because a westward movement upsets the basic power realities in the organization. If your head is in the noose, if things don't work out, then it is hard to turn the decisions totally over to your subordinates.

5. *If subordinates' expectations are not met, morale can suffer.* What if your subordinates expected you to use a (50, 90) process and instead you made the decision using a (90, 10) style? That's right—dissatisfaction and morale problems. As I mentioned before, the decision-making process can be as important as the outcome, especially from the standpoint of motivating subordinates.

6. *Be flexible.* A successful manager is autocratic when he needs to be, consultative when necessary, and consensual when the situation calls for it. Move around the leadership space to fit the needs of the situation. Unsuccessful managers are inflexible and try the same style in all situations. Most managers feel that their score on the Jerrell/Slevin Management Instrument is a function of the particular job they have been in for the last few months. Be flexible and match your leadership style to the job.

LEADERSHIP CHECKLIST

Let us now see how well your leadership style squares with your organization.

	Yes	No
1. *Dominant leadership style*		
Should I try to change my own style?	☐	☐
Should I become more autocratic?	☐	☐
Should I become more consensual?	☐	☐

	Yes	No
2. *Fit*		
Is my leadership style inappropriate for my organization?	☐	☐
Am I an autocratic peg in a participative hole?	☐	☐
3. *Flexibility*		
Do I fail to move my leadership style around the graph to match the different problems I face?	☐	☐
Am I sometimes too inflexible for my responsibilities?	☐	☐
4. *Subordinate fit*		
Do my subordinates have expectations and needs that are not in line with my leadership style?	☐	☐
If so, do I need new subordinates?	☐	☐
5. *Information*		
Do I receive insufficient information for making decisions?	☐	☐
Do my subordinates fail to regularly send me meaningful reports?	☐	☐
6. *Decision-making authority*		
Do I fail to share authority appropriately?	☐	☐
Am I stifling my subordinates by not letting them participate in decisions affecting them?	☐	☐

If you answered no to all the questions, you're OK in all six areas and are in excellent shape. If you answered yes to any question, the respective heading is a problem area and you should examine it. For example, if your subordinates don't seem to fit your own leadership style, maybe you need some new subordinates. Or you need to change. If you just don't seem flexible enough to take on the broad range of problems you face, maybe you need to reexamine your leadership style. If you have three or more problem areas, it's undoubtedly time to give that corporate headhunter a call. (Or maybe you'd better engage in a serious, high-priority program of leadership therapy.)

SUCCESS STORIES

Does the leadership model really work? We have applied it in a number of research, training, and field management settings. Here are what some practicing managers have told us about it.

Production Supervisor, Polyurethane Division, Large Chemical Corporation

This manager kept a running diary over a three-week period of forty-one decision-making situations he faced on the job. Later he plotted them on the model. He found a strong divergence between the way he thought he behaved and the way he actually behaved in most leadership situations. It became obvious to him that his dominant leadership style was not that of a consensus manager but more that of a consultative autocrat; when he plotted his flexibility space on the basis of actual behavior, he found that the only direction in which he was flexible was vertical (that of allowing increased input from subordinates). In no case did he share any decision-making authority, as he had previously supposed he did.

He concluded: "The merit of the Bonoma-Slevin leadership model was in its simplicity, since it uses only two dimensions to describe alternative leadership styles. The model confirmed that my actual leadership style was inconsistent with my preconceived image of my leadership style. It presented a visual conception of changes necessary for me to alter my present leadership style as that of a consultative autocrat to become a consensus manager."

Anyone wanting to use the leadership model for self-analysis should keep a diary of decision-making situations faced over a period of time. At the end of each day, the individual should analyze each situation that involved his subordinates. In each case, the individual should ask himself the two key questions that are the basis of the leadership model: (1) Where did I get my input? and (2) where did I place the decision-making authority for this problem?[1]

Vice-President, Largest Division of International Manufacturing Firm

This manager supervises approximately five other managers and five people not holding managerial status. He asked each of his subordinates, first, to estimate his dominant decision-making style over the last twelve months, and, second, to recommend how he should change. As a result he learned that his subordinates rated him approximately 20 percent more autocratic than he had rated himself. However, he also found that his subordinates were quite

---

[1] R. L. Sarson, personal communication, 25 February 1977.

happy with his leadership style, and desired only slightly less autocratic decisions and slightly more input.

He comments: "I think my guys thought, 'Here's a chance to give my boss a performance appraisal,' and they did."[2]

Division Superintendent, Primary Operations, Producer of Specialty Steel

After ten years of job assignments with gradually increasing responsibilities, this manager was unexpectedly promoted to this new position, one of great importance; he had never before managed an area with so many supervisors. He quickly realized that he knew very little about the hierarchy of command or the leadership style of his new organization. He, therefore, undertook an entire leadership audit of all his new supervisory personnel at the level of general foreman or above, and asked them to fill out a leadership survey anonymously.

Later he wrote: "As of this date, six weeks have elapsed. Often during this period I have been confronted with difficult problems. The survey conducted has aided considerably in 'deciding how to decide.' For someone like me, new in a position, this technique is super for helping me understand where I stand with my supervisors, peers, and subordinates. I feel comfortable with the results of this survey and the pragmatic approach it offers. I also plan to file this data and to resurvey on a yearly basis to note changes in the leadership profile."[3]

TAKE CONTROL OF YOUR STYLE

It is possible to manage your leadership style by consciously choosing your position in the leadership space. You can choose to be autocratic, consultative, or consensual. Witness the following experiences of one of my executive students as he demonstrated leadership flexibility by modifying his style to fit the various projects for which he was responsible.[4]

---

[2]R. B. White, personal communication, February 1977.
[3]M. Kosanovich, personal communication, February 1977.
[4]William Sprecher, personal communication, April 1988.

Project: Determine if the companies should take cash discounts where economically feasible and ensure these discounts are passed through to the customer.

Leadership style: Autocratic (100, 0).

Basis for leadership style: The question lends itself to a logical solution (which I am qualified and have the authority to make). Implementation is primarily focused on adequate contacts versus a group consensus or commitment.

Project: Initiate a study to consider involving the salesmen in overall company profitability.
1. Should the formula for salesmen's compensation take into consideration the level of gross margin achieved on each sale?
2. What expenses are controlled by salesmen? How should these expenses be monitored?
3. Should salesmen be involved in collection of accounts receivable?

Leadership style: Consultative autocrat (80, 80).

Basis for leadership style: Similar to item 1, this question represents a financial control decision to the organization. Implementation of the decision can be performed by focusing on adequate controls and does not require a group consensus. Unlike item 1, this decision is one I do not feel qualified to automatically make. It requires a detailed knowledge of current procedures, industry norms, and individual corporate cultures. Accordingly, considerable consultation and data collection will have to be performed prior to making and implementing a decision.

Project: Coordinate efforts when a new product is introduced and manufacturer support is not adequate, to ensure sales and services training is appropriate.

Leadership style: Consensus manager (10, 80).

Basis for leadership style: The subject is one that requires information from the group as well as a group commitment for successful implementation. The group process will likely generate various alternatives that will be incorporated into the final decision. Equally important as the leadership style (consensus manager) is the composition of the group. Accordingly, members of management and sales and several technicians will be asked to participate in this process.

OVERVIEW: ORGANIZATIONAL IMPLICATIONS

The leadership framework presented in our model forces the manager to ask two key questions concerning decision making: (1) Whom do I ask? and (2) Who makes the decision?

Obtaining accurate input from one's subordinate group is crucial to effective management. Similarly, decision-making authority must be located in the right place vis-à-vis the leader's group.

In addition, this model might be broadened to apply to even more fundamental questions of the managerial job. Forget for a moment that you are the leader of a subordinate group, and answer the following questions, considering both vertical and horizontal relationships in your organization:

1. *Where do I get my information?* Every manager needs accurate information to make effective decisions. Do you get sufficient information:

    - From your boss
    - From your peers
    - From the formal information system
    - From all sources in the organization that can aid you in your job

2. *Who makes the decisions?* Is the decision-making authority vested in the right people—not just concerning your subordinates but also upward and laterally? Should other departments be making decisions that you now make or vice versa?

The answers to these questions have broad implications for the management information system and the power structure of your organization. If you are not getting necessary information, perhaps the management information system should be modified to provide it. If you have a problem of misplaced decision-making authority (downward or upward), this problem should be addressed. If the answers to these fundamental questions are satisfactory, then only one important question remains, which cannot be addressed here: Are the decisions good ones?

JERRELL/SLEVIN MANAGEMENT INSTRUMENT

Circle the number for each item that represents your best estimate.

	Strongly Disagree	Disagree	Neutral	Agree	Strongly Agree
1. I don't like it when others disagree with me.	1	2	3	4	5
2. I like quick results.	1	2	3	4	5
3. I find it hard to accept others' decisions.	1	2	3	4	5
4. I have a strong ego.	1	2	3	4	5
5. Once I make up my mind, I stick to it.	1	2	3	4	5
6. I enjoy giving orders.	1	2	3	4	5
7. The work group should determine its own vacation schedule.	5	4	3	2	1
8. The work group should determine its own work schedule.	5	4	3	2	1
9. I feel comfortable being placed in a powerful position.	1	2	3	4	5
10. I like working in a group situation.	5	4	3	2	1
TOTAL D SCORE (Items 1–10 above)		D = _____			

	Strongly Disagree	Disagree	Neutral	Agree	Strongly Agree
11. It is easier to make a decision in a group.	1	2	3	4	5
12. Groups usually take up more time than they are worth.	5	4	3	2	1
13. I often ask for information from subordinates.	1	2	3	4	5
14. Groups give a deeper analysis of a problem.	1	2	3	4	5
15. I often use what subordinates have to say.	1	2	3	4	5
16. No one else can know as much about the problem as I do.	5	4	3	2	1
17. I usually make my decision before calling a staff meeting.	5	4	3	2	1
18. Better decisions are made in group situations.	1	2	3	4	5
19. A group is no better than its best member.	5	4	3	2	1
20. Group decisions are the best.	1	2	3	4	5
TOTAL I SCORE (Items 11–20 above)		I = _____			

Scoring Instructions

1. Record your D score (the sum of the answers to items 1–10 on the previous page).

    D = _____

2. Record your I score (the sum of the answers to items 11–20 on the previous page).

    I = _____

3. Determine your percentile score from the table below.

D			I	
Raw Score	Percentile		Raw Score	Percentile
19	1		22	1
20	1		23	1
21	1		24	1
22	3		25	2
23	5		26	2
24	6		27	4
25	9		28	6
26	12		29	7
27	15		30	8
28	22		31	15
29	27		32	18
30	37		33	26
31	42		34	39
32	53		35	48
33	64		36	56
34	72		37	69
35	81		38	78
36	85		39	84
37	91		40	87
38	94		41	92
39	97		42	96
40	98		43	98
41	99		44	99
42	99		45	99
43	100		46	100

4. Plot yourself on the grid on the following page.

    Percentiles are estimates based on data collected from 191 American managers.

FORM 9-1.

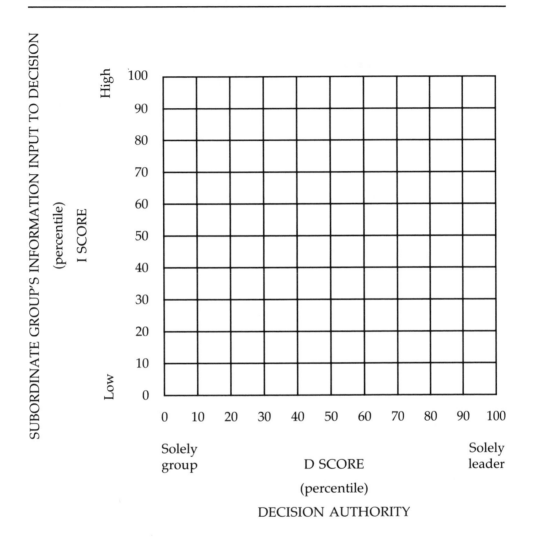

Chapter 10

Motivation

2:15 P.M. Harry is interrupted by a steady stream of people with one or another need, question, progress report, complaint:

Randy Johnson, vice-president, finance.

"I hear you're zipping off to the West Coast this evening with Ron. You realize it's going to play havoc with our financial planning later this week?"

"Yeah, I know," replies Harry. "Ron wants me to help him close the Calloway deal."

"Why don't you tell him to shove it, Harry? You've got at least a half-dozen more important projects pending right here at home."

"Ron seemed to feel quite strongly about this issue."

"Ron feels strongly about a lot of issues, especially if they involve leaping on an aircraft and dragging his subordinates around with him," says Randy.

"Look," replies Harry sternly, "like it or not, he's our boss and I respect that."

"OK, it's your life."

Pete, from accounting.

"Hi, Harry, are we still on for golf on Saturday? Joe and I would like to double the stakes—if you're game, that is."

"I hate to take your money," says Harry. "But if you insist, you're on. Ralph and I will show you some of the finer points of the game."

Jim, the union steward.

"Harry, Tom is up to his old tricks; he is threatening to use Bill instead of Clarence, even though Clarence has greater seniority. Will you please talk to him? Else I'm sure there will be a grievance hearing."

"Gee, Jim, I know he knows better."

"I know," agrees Jim, "but he seems to need to hear it from you every now and then."

Deborah Walters, production manager.

"Harry, I'd like you to reconsider the decision we made this morning concerning overtime. I just don't think I can meet my target without it."

"Deborah, that decision has been made for this week and I am sticking by it. You had your chance this morning to give all your arguments, which I presume you did. We'll discuss it next week, if you like, but until then, no overtime."

Carol Richards, from personnel.

"Mr. Thorpe, you know Mr. Greene died over the weekend. He served the company well for over thirty years, and we wondered if you were going to attend his funeral tomorrow? It's at 2:00 at Whitehall Chapel. I know it would mean a lot to his family."

"Carol, I'd like to go, but I'm leaving for the West Coast this evening. Why don't you talk with my secretary and make sure that we send flowers, and ask Quentin Hill if he can attend in my place?"

Harry's secretary.

"Dan Hall, the manager of the Dallas office, called while you were tied up. He wanted to tell you that the budget plan will be a week late."

"Did he now?" asks Harry. "Well, he's going to be the only branch office that is late and there's no excuse. Have him call me in L.A. tomorrow at 12:30 P.M., L.A. time."

2:27 P.M. Harry is staring morosely out of his window. His thoughts go like this: "Boy, it was easier before my promotion. Do I want this job? Sometimes the job seems to handle me more than I handle it. Do I have the right stuff to be a manager?"

The right stuff is not limited simply to skills. There is also the motivation to manage (MTM). And it is not a motivation that is inherent. Everybody does *not* have it. Do you?

According to research conducted over the past two decades, MTM and its associated attitudes and motives are likely to cause a person to:

- Choose a managerial career
- Be successful in a managerial position
- Move rapidly up the managerial ladder

In other words, the motivation to manage is essential for managerial success. The six components included in MTM, as outlined by John B. Miner, follow.[1]

1. *Favorable attitude toward authority.* Managers are expected to behave in ways that do not provoke negative reactions from those to whom they report; ideally, their behavior elicits positive responses. Equally, a manager must be able to represent his group upward in the organization and to obtain support for his actions at higher levels. This requires a good relationship between a manager and his superior.

2. *Desire to compete.* There is, at least insofar as peers are concerned, a strong competitive element built into managerial work; a manager must compete for the available rewards, both for himself and for his group. Certainly, without competitive behavior, rapid promotion is improbable. On occasion a challenge may come from below, even from among a manager's own subordinates.

3. *Assertive motivation.* There is a marked parallel between the requirements of the managerial role and the traditional assertive requirements of the masculine role as defined in our society. Although the behaviors expected of a father and those expected of a manager are by no means identical, there are many similarities: Both are supposed to take charge, to make decisions, to take such disciplinary action as may be necessary, and to protect the other members of their group . . . . When women are appointed to managerial positions, they are expected to follow an essentially assertive behavior pattern. (See Figure 10-1.)

4. *Desire to exercise power.* A manager must exercise power over his subordinates and direct their behavior in a manner consistent with organizational (and presumably his own) objectives. He must tell others what to do when this becomes necessary and enforce his words through positive and negative sanctions. The individual who finds such behavior difficult and emotionally disturbing, who does not wish

---

[1] John B. Miner, "The Real Crunch in Managerial Manpower," *Harvard Business Review*, Vol. 51, no. 6 (1973), p. 153. Copyright © 1973 by the President and Fellows of Harvard College. All rights reserved, reprinted by permission.

Figure 10-1. Assertive rights and behaviors.

Some Basic Assertive Rights

I have the right to:

1. Act in ways that promote my dignity and self-respect
2. Be treated with respect
3. Make my own decisions
4. Be recognized
5. Take time to think
6. Change my mind
7. Ask for what I want
8. Do less than I am humanly capable of doing
9. Ask for information
10. Make mistakes
11. Ask for another's time
12. Choose not to assert myself

Some Basic Assertive Behaviors

Eye contact—Looking directly at another person indicates that you are sincere about what you are saying and that the remarks are directed at him.

Body posture—Your message will be clearer if you face the person, sit or stand appropriately close to him, lean toward him, and hold your head erect.

Gestures—Use of hands and body are meant to accent the message, not be a distraction from it.

Facial expression—Effective assertions demand that the facial expression agree with the message; angry looks go well with angry words, etc.

Voice tone—Whispers and shouts bring about disbelief and defensiveness, respectively. A well-modulated, conversational tone is most often convincing without being intimidating.

Timing—Spontaneous expression is most assertive. At-the-time responses are more apt to be believable than those delayed and rehearsed. Caution: timing is greatly modified by circumstance; do your disagreeing in private as much as possible.

---

to impose his wishes on others or believes it wrong to do so, probably cannot be expected to meet this requirement.

5. *Desire for a distinctive position.* The managerial job tends to require a person to behave differently from the ways his subordinates behave toward each other. He must be willing to take the center of the stage and assume a position of high visibility; he must be willing to do things that invite attention, discussion, and perhaps criticism from those reporting to him; and he must accept a position of considerable importance in relation to the motives and emotions of others.

6. *A sense of responsibility.* The managerial job requires getting the work out and staying on top of routine demands. The things that have to be done must actually be done: constructing budget estimates, serving on committees, talking on the telephone, filling out employee rating forms, making salary recommendations, and so on. To meet these requirements, a manager must be capable of dealing with this type of routine and, ideally, of gaining some satisfaction from it.

RESEARCH RESULTS

Can you predict your degree of success and satisfaction with your job choice by knowing your MTM? It appears that you can. Research has compared the initial MTM with subsequent promotions over a five-year period in two departments. The results are presented in Table 10-1. Numerous other results have suggested the basic premise: To be a successful manager, you must have the motivation to manage.

How does this relate to you? Many managers evolved into their managerial positions with technical expertise in areas such as accounting, finance, marketing, and engineering. It is not uncommon to have a highly qualified individual promoted to managerial ranks. The change is dramatic. In his previous role he communicated primarily with things. He now must communicate primarily with people. Previously he could spend long uninterrupted hours reading, reflecting, collecting data, and working on technical projects. He now must spend large amounts of time in group meetings, talking on the telephone, being interrupted by subordinates, and doing the other frenetic activities that encompass a typical manager's day. Before, he could self-actualize by coming up with good technical solutions. Now he must engage in the sometimes unpleasant process of exercising power over others and engaging in competition for key resources.

Management is recognized as a step up the career ladder. It is noted

Table 10-1. *Motivation to manage.*

Initial motivation to manage and number of subsequent promotions over next five years in the R & D department of an oil company.

Motivation to Manage	No Promotions	One Promotion	Two or More Promotions
High	3 (25%)	6 (38%)	15 (71%)
Low	9 (75%)	10 (62%)	6 (29%)

Initial motivation to manage and rate of subsequent promotion over next five years in the marketing department of an oil company.

Motivation to Manage	No Promotions	Slow Promotion Rate	Fast Promotion Rate
High	13 (32%)	14 (64%)	16 (89%)
Low	28 (68%)	8 (36%)	2 (11%)

Source: John B. Miner, *The Human Constraint* (Washington, D.C.: Bureau of National Affairs, Inc., 1974), pp. 28–29. Reprinted with permission.

as a logical progression in one's professional advancement. Nevertheless, for the talented specialist with a low MTM, it may be a traumatic metamorphosis, indeed. A crucial question every manager should ask himself is: "Do I have sufficient MTM to ensure that I will be satisfied and successful in this position?"

DIAGNOSING YOUR MOTIVATION TO MANAGE

Now it's time to give you an opportunity to see where you stand on MTM. Complete the Motivation to Manage Audit (Form 10-1). This is a subjective assessment, and you may have some error, but at least it will sensitize you to the key variables and encourage you to think about these issues.

MTM AND JOB CHARACTERISTICS

Activities that are preferred and enjoyed are very different for the person with a high versus a low motivation to manage. Jobs with given characteristics are better or less well suited to each managerial type. Table 10-2 indicates those job characteristics that are best matched to people with high MTM and low MTM.

Table 10-2. *Job characteristics associated with MTM.*

Low MTM	*High MTM*
Relatively small span of control	Large span of control
Small number of subordinates	Large number of subordinates
High technical or engineering component	High people and budgetary component
Requires "hands on" expertise	Surrounded with technical experts
Limited number of activities per day	As many as 200 activities per day
Few interruptions	Many interruptions
Time for reading, analyzing	Time for interactions
Serves as facilitator to staff	Serves as "boss" to staff
Career progression increases technical expertise	Career progression equals managerial advancement
Little exercise of power required	Much intervention in lives of others
Lower-stress position	High-stress position

For you to be satisfied and successful in an organizational role, you must first attempt to match your basic motivation to the job. Does your job fit your motivation to manage? Different jobs require different levels of MTM. Look at Table 10-2 to determine if you are in a high- or low-MTM job.

Suppose you have just concluded that you have low MTM. What should you do? You have two alternatives:

1. Select jobs that are more appropriate to your MTM.
2. Attempt to change your MTM.

For you to be happy, feel fulfilled, and be successful in your job, you must fit the job requirements. There must be a match between your motivation and the characteristics of the job—the activities you like to do and those demanded by the job. Thorough and accurate self-assessment regarding your motivation to manage is very important as you make your career choices.

CHANGING YOUR MTM

It is generally accepted in psychology that a certain amount of motivation is learned. David McClelland has claimed the ability to teach people to increase their need for achievement.[2] He has also concluded that successful managers have a higher need for power than for affiliation.[3] This seems compatible with MTM, in that a manager must be prepared to exercise power over others in order to succeed.

Is it possible to increase a person's motivation to manage? Little research has been done in this area; there are no figures to cite. However, look at the six components of MTM. They are learned motives; therefore someone should be able to change them. Is it possible to change your MTM? Definitely! If you want to.

Do you want to change your MTM? If yes, you will need to formulate an action plan for changing each of the components of managerial motivation.

Return to the Motivation to Manage Audit (Form 10-1). Look at your desired level for each of the factors in your present position. The difference between the desired level and your actual level provides a managerial motivation deficit for each factor. Then specify on the Motivation to Manage Action Plan (Form 10-2) the specific steps you might take to increase your MTM on each factor and thus remove the deficit.

MOTIVATING OTHERS

So far we have focused on what motivates you, on diagnosing your internal motivational structure. As a successful manager, you must be able to effectively motivate others. I have attempted to provide a pragmatic approach to the problem of motivating others. In the old days this was easier, or it at least appears to have been easier from today's perspective. To dramatize this, let's go back to the Bethlehem Steel Company labor yard in Bethlehem, Pennsylvania, in the spring of 1899. Frederick Winslow Taylor, the father of scientific management, comes over to the laborer Schmidt, whose job it is to load pig iron onto gondola cars. (His real name was Henry Noll, but Taylor thought "Schmidt" sounded better in his historical record.) Schmidt's job was quite simple: Pick up a 91-pound pig of iron, walk horizontally across the yard and

---

[2]David C. McClelland, "Toward a Theory of Motive Acquisition," *American Psychologist*, Vol. 20 (1965), pp. 321–333.
[3]David C. McClelland and David H. Burnham, "Power Is the Great Motivator," *Harvard Business Review*, Vol. 54, no. 2 (March–April 1976), pp. 100–110.

up an inclined ramp with it, and deposit it in the gondola car. He would then return to the pile for another pig of iron and continue to do this throughout the day. During a typical day, Schmidt would load between 12 and 13 tons (long tons = 2,240 pounds each) of pig iron. For doing this he earned his daily wage of $1.15. Taylor studied him "scientifically." He carefully timed how long it took to pick up a pig, the speed with which he could walk horizontally up the incline with a load and back down the ramp unloaded, and so forth. He then made Schmidt a proposition: "Follow my instructions and increase your output and pay." Schmidt agreed, since he was put on a piece-rate system under which he could now earn $1.85 per day providing he reached his target. His target amounted to 45 to 48 tons of pig iron per day. According to Taylor, Schmidt reached his target and continued to perform at this rate on a regular basis.[4]

The enormity of his task is hard to contemplate in today's world. To accomplish his 45 tons per day, Schmidt had to walk the equivalent of eight miles each day with a 91-pound pig of iron in his arms. He then had to run eight miles back to the pile. According to Taylor's reports, Schmidt was not a large man, he weighed about 130 pounds, but was particularly suited to his work. Based on discussions I have had with the Human Energy Laboratory at the University of Pittsburgh, Schmidt's caloric energy output amounted to at least 5,000 to 6,000 calories per day. The poor man would have had to spend much of his waking hours eating just to keep from slowly disappearing over time.

As an interesting human-interest side of this story, although Taylor reported Schmidt as happy with his work, later reports indicate that Henry Noll became an excessive drinker and lost both his home and his job. Also, although Taylor's own reports seem to indicate great success and relative ease of implementation, such was not the case. The excellent history written by Daniel Nelson demonstrates some extremely difficult problems such as worker resistance, lack of cooperation from top management, political infighting, and other problems of modern-day organizational change.[5]

The moral of this story is that it is much easier to motivate an extremely deprived and hungry worker. Taylor's writings include stories of tremendous accomplishments with his "first-class men," individuals

---

[4]Frederick W. Taylor, "Time Study, Piece Work and the First-Class Man," *Transactions of the American Society of Mechanical Engineers*, Vol. 24 (1903), pp. 1356–1364. Reprinted in Harwood F. Merrill, *Classics in Management* (New York: American Management Association, 1960).

[5]Daniel Nelson, *Frederick W. Taylor and the Rise of Scientific Management* (Madison, Wisc.: University of Wisconsin Press, 1980).

willing to work at extremely high physical rates. He was able to accomplish these feats because the workers were at near subsistence levels and were willing to work quite hard to get that potential 60 percent increase in pay. Imagine the difficulties Taylor might have in a modern-day steel yard!

MASLOW'S HIERARCHY OF NEEDS

One very useful model for explaining the changes that have occurred in human motivation over the years is that developed by Abraham Maslow. Maslow's hierarchy argues that man's needs come in an ordered sequence, arranged in the following five needs categories:[6]

1. *Physical needs:* The need for food, water, air.
2. *Safety needs:* The need for security, stability, and freedom from threat to physical safety.
3. *Love needs:* The need for friends with whom one may affiliate.
4. *Esteem needs:* The need for self-respect and esteem of others. This includes recognition, attention, and appreciation from others.
5. *Self-actualization needs:* The need for self-fulfillment, to be able to grow and learn.

Maslow asserted that these needs were arranged on a "hierarchy of prepotency." In other words, they must be fulfilled in sequential fashion, starting with the lower order needs and progressing up the needs hierarchy. Someone who is dying of dehydration in the desert is not interested in esteem needs; a person being threatened by a criminal is not interested in self-actualization and so forth. Substantial follow-up research (and even Maslow's original speculations) indicate that the needs do not always have to be fulfilled in a lockstep fashion. At times the artist may be willing to starve in order to create, and such. But, in general, the hierarchy is a useful managerial model when we consider how to motivate workers. During the eight decades since Taylor's initial success, society at large has moved dramatically up the needs hierarchy. It would be quite difficult today to get a worker to triple output in return for a 60 percent increase in wages.

The manager of today must be able to assess where each of his subordinates and coworkers are on the hierarchy, and attempt to appeal to

---

[6]A. H. Maslow, "A Theory of Human Motive Acquisition," *Psychological Review*, Vol. 1 (1943), pp. 370–396.

their appropriate needs. Some people crave status and recognition. Others want strongly to be a member of a cohesive team and "to belong." Others have a tremendous need to be creative, be innovative, and learn new skills. If you have a motivational problem with a worker, attempt to answer these three questions:

1. Where is he on Maslow's needs hierarchy?
2. What needs will motivate him?
3. How can you help him to satisfy those needs?

HERZBERG'S MOTIVATIONAL HYGIENE THEORY

Frederick Herzberg has suggested that there are two types of motivational factors: hygiene factors and motivators.[7] He suggests that the hygiene factors are necessary conditions for a satisfied worker, but they do not guarantee satisfaction. If they are absent, you will have an unhappy worker; but their presence does not guarantee contentment. The hygiene factors include:

- Company policy and administration
- Supervision
- Relationship with supervisor
- Working conditions
- Salary
- Relationship with peers
- Personal life
- Relationship with subordinates
- Status
- Security

The hygiene factors satisfy the lower level Maslow needs. On the other hand, there are motivators that account for satisfaction in the worker. The motivators include:

- Achievement
- Recognition
- Work itself
- Responsibility

---

[7]Frederick Herzberg, "One More Time: How Do You Motivate Employees?" *Harvard Business Review*, Vol. 65 (1987), pp. 109–120.

Figure 10-2. Maslow and Herzberg compared.

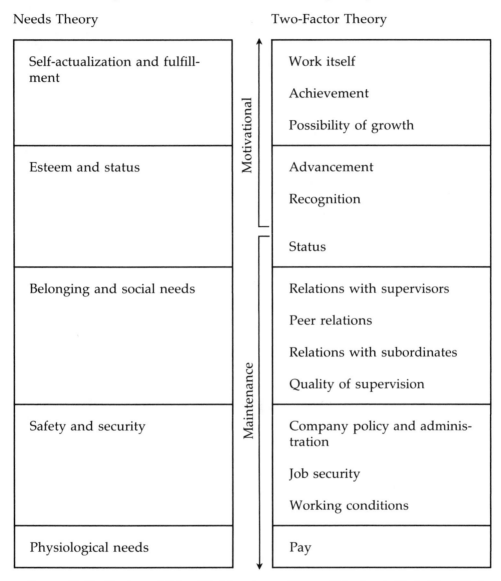

Needs Theory

Two-Factor Theory

Source: Keith Davis and John W. Newstrom, *Human Behavior at Work* (New York: McGraw-Hill, 1985), p. 77. Used with permission.

- Advancement
- Growth

In other words, the motivators are found at the higher levels of Maslow's hierarchy, as can be seen in Figure 10-2.

Herzberg's model has been challenged on both empirical and conceptual grounds. However, it has been demonstrated to be quite powerful as a general guide to the process of "job enrichment." The basic philosophy is that you can enrich someone's job and induce that individual to work harder by making the work more interesting and satisfying.

If you would like to explore the possibility of job enrichment, perform the following steps:

1. Remove serious dissatisfiers. For example, make sure working conditions are pleasant, pay is equitable, and supervision is fair.
2. Vertically load the job content on the satisfiers. For example:
   • Push responsibility downward.
   • Push planning upward.
   • Provide meaningful modules of work.
   • Increase job freedom.
   • Introduce new and difficult tasks.

It is well known that individuals tend to do what is satisfying to them. They are more likely to repeat behaviors that result in rewards and to not repeat behaviors that do not. Consequently, if you can design a work environment in which individuals are reinforced by the work itself, you will experience much greater effectiveness as a manager.

MOTIVATION AND OTHER THEORIES

Motivation is a complex phenomenon, and there is no panacea for getting people to work harder and with more enthusiasm. But it is possible to draw on material mentioned in other chapters to help you attain higher levels of motivation in your work and in the work of your subordinates. In addition to the standard motivational theories, look at these issues:

Being a Good Leader

A good leader by definition generates followers. If you lead with integrity, enthusiasm, concern, and support for your employees, if you make correct decisions and communicate with them effectively, you will have more motivated subordinates. Use the leadership principles presented in Chapter 9 to fit your style to the situation. If you do, you will be perceived as a sensitive leader who gets extra motivation from his followers.

Rewarding Desired Behavior

People tend to repeat behaviors that are reinforced and not repeat behaviors that are not reinforced. It's a simple, fundamental behavior-modification principle. How many times have you seen a reward system that is just not working? Use your position as a manager to provide praise, recognition, and a variety of reinforcements for desired behavior. To a certain extent, the successful manager is a cheerleader for his team. Take the time to reward, and you will have more motivated subordinates.

Using Management by Objectives (MBO)

Often there is nothing more satisfying than attaining a challenging goal. If your MBO system is working properly, the goals themselves will become motivators. Set goals intelligently and in such a way that they are a challenge, keep your subordinates' attention focused on their goals and achievement, show them that you care, and you will have motivated subordinates.

Motivation is an important variable in executive survival. Integrate the material in this chapter with the rest of the book to get maximally motivated employees and to stay motivated yourself.

CONCLUSION

You have now had an opportunity to assess in a personal way your motivation to manage (MTM). The logical steps in this assessment are portrayed in the flowchart shown in Figure 10-3. Try to accomplish this in as perceptive a way as possible. It's fun to consider your personal motivational structure and to talk to others about career, job, and personal needs. If you can better understand where you are concerning your motivation to manage, you will be in a better position to perform your job at peak efficiency. If your MTM is insufficient for your current or future job prospects, then you must seriously consider changing these needs or changing your career. Millions of people get matched to millions of jobs through ad hoc and almost accidental sequences of events. In this chapter you have been provided with a framework for consciously and analytically assessing the match between your motivational structure and the manager's job.

The second aspect of this chapter is your attempts to motivate others.

Figure 10-3. Motivating yourself and others.

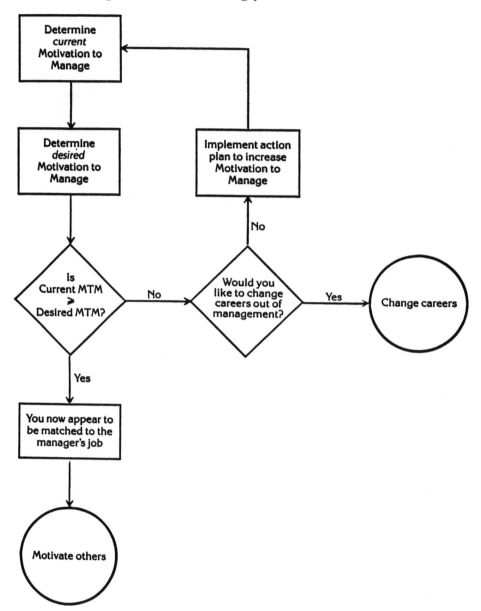

Remember that different people have different motivational needs. You may have to respond in a very contingent manner to individuals on your team. Entire books have been written on this topic, and human motivation is indeed a complex area. In brief, you should try to assume the role of a facilitator who links up needed satisfactions with desired job performances. If you can structure an environment in which diverse individual needs are met through job performance, you will find yourself with a more cohesive and dedicated work group. If you can master these techniques, you will be well on your way to becoming a highly effective and successful manager.

MOTIVATION TO MANAGE AUDIT

How motivated to manage are you? Circle the number for each item below that best represents your estimate of your current level.

	Well Below Average		Average		Well Above Average	
1. Favorable attitude toward authority	0 1 2 3	4 5 6	7 8 9 10
2. Desire to compete	0 1 2 3	4 5 6	7 8 9 10
3. Assertive motivation	0 1 2 3	4 5 6	7 8 9 10
4. Desire to exercise power	0 1 2 3	4 5 6	7 8 9 10
5. Desire for a distinctive position	0 1 2 3	4 5 6	7 8 9 10
6. A sense of responsibility	0 1 2 3	4 5 6	7 8 9 10

TOTAL MOTIVATION TO MANAGE = _____

Now place a check mark next to the number for each item that represents your best estimate of where you would *like to be*. The difference between your *desired* and *actual* scores for each item is your MTM deficit on that factor. It will be used in completing your Motivation to Manage Action Plan (Form 10-2).

MOTIVATION TO MANAGE ACTION PLAN

Record your MTM deficit (desired–actual) for each factor below. Then specify appropriate steps you can take to increase your MTM on each factor and remove the deficit.

1. FAVORABLE ATTITUDE TOWARD AUTHORITY   Deficit: _____

    Action plan: _____

_____

_____

_____ Probability of success: _____

2. DESIRE TO COMPETE   Deficit: _____

    Action plan: _____

_____

_____

_____ Probability of success: _____

3. ASSERTIVE MOTIVATION   Deficit: _____

    Action plan: _____

_____

_____

_____ Probability of success: _____

4. DESIRE TO EXERCISE POWER   Deficit: _____

    Action plan: _____

_____

_____

_____ Probability of success: _____

5. DESIRE FOR DISTINCTIVE POSITION   Deficit: _____

   Action plan: _____

   _____

   _____

   _____ Probability of success: _____

6. A SENSE OF RESPONSIBILITY   Deficit: _____

   Action plan: _____

   _____

   _____

   _____ Probability of success: _____

Chapter 11

Organizational Design

3:05 P.M.   Harry has a meeting with Ralph Kingsley, the production manager, and Henry Carothers, the sales manager. Harry dreads these meetings. They are held monthly and should be held weekly, but they always seem to result in harsh words and unpleasantness.

"Good afternoon, Henry, Ralph. I think we've had an excellent month," begins Harry.

"Well, production cut down markedly on its scrap this month, which was one of my goals," says Ralph.

"And sales are up five percent over this month last year," says Henry. "It really has been a good month."

"I've been meaning to talk to you about that," says Ralph. Harry grits his teeth; here it comes. . . .

"Oh, really?" says Henry. "Surely you don't have any complaints about increased sales."

"Well, of course not," says Ralph, "but I am concerned about the delivery dates your men are promising customers. Do you think we are magicians on the line? There are physical limits as to what people and machines can produce, you know."

"Sometimes, you drive me crazy!" growls Henry. "Do you want this

221

company to be profitable or not? Do you want to increase our market share or not? I am really tired of fighting with you. I used to think we were on the same side, but I find dealing with you harder than dealing with any of my customers."

"Harry, you are going to have to do something," they say in unison. "This can't continue."

Harry allows himself the luxury of withdrawal. These are both very good employees. They are highly motivated and excellent performers. He basically gets along well with both of them, even if Kingsley does get a little hung up on details. But Harry is concerned that they're so often at each other's throats. Is it just because one man is sales and one man is production? Even though this conflict is age old and common to many industries, he still feels that he should be able to resolve it or at least handle the problem better. "If I am a good manager," he says to himself, "I should be able to handle their problems and get them to work together smoothly."

Harry is experiencing a problem in organizational design. Next to staffing an organization, the most important function of a manager is to design that organization so that people can work together effectively. This chapter provides you with some basic tools for solving your organizational design problems.

"But," you may say, "I can't redesign the organization. I'm just a manager, not the CEO." Or you may think, "I don't need this, I'll read this chapter sometime later if I have a real organizational design problem."

However, you don't need to be president in order to find an understanding of organizational design useful. You already practice organizational design if you have hiring and firing authority and responsibility for planning the work of others. Chances are, you do design activities continually.

TWO KEY CONCEPTS: DIFFERENTIATION AND INTEGRATION

You can become an organizational designer and do as good a job as Booz-Allen or McKinsey, perhaps even better, if you keep two key concepts in mind:

1. Differentiation means different people doing different things. Every firm has accountants, salespeople, clerical staff, production workers,

and so on. This results in a differentiation between corporate sub-units. Differentiation is the degree to which specialization in task activities occurs.

2. Integration is the quality or state of collaboration that exists among departments. Integration provides the coordination between the various differentiated subunits necessary to get the job done.[1]

Organizational design, then, means simply specifying the differentiation necessary and providing the integration required to coordinate the diverse and differentiated subunits. In this chapter you will discover the methodology for accomplishing these two tasks.

The central problem facing any organizational designer is that differentiation and integration are often antagonistic. This fact is demonstrated in Figure 11-1. If your company is totally integrated (point A), then it is more difficult to have the diverse and differentiated specialists essential to provide necessary management services. If you have a lot

Figure 11-1. The antagonism of differentiation and integration.

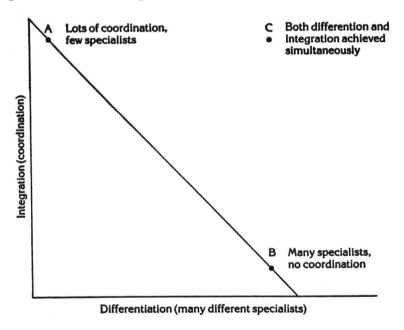

[1] Adapted from P. R. Lawrence and J. W. Lorsch, *Organization and Environment* (Cambridge, Mass.: Harvard University Press, 1967).

of differentiation (point B), integration is more difficult. It is possible to reach point C, where you have both, but it is difficult. It requires both a knowledge of organizational design and a lot of organizational energy.

When do you need differentiation and when do you need integration? Behavioral researchers have been working on this problem for over two decades, and their findings can be summarized quite simply:

- The more dynamic the environment faced by the firm, the more differentiation required. High-technology firms and firms in environments of rapid change must have differentiated specialists in order to survive.
- The higher the level of integration achieved in a firm, the better its performance. Regardless of its environment, the better integrated (coordinated) the company, the more successful it will be.

DIFFERENTIATION AND THE ENVIRONMENT

How tough is your business environment? Is it turbulent, demanding, hostile, complex, and ever changing? There are a variety of models for looking at the nature of a company's external environment. A number of researchers have articulated them in some detail.[2] From their work, two important fundamental dimensions of environment emerge.

1. *Complexity.* This refers to the homogeneity-heterogeneity dimension of the environment. You might visualize it as simple versus complex. It relates to the number of different components that exist in the environment. The more identifiable and different the components, the more the heterogeneity and thus the greater the complexity.

2. *Dynamism.* This refers to the rate of change over time, or "movement," that occurs in the environment. It often consists of two subcomponents: (1) A higher rate of change makes an environment more dynamic; and (2) The greater the unpredictability of the change, the more dynamic the environment. For example, in the agricultural industry the harvest occurs every September, and even though there is a high rate of change during that time, it can be anticipated. This is in contrast to a high-tech environment, where the next change is highly unpredictable.

---

[2] Robert H. Miles, *Macro Organizational Behavior* (Glenview, Ill.: Scott Foresman, 1980).

Figure 11-2. Organizational elements.

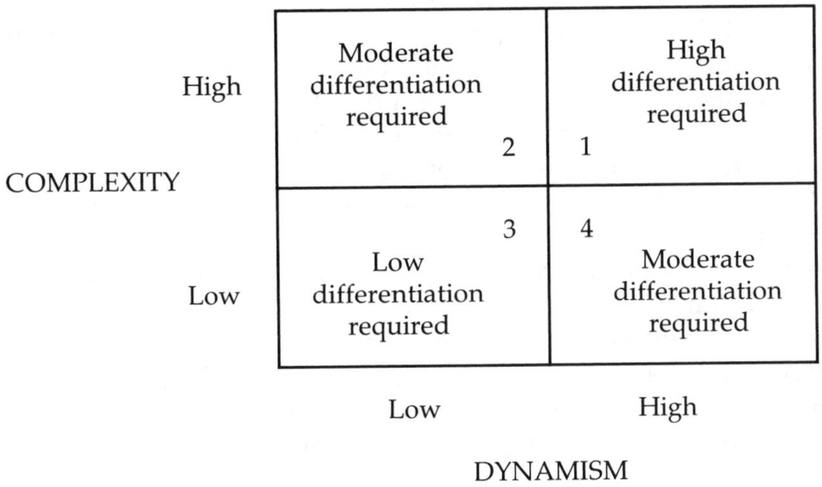

	Low	High
High	Moderate differentiation required 2	1 High differentiation required
Low	3 Low differentiation required	4 Moderate differentiation required

COMPLEXITY (vertical axis: High / Low)

DYNAMISM (horizontal axis: Low / High)

These two dimensions of complexity and dynamism can be used to define the environment and indicate how difficult and challenging it is for the company. As you can see from the model shown in Figure 11-2, we can look at environments that are high and low on each of these two dimensions.

Cell 1 represents the most difficult environment in which to operate, because it is high on both complexity and dynamism. This type of environment is quite challenging and requires the highest level of differentiation.

In contrast, cell 3 represents a much more benign environment with low complexity and low dynamism. This environment requires the least degree of differentiation.

The remaining cells (2 and 4) require moderate levels of differentiation. They are high on one of the environmental dimensions and low on the other.

Where do you find your company? The more difficult the environment in terms of complexity and dynamism, the more likely you are to need higher levels of organizational differentiation.

DIFFERENTIATION: HOW TO SET IT

The differentiation of a company or department is very simple to regulate. First, you hire the specialists you need to cope with this differentiation. Second, you manage them after they arrive.

The most important function for correct differentiation is staffing. As a manager you hire people with diverse skills. If you hire a patent attorney, a CPA, a robotics specialist, and a computer analyst along with a couple of quality-control wizards, you will have a differentiated group of individuals. You presumably are hiring them to fill the jobs necessary to accomplish essential tasks in your work group. The choice of which specialists to hire and the decision as to which special skills are necessary for effective production are part of manpower planning and are covered in more detail in Chapter 13.

After these people are hired, job design, control systems, reward systems, and training and development programs either emphasize or minimize their differentiation. The major task of management relative to differentiation is handled during strategic planning. The selection of organizational goals dictates the need for specialists. The remaining and ongoing problem for management is integration. How do you coordinate these differentiated task functions into one smooth-flowing operation?

ORGANIZATIONAL INTEGRATION: HOW TO SET IT

There are five possible conditions of organizational integration:

D = Dis-Integration (no information exchange)
U = Unstable (information exchange but no agreement)
I = Instantaneous (stage I—modest short-term integration)
II = Process (stage II—moderate integration)
III = Composite (stage III—highest level of integration)

The key variables that define the integration stage are (1) information exchange, (2) agreement on decision, and (3) agreement on decision-making authority. As you can see from Figure 11-3, each of these variables can have either a high or low position. This leads to eight possible states of the world, as shown in Figure 11-3.

The first four positions are entitled Dis-Integration. This is because there is no information exchange. Integration is impossible without information exchange, and hence the Dis-Integration, or D position, is the least integrated possible. Dis-Integration occurs when organizational subunits are not talking with each other at all. This may or may not be bad. If they have no need to talk, then there is perhaps no problem.

Figure 11-3. Stages of integration.

DIS-INTEGRATION

	D							
	Low	*High*	*Low*	*High*	*Low*	*High*	*Low*	*High*
Information exchange	☑	☐	☑	☐	☑	☐	☑	☐
Agreement on decision	☑	☐	☐	☑	☑	☐	☐	☑
Agreement on decision-making authority	☑	☐	☑	☐	☐	☑	☐	☑

	UNSTABLE		INTEGRATION					
	U		I		II		III	
	Low	*High*	*Low*	*High*	*Low*	*High*	*Low*	*High*
Information exchange	☐	☑	☐	☑	☐	☑	☐	☑
Agreement on decision	☑	☐	☐	☑	☑	☐	☐	☑
Agreement on decision-making authority	☑	☐	☑	☐	☐	☑	☐	☑

However, if performance is being negatively impacted, then the Dis-Integration position can be highly undesirable.

The next integration position is called Unstable. This occurs when a lot of information is being exchanged and yet there is no agreement: Individuals are not agreeing on the decisions, and they are not agreeing on the decision-making authority. Consequently, this position is most likely unstable because the conflict resulting either will provide enough tension to change the status or, perhaps more likely, may cause communication to break down as the system moves back into the Dis-Integration position. The Unstable position is not all bad, because at least people are talking, and some solutions may arise if they move into the stages of integration.

The true levels of integration are stages I, II, and III. Each of these has various levels of application and may be appropriate to different situations. Each will be discussed in more depth. But first, how you set each variable is crucial to organizational design success. An example might be useful.

Six months earlier, Harry had observed a minor fire storm occurring between Kingsley and Carothers with regard to the Prentice account. It was the usual "production versus sales" issue. Sales wanted to give the customer the earth and production wanted to provide minimal flexibility on product design and scheduling. The communications were almost a source of humor in the organization. There was a furious exchange of memos and Harry got copies of every one. There were a few meetings, but all that seemed to result was the elevation of the conflict rather than a resolution. The system was in an Unstable mode, as follows:

	Low	High
Information exchange	☐	☑
Agreement on decision	☑	☐
Agreement on decision-making authority	☑	☐

This conflict bothered Harry greatly. The system was in an Unstable mode and something had to be done. Three months earlier, Harry had a meeting with Kingsley and Carothers about the Prentice account. As sales manager, Carothers had approved an order for a special set of red stampings for Prentice Manufacturing Company, even though the standard product was blue. The order was a rush. Kingsley, as production manager, did not want to retool the paint room for this special run. They met in Harry's office to resolve the conflict. It went like this:

CAROTHERS: Prentice is one of our best customers, and competitive pressures are increasing. They have recently made a model change in their equipment and would like our product painted red instead of blue. They need these parts in three weeks. I have already given a verbal commitment that we would accommodate them in this matter. It seems to me it's a minor request that means a lot to an important customer and we should be able to fulfill it.

KINGSLEY: Harry, I know it seems like a small request on the customer's behalf, but it's going to wreak havoc with our production output this month. The reason we standardized on the blue paint was that every time we change to another color, the complete paint line has to be shut down, nozzles cleaned, new paint reservoirs added, and so on. Then we go back to the standard blue and the same process must be repeated. In addition to this we are supposed to bump other orders and put a high priority on the shipping schedule to Prentice. I don't like what this request is going to do to my production output. I would rather that we explain to Prentice why we can't do it.

After a lengthy and heated debate, and evaluation of the pros and cons, Harry decided they should provide Prentice with their requested red stampings on a priority shipping schedule; everyone left ready to move forward to other problems. Harry felt relieved that the problem had been solved and that everyone was in agreement, but something still bothered him. What was it?

Stage I: Instantaneous Integration

Was Harry solving a design problem in what he had accomplished? He was, but in a rather narrow way. The scale below indicates the level he reached on each of the three critical integration dimensions:

	Low	High
Information exchange	☐	☑
Agreement on decision	☐	☑
Agreement on decision-making authority	☑	☐

Harry got a lot of information out on the table and persuaded Carothers and Kingsley to agree on the paint decision, but he still felt uneasy. Why? Because he had provided a one-time solution to a recurring problem. The next time a similar problem comes up, it will generate the same hostility, aggression, and anger, and it will have to be solved all over again. Therefore, this stage of integration is called Instantaneous Integration; a decision is reached that is satisfactory in this instance only.

Stage II: Process Integration

Two months after the first meeting, the Prentice problem reappeared. This time Harry solved it differently. After Carothers and Kingsley had given their arguments, Harry decided that Carothers could have 10 percent of the monthly output in any color he wanted. This solution would allow sales to become more responsive to customer needs by being able to react quickly and with more flexibility. Kingsley, however, left Harry's office somewhat unhappy. Although he basically agreed that Harry had the right to make such a decision, he was concerned about future decisions (promises) that Carothers might make.

Harry's organizational integration profile this time is as follows:

	Low	*High*
Information exchange	☐	☑
Agreement on decision	☑	☐
Agreement on decision-making authority	☐	☑

Harry has achieved information exchange and agreement on decision-making authority, but he has not accomplished agreement on the decision. Kingsley and Carothers understand each other's problem, and both agree that Carothers has decision-making authority for 10 percent of production output, but neither man has changed his feelings on the decision itself. Kingsley wishes that none of the output need be specially painted. Carothers wants more than 10 percent of the output to be available for custom jobs.

What happened in this meeting is an example of stage II, Process Integration. Harry tried to set up a process, or system, for solving integration needs in the future. By providing others with decision-making authority to solve future problems of this same type, he hoped to be able to avoid time-consuming Instantaneous Integration meetings and solve the "special paint" problem in a more systematic fashion. The benefits of this approach are obvious: If Harry can solve this problem in a systematic fashion through Process Integration, the next time a similar problem arises, it will automatically be solved by the mechanisms Harry has constructed. In other words, Harry will not have to rediscover a solution each time the problem recurs. However, the major pitfall of Process Integration is that it does not guarantee agreement on decisions. Kingsley left Harry's office upset and skeptical of the decisions the sales manager might be making. Carothers, on the other hand, still had authority over only 10 percent of the production and felt he might need more for special orders.

Stage III: Composite Integration

Two weeks later, Harry tries to solve the problem in a more long-term fashion. Kingsley comes into the 2:00 P.M. meeting in a state of great agitation, waving a sheet of paper.

KINGSLEY: Harry, look at this. Sales stayed under their 10 percent quota on color changes last month, but they specified color changes to seven different customers! I had to shut down the production line fourteen times for paint changes! In other words, Carothers has split up the total 10 percent into smaller lots of 1.5 percent output, each one requiring shutdown time for a paint change.

CAROTHERS: Look, I'm only trying to be responsive to my customers' needs. It's a very competitive world out there, Ralph, and many customers are experiencing the same sort of problems in product development as Prentice. I stuck to the guidelines of our agreement, and have requested color changes on less than 10 percent of last month's output.

KINGSLEY: Sure, you stuck to the guidelines, but you're still strangling my production output. We can't shut down the paint line all the time and still reach our quotas. Harry, when I agreed with you about the 10 percent, I thought sales would request one or two orders that would use up the entire 10 percent. This current approach may be more responsive to customers, but it's driving us crazy on the shop floor.

HARRY: OK, look, we're all working toward the same goal. We want to achieve the level of collaboration required to function effectively. However, we want to do it the quickest way possible, and we can't spend our lives in meetings deciding production and sales policy. Whenever we sit down at one of these meetings, we want to make sure three things happen: one, that information is exchanged; two, that agreement is reached on the decision; and three, that agreement is reached on decision-making authority. I propose to you that sales have the discretion to modify the paint color of up to three orders per month amounting to a total of no more than 10 percent of the monthly output. I will check with each of you on a monthly basis to make sure that we are achieving our goal of responsiveness to customers without handicapping production efficiency. Can you both agree on this?

KINGSLEY: Yes, I can live with it.

CAROTHERS: Yes, it looks like the best solution.

What has Harry accomplished in his meeting today?

	Low	*High*
Information exchange	☐	☑
Agreement on decision	☐	☑
Agreement on decision-making authority	☐	☑

That's right. Harry has just accomplished stage III: Composite Integration. Both Kingsley and Carothers (1) understand each other's problem, (2) agree on who has authority for what production decisions, and (3) can live with the decision reached. Although it can sometimes be costly, in the right situation (an important enough and repetitive problem) Composite Integration can be both efficient and effective. It can be efficient because agreement on decision-making authority is often necessary in the organization in order to minimize time spent in debating decisions. It can be effective because full consensus and cooperation of specialists is achieved.

As shown in Figure 11-4, as you move from stage I to stage III integration, the time frame becomes longer and more resources are required. Ask yourself the question, "Do I need a quick fix or a long-term solution?"[3] Then position yourself on the continuum as shown in the figure.

Figure 11-4. Stages of integration vs. time frame
and resources required.

TIME FRAME

Short term ⟵————————————⟶ Long term

	I Instantaneous	*II Process*	*III Composite*
Information exchange	high	high	high
Agreement on decision	high	low	high
Agreement on decision-making authority	low	high	high

Low ⟵————————————⟶ High

RESOURCES (Time and Energy) REQUIRED

---

[3]Ralph H. Kilmann, L. Pondy, and Dennis P. Slevin, eds., *The Management of Organization Design, Vols. I and II* (New York: American Elsevier, 1976).

FIVE POSSIBLE INTEGRATION POSITIONS

Remember, there are three dimensions of organizational integration—information exchange, agreement on decision, and agreement on decision-making authority—with two positions on each—high or low. There are, therefore, eight possible integration positions. But the low-information-exchange situation is unworkable because obviously there can be no integration without adequate information exchange. Therefore, the four positions characterized by low information exchange will be treated as one.

It is important to understand where your organization is and in which direction you would like to move on these three dimensions for optimal organizational integration. Let's try to find out.

D = Dis-Integration (no information exchange)

	Low	High
Information exchange	☑	☐
Agreement on decision (irrelevant)	☐	☐
Agreement on decision-making authority (irrelevant)	☐	☐

You have experienced numerous situations in which a lack of information exchange has been costly and inefficient. For example, your southern division needs a spare unit for a customer, and they order it from the original manufacturer, paying a premium price and waiting two weeks for delivery. But your northern division already had three of these same parts in stock.

Information exchange is essential to effective management! Integration is impossible without adequate information exchange. No effective coordination can take place without information flow. Therefore, the remaining four positions assume a high level of information exchange.

U = Unstable (information exchange but no agreement)

	Low	High
Information exchange	☐	☑
Agreement on decision	☑	☐
Agreement on decision-making authority	☑	☐

This position represents an organization with adequate information exchange but in a high state of instability and potential conflict. Thus, no matter how hard the people work, the organization will fail! No agreement exists on who has authority to make decisions or on the decisions themselves. A great deal of conflict is likely. In fact, war between nations (as well as within corporations) occurs when there is absolutely no agreement on either decisions or decision-making authority.

I = Instantaneous (stage I—modest short-term integration)

	Low	High
Information exchange	☐	☑
Agreement on decision	☐	☑
Agreement on decision-making authority	☑	☐

Many of the case examples used in the participative management literature reflect this type of organizational system. A great deal of time is spent achieving consensus on particular decisions and generating high levels of motivation. But an organization may run into difficulties when its environment becomes more unpredictable. Under such circumstances, time and resource pressures become more severe.

The problem with this stage I Instantaneous Integration is that each new problem must be solved in an ad hoc fashion. This wastes time and requires renegotiation each time a new (or old) problem crops up.

II = Process (stage II—moderate integration)

	Low	High
Information exchange	☐	☑
Agreement on decision	☑	☐
Agreement on decision-making authority	☐	☑

In this position, routine integrative problems can be handled in an efficient manner. Less time is spent on achieving consensus, because the lines of decision-making authority are clear and agreement on particular decisions is less necessary. However, if people do not basically agree on decisions, they will eventually develop a low level of morale and motivation. Stage II Process Integration is best illustrated by the watercooler wisdom, "The boss may not always be right, but he's always the boss." But in the long run, he'll only stay boss if he's right in the majority of instances. Thus, Process Integration can be efficient, but it must be used sparingly.

III = Composite (stage III—highest level of integration)

	Low	High
Information exchange	☐	☑
Agreement on decision	☐	☑
Agreement on decision-making authority	☐	☑

Composite Integration represents the fully integrated organization. A high level of information exchange takes place. The lines of decision-making authority are clear cut, understood, and accepted. There is basic agreement on the decisions made in the organization. The system achieves both effective decision making and high motivation; true collaboration and unity of effort are achieved.

THE INTEGRATION MODEL IN ACTION

The integration model can be quite effective in a variety of settings. The following true case, implemented by one of my executive MBA students, shows how organizational design can be an effective management tool in a health-care environment.

Statement of Problem[4]

In my new position, I have administrative responsibility for nearly $11 million and the daily operations of five major clinical departments. As I assumed my new responsibilities, the capital and operating budgets were being implemented for the new fiscal year. One problem with the span of control I had in my new position became very evident: Although I was responsible for the operations of my clinical areas, the bulk of the money budgeted for capital expenditures in these departments was controlled by nursing cost centers.

Application of Model: Organizational Integration

Further investigation made it clear that:

- Cost-center managers had not received complete information.
- There was no understanding of the decision that had placed money in their cost centers.

---

[4]Betsy Boland Murdock, personal communication, April 1988.

• There was no understanding of who had the authority to decide when the money was to be expended.

This year the problem was solved. Stage I Instantaneous Integration was achieved by my explaining the need for the equipment and requesting that it be ordered. These requests were agreed to without incident. The money was spent, the equipment was ordered. The problem, however, was not solved for the long term. The organizational integration model [in this book] suggested a solution for the future.

Process for Achieving Integration

The capital-budgeting process at the hospital begins in November, when all cost-center managers are asked to submit listings of equipment they desire for the coming year. These lists are sent to purchasing, which prices the equipment and returns the lists to the cost centers. The cost-center managers then prepare justifications explaining the need for the equipment, its impact on other areas, staff additions required to operate, and so on. The AVPs are responsible for reviewing and approving these justifications, which are then submitted to the VPs.

A capital equipment committee ranks requests, and eventually deletes many of them. When the budget is finally approved, the funds are assigned by finance staff to the cost centers that appear to be where the equipment will be housed—hence the lack of knowledge by cost-center managers of the timing of expenditures.

My plan in applying the organizational integration model was to share information among all cost centers that would be impacted by a department's plans. For ease of presentation, I use the department of OB/GYN as an example.

Step 1. I determined that six cost centers would be impacted by OB/GYN's plans: OB/GYN clinic, chairman's office, labor and delivery, nursing floor, operating room, and intensive care nursery.

Step 2. I invited all the cost-center managers, the AVPs they reported to (two, besides me), and the chairman of the department of OB/GYN to the meeting.

Step 3. I explained that the purpose was to make sure the chairman had a complete picture of all equipment being requested that would affect his service.

The first topic raised regarded decision-making authority. Did this mean I intended to "take over" responsibility for their cost centers? I assured them that was not the intention and I reviewed with them the problem I had noted during the current year. The agreement on decision-making authority was thereby reaffirmed.

> *Step 4.* Each cost-center manager reviewed the equipment requests submitted that were intended for use by OB/GYN staff. The chairman explained what his plans were, especially for the items in his budget plan. This was particularly important information, since 90 percent of the funds for this equipment would end up in one of the cost centers. Now they will know what it is for.

At this point, a totally unexpected benefit of this information sharing occurred. Some of the cost centers had requested funds for equipment that was sitting idle in other areas. For instance, the ambulatory clinic had requested two Dopplers. The labor and delivery room had one they did not need. The intensive care nursery needed a centrifuge. The ambulatory clinic had one they did not need, since they had been moved next to the pediatric clinic, which had one. The chairman had requested a two-headed teaching microscope. The manager of the OR had enough money left in her huge budget, owing to unexpected discounts on equipment she had ordered, to buy it for him this year. All of these items were stricken from the new requests.

> *Step 5.* I committed to all present that I would routinely share program-development plans with them, including advance notice of when new physicians were arriving.

Analysis of Results

The meeting produced the results I had hoped for but hardly believed possible:

	Low	High
Information exchange	☐	☑
Agreement on decision	☐	☑
Agreement on decision-making authority	☐	☑

The camaraderie begun at this meeting has continued and appears to be growing stronger. I have heard that cost-center managers who never used to communicate are now visiting each other's areas and beginning to share expertise, equipment plans, and the like. Composite Integration has been achieved in this department. Better yet, the positive feeling of the cost-center managers and AVPs involved has been infectious, and I understand they are encouraging a similar system in other areas.

INTEGRATION DEVICES

There are a variety of ways of achieving organizational integration, as shown in Figure 11-5. For instance, goals provide a community of interest that helps foster integration. Policies often are the logical outcome of goals. Plans often have a strong coordinative element to them. The management information system is frequently a major source of data for integrative purposes. Hierarchy and departments are both ways of accomplishing coordination. Some people have jobs designated specifically as integrators and some teams work together for the purpose of integration. The founding rules and roles can help achieve the commonality of action necessary for an integrated organization.

All of these techniques are crucial to an organization as differentiation increases. One possible explanation for the downfall of People Express may be expressed in the terms of organizational integration. As a small, regional, "niche" carrier, the operation was a highly regarded success. However, it differentiated rapidly. It expanded routes dramatically. It purchased a variety of used aircraft from other carriers, which greatly complicated maintenance issues because each plane was built slightly different. In short, organizational differentiation increased very rapidly while the company appeared to have a philosophical objection to organizational integration. It seemed to enjoy its somewhat renegade status. It had a particular dislike of hierarchy, departmentalization, rules, policies, and other integration devices. Differentiation soared and integration was not provided to bring things back together. The results are known. In the first quarter of 1986, complaints filed with the U.S. Department of Transportation soared to 10.3 per 100,000 passengers. This is more than double the rate of the second worst carrier and triple the rate of the industry average. Remember, if you are increasing the differentiation in your organization, you must also provide the necessary integrative mechanisms to make it work.

Figure 11-5. Integration devices.

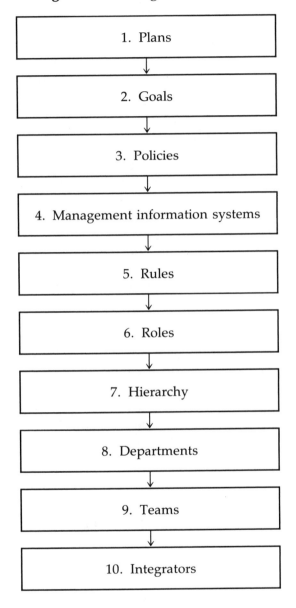

ORGANIZATIONAL INTEGRATION: WHERE ARE YOU?

Take a few minutes to diagnose where you are in achieving organizational integration for your department, your division, or your company. You don't need to be in complete charge of your unit in order to benefit from this exercise.

Typical integration problems are as follows:

- Lack of information exchange. There just isn't the kind of information exchange between departments to allow you to coordinate your activities with others effectively. Integration, of whatever kind, is impossible.
- Wasteful use of information-exchange mechanisms (such as meetings and memos). When information-exchange mechanisms are used to excess, the effects are either information overload or information dilution. The net result in either case is reduced integration.
- Lack of agreement on decisions. Individuals constantly complain about decisions.
- Units work at cross-purposes. Usually this is due to no information exchange, political differences, or lack of shared goals.
- Lack of awareness as to who has the decision-making authority. Individuals are insensitive to organizational power realities, which may not parallel the organizational chart.
- Ambiguous decision-making authority lines. No one is clear as to who has the authority to make a particular decision, and disintegration and inaction results.

Now complete the Stages of Integration Survey (Form 11-1).

Your Action Plan

Harry Thorpe solved the sales/production organizational design problems, but he did it unknowingly. Wouldn't it have been much nicer and more rewarding if he had done it consciously, as shown in Figure 11-6, knowing precisely what he was trying to do at each step of the process? The design methodology presented here can probably do as much to increase your long-term managerial effectiveness as any other chapter in this book.

Remember, there are two basic steps to any organizational design problem:

Figure 11-6. The organizational design process: setting differentiation and integration.

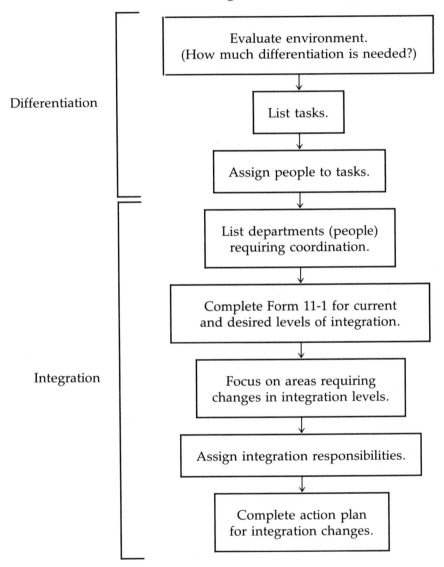

1. You need to achieve the level of differentiation required by your task environment (hire the specialists and get them to do the necessary tasks).
2. You need to accomplish the integration necessary by consciously selecting among the three stages just described (coordinate the decision-making activities).

The process is not easy. In fact, organizational design problems probably produce as much conflict as any set of management problems. You may find yourself faced with organizational politics, resistance to change, and entrenched self-interest. But don't dismay. Start in your own sphere of influence and demonstrate that you can do a good organizational design there. From there, you can branch out to your relationships with other areas in the organization, using negotiation skills described in Chapter 12 and other techniques.

The Organic Issue

In addition to deciding how much differentiation and integration you would like in your organization or subunits, you may also wish to consider what type of integration is most appropriate. This is anticipating material in Chapter 16, and perhaps you would like to flip to Table 16-1 for a quick introduction.

Organizations may vary structurally on the mechanistic-organic dimension. As you can see from the table, organic structures are much more open in their communication patterns and much more adaptable. But that does not necessarily mean the organic form is always preferred. There are various industrial settings in which a mechanistic structure might be more appropriate. As you can see from Figure 11-7, before completing your action plan on integration you may also wish to ask yourself on which side of the figure you would like to find yourself. Do you want to achieve your integration through organic means, or do you think a mechanistic approach is more appropriate? The bottom line is that there is a variety of ways to achieve integration, and you should match your integrative mechanism to the needs of your environment.

On Form 11-1, you were asked to diagnose the stage of integration that *currently exists* in your company or work group. Then you indicated the level of integration you *would like to have* with each department with which you interface.

First, review Table 11-1, which shows when you should seek stage I, II, or III integration, as well as their operational results, benefits, and liabilities. In general, the more important the organizational problem, the higher the integration stage should be, although the cost will be higher.

Now refine the Integration Action Plan in Form 11-1. Look at the Integration Matrix you have developed. Formulate an action plan to achieve the best possible fit between desired and actual organizational integration. The better you design your organization, the more successful you will be as a manager.

Figure 11-7. A general contingency model of organization-environment relations.

STRUCTURAL FLEXIBILITY

	High (organic)	Low (mechanistic)
High (differentiated)	*Complex and Dynamic Environment* Description: Organization operates in an environment consisting of a large number of different components, all rapidly changing. Examples: aerospace firm, university	*Complex and Stable Environment* Description: Organization operates in an environment consisting of a large number of different but relatively stable components. Example: multiple-line insurance company
Low (undifferentiated)	*Simple and Dynamic Environment* Description: Organization operates in an environment consisting of a few basically similar components, all rapidly changing. Example: custom-handling-systems producer	*Simple and Stable Environment* Description: Organization operates in an environment consisting of a few basically similar but relatively stable components. Example: container manufacturer

STRUCTURAL DIFFERENTIATION *(row label spanning left of table)*

Source: From *Macro Organizational Behavior* by Robert H. Miles (Glenview, Ill.: Scott Foresman, 1980), p. 279. Copyright © 1980 by Scott Foresman and Co. Reprinted by permission.

Table 11-1. Three roads to organizational integration.

You Should Seek . . .	When . . .	You Get . . .	The Benefits	The Liabilities
STAGE I: Instantaneous Integration	Problem is nonroutine	Agreement on decision	Consensus, agreement	May degenerate into crisis management with repeated use
	One-time agreement is necessary		Short-term problem solution	Consensus may not be appropriate or possible
	Agreement of subordinates is critical		Low one-time cost	No systemization of decision-making rules
STAGE II: Process Integration	Problem is or can be routinized	Agreement on decision-making authority	Systemizes problem solving	Does not address agreement on decision issue; no consensus occurs
	Repetitive decisions are necessary		Identifies decision responsibilities	May serve as cover for lack of managerial coherence
	Agreement on any particular decision is not necessary for implementation		Moderate cost	May result in overbureaucratization
STAGE III: Composite Integration	Maximal integration is desirable or necessary	Agreement on decision and authority	High morale; clear organizational decision lines	Hard to implement
	Final and continuing resolution is desired		Full integration of cross-cutting corporate specialists	Requires real commitment to organizational goals
	Consensus and clear decision-making responsibility is central to implementation		High continuity of managerial efforts	High cost

STAGES OF INTEGRATION SURVEY

This exercise is designed to help you define the relationships among key departments or subunits in your company. List the departments (or smaller subunits) that you would like to consider below:

Target department 1 _____

Target department 2 _____

Target department 3 _____

Target department 4 _____

Target department 5 _____

Target department 6 _____

Use the table that follows to diagnose the levels of integration (or dis-integration) between each pair of your departments or subunits, then complete the accompanying Integration Matrix. Refer to the definitions, as follows:

D = *DIS-INTEGRATION.* Represents a low level or lack of information exchange. Integration is impossible without information flow.

U = *UNSTABLE.* An unstable stage because high information exchange is likely to lead to agreement on decision and/or decision-making authority, or the low levels of agreement are likely to lead to a reduction in information flow.

I = *STAGE I—INSTANTANEOUS INTEGRATION.* When time and resource pressures are severe, low agreement on decision-making authority may be acceptable but negotiation will be required each time a problem arises.

II = *STAGE II—PROCESS INTEGRATION.* Requires less time to achieve consensus but in the long run may lead to motivation problems.

III = *STAGE III—COMPOSITE INTEGRATION.* Achieves both effective decision making and high motivation. It represents full integration.

Stages of Integration

DIS-INTEGRATION

	D							
	Low	High	Low	High	Low	High	Low	High
Information exchange	☑	☐	☑	☐	☑	☐	☑	☐
Agreement on decision	☑	☐	☐	☑	☑	☐	☐	☑
Agreement on decision-making authority	☑	☐	☑	☐	☐	☑	☐	☑

	UNSTABLE U		INTEGRATION I		II		III	
	Low	High	Low	High	Low	High	Low	High
Information exchange	☐	☑	☐	☑	☐	☑	☐	☑
Agreement on decision	☑	☐	☐	☑	☑	☐	☐	☑
Agreement on decision-making authority	☑	☐	☑	☐	☐	☑	☐	☑

Integration Matrix

1. Fill in names of the subunits along the top left-hand side of the matrix.

2. In the upper left of each box, fill in the symbol
   D = DIS-INTEGRATION
   U = UNSTABLE
   I = INSTANTANEOUS
   II = PROCESS
   III = COMPOSITE
   for the *current* level of integration.

3. In the upper right of each box fill in the symbol D, U, I, II, or III for the *desired* level of integration.

4. Below the symbol for the current and desired levels of integration place a star for each level of integration you must go up to reach your desired level. For example,

5. Refer to the table showing the various stages of integration, as necessary.

Integration Matrix

	1. _____	2. _____	3. _____	4. _____	5. _____
1. _____					
2. _____	→				
3. _____	→	→			
4. _____	→	→	→		
5. _____	→	→	→	→	
6. _____	→	→	→	→	→

Integration Action Plan

| Target Units | Integration | | Action Plan to Achieve Desired Results |
	Current Level	Desired Level	

Key Issues

Level	Benefits	Costs
D	None	None
	Use when no interaction is necessary or desired.	
U	Some information exchange	Conflict
	Never use—this is unstable. Either some agreement will occur (moving to I, II, or III) or information exchange will cease.	
I	Consensus, agreement Short-term solution	Low—but may become crisis management
	Use when one-time agreement is necessary.	
II	Identifies responsibilities	Moderate—may generate over-bureaucratization
	Use when decision must be made and focused in proper place in hierarchy.	
III	Consensus, high morale	High—lots of organizational time spent
	Use when implementation issues are important and decision quality is crucial.	

Chapter 12

Negotiation Skills

3:45 P.M.   John Roberts phones. He's head of the management negotiating team for the upcoming labor-management negotiations.

"Harry," asks John, "have you had a chance to look at the position papers I left with you last week?"

"No," says Harry, "I've been swamped lately."

"No problem," says John, "but I'll need your input soon. We meet next week with the union. Could you give special thought to, one, what our position should be on pay, vacation time, pension benefits, holidays, and safety equipment; and, two, what labor's initial demands will be?"

"OK," says Harry. "I'll get back to you in a day or two."

3:52 P.M.   Harry sits staring blindly at the position paper for the negotiations. "Why did they put me on this damn committee? I know absolutely nothing about negotiations," he says to the paper. He doesn't know where to start. His mind wanders to other negotiations in which he's recently been involved, and he's not encouraged by his memories. Last Monday, he bought a new BMW. Today he read in *Consumer Reports* that he paid $1,800 more for it than he needed to. On Tuesday, he got talked into letting his 15-year-old daughter go on a weekend trip with her boyfriend and his family; he really did not approve, but she insisted.

4:04 P.M. Harry tosses the position paper in the "action pending" file and turns to other things. He feels at a total loss about what to do in regard to the upcoming negotiations. He feels inadequate, ill prepared, and ignorant. "Frankly, I don't think I'm the right man for this assignment," he says to himself.

Harry should be concerned. He doesn't know much about negotiating. His lack of skill could cost the company hundreds of thousands of dollars over the next twelve months. What makes us leery of Harry's appointment to the labor-management negotiating team is not his lack of formal knowledge but his general poor performance in negotiation. But he can improve. He can develop his skills to the point that he performs quite effectively in the negotiating situations he faces both managerially and personally.

How about you? Are you a good negotiator? When was your last negotiation? I'll bet that you had at least an implicit negotiation within the last twenty-four hours. It may have been on the job; it may have been with your spouse; it may have been with the kids. Negotiations are pervasive in everyday life. In fact, most of the negotiations you enter into are not even identified or thought of as bargaining situations. You don't need a labor negotiation team sitting across the table from you in order to get taken to the cleaners. The material that follows can help you capitalize on your basic skills, to make the best of all the negotiation situations you face.

WHEN TO NEGOTIATE

The first skill required is to correctly diagnose a situation as a potential candidate for negotiation. Negotiation is possible when there are two or more parties with incompatible goals and each party can block the other's goal attainment to some extent.

You can see that a tremendous amount of human interaction is characterized by these three elements. Collectively, they define social conflict. Negotiating is one way to resolve conflict. As a manager, a spouse, a parent, and a citizen, you are constantly negotiating. You negotiate with your wife, your children, your subordinates, your peers, your boss, and numerous people on a daily basis. One of the fundamental lessons of negotiating is to correctly diagnose a situation as negotiable. Here are some signs that tell you to negotiate rather than to fight, withdraw, or problem-solve.

There Are No Gross Power Differences

If you are much stronger than your opponent, ordinarily you won't bother negotiating, but will take what you want. If you are much weaker than your opponent, he will take what he wants. When you are about equal in power, negotiation may be the best way to resolve conflict. It avoids costly confrontation, and it allows both of you to satisfy some of your goals.

You Want What He Has, and Vice Versa

Obviously, if there is nothing the other has that you want, there can be no negotiation. Or, if you have nothing to trade, no bargaining can occur. There must be mutual interest in each other's horses for horse trading to occur.

There Are No Limiting Restraints

Geography, time, legal considerations, competitive information, or other restraints can prevent you from bargaining.

It is important to realize that negotiating isn't bargaining. That's right! Bargaining is not negotiation—only a small part of it. Bargaining is what goes on during the compromise period, during the horse trade, at the table. Negotiations include all those things that occur before and after as well as during bargaining.

It is also important to note that negotiations are not the only approach to resolving conflict. As you can see in Figure 12-1 there are many conflict-resolution approaches you can use. When faced with a conflict, a person can choose from at least six different approaches:

1. *Withdraw.* Leave.
2. *Comply.* Do it.
3. *Smooth.* Minimize; don't admit it.
4. *Negotiate.* Compromise.
5. *Force.* Make them do it.
6. *Problem-solve.* Find new and better ways.

Figure 12-1. Impact of power, time, and trust on decision to negotiate.

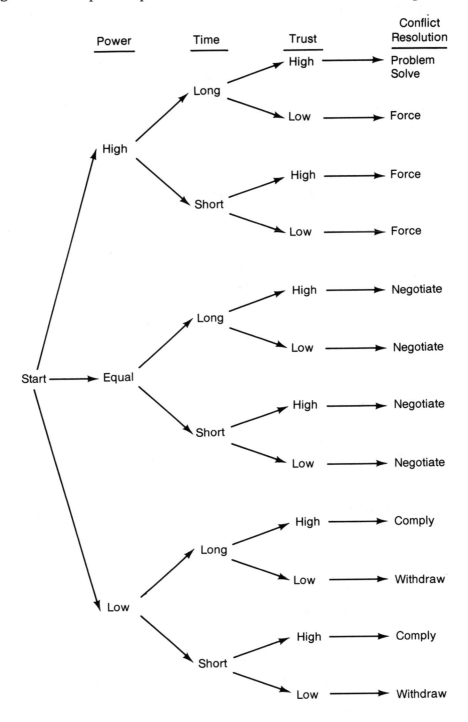

When deciding which conflict-resolution technique you will use, focus on the following three variables:

1. Power—How much do you have?
2. Time—What sort of pressures are there?
3. Trust—Do you trust your opponent?

As Figure 12-1 shows, these three variables interact to point you toward a preferred conflict-resolution technique. Study this model of the conflict before you decide to negotiate.

NEGOTIATION SPACE

For a successful negotiation to occur, there must be a "negotiation space." For example, suppose you are on the management team attempting to negotiate a contract with a union. The total cost of the contract will be somewhere between 0 and $1 million per year. You obviously want to minimize the labor costs while the union bargainers want to maximize the contract value. Figure 12-2 shows target and cutoff points for both labor and management in this hypothetical case. The target and cutoff points are defined as follows:

- The target point is the best possible settlement you can hope to get: what you hope to get, ideally.
- The cutoff point is the most you will pay and still settle. If you cannot reach an agreement at a price lower than your cutoff point, you will take the consequences of not settling (such as a strike and lost business).

The negotiation space is the area between the cutoff points of labor and management. Labor will strike if it does not get at least $350,000 per year. Management will take a strike if it cannot settle below $650,000 per year.

To be a good negotiator, you need to do three things:

1. Discover your opponent's cutoff point.
2. Conceal your own cutoff point.
3. Move your opponent's cutoff point in your direction.

Your objective is to get as much as possible for your side.

Figure 12-2. The negotiation space. If either party does not achieve its cutoff point, a strike will occur.

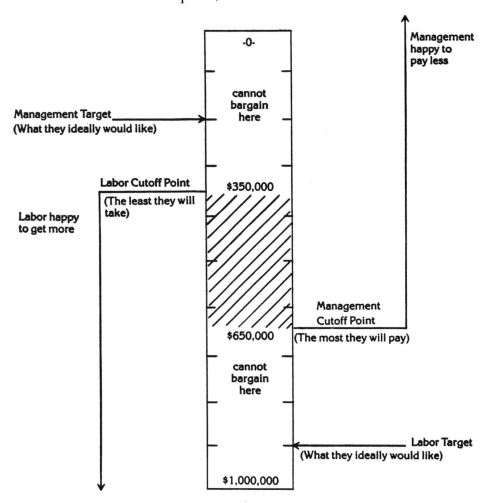

NEGOTIATION RESEARCH

A lot of behavioral research has been conducted on the process of negotiation. Some of it is of immediate interest to you as a negotiator. It points out management behavior that is critical to negotiation success.

Recognize That Satisfaction Is Not Necessarily Success

Satisfaction is not related to negotiation success. Both "winners" and "losers" show equal satisfaction. If you don't know how much money you left on the table, you will be satisfied with a settlement even though it might have been a disaster for your company.

For example, Herbert Ganz was elated when he sold his company to Plimpton Optical for $1.75 million. He felt he had been quite successful as a negotiator. Little did he know that Plimpton was prepared to pay up to $4 million for this choice acquisition.

Avoid Misperception of Your Opponent's Goals

This is perhaps the most important message of all. We always view our opponent's goals in terms of our own. This, unfortunately, is a perceptual fact of life (as discussed in Chapter 8). It is impossible to get out of your own perceptual filter. However, for negotiation success you must be able to think like your opponent, to anticipate his goals, options, and moves. If you are using a bargaining team, it is helpful to assign one of the members to deliberately "think like the opposition." Misestimation of your opponent's goals can cause disastrous results.

For example, a radical "Stop the War" student group in the 1960s took over a college president's office. They presented him with a list of twenty demands, including a halt to military research on campus, abolition of ROTC, and the like. Misperceiving their real goals (antiwar and personal publicity), the president granted eleven of their demands. Saying, "What a clod," they returned the next week with another list of twenty demands. The president's inability to perceive their true goals cost him his job.

Set High Targets

People with high targets get high rewards. One of the most important steps you can take as a negotiator is to set your target as high as possible. However, a high target also increases your likelihood of a deadlock.

For example, when Leonard Sanz finally approached his boss for a raise, he was asked, "How much do you want?" "Twenty-five hundred dollars a year would be great," said Leonard. His boss quickly gave him the raise, relieved that Leonard's target was much lower than the $7,500 he would have paid to keep him.

Plan Ahead

Planning is crucial. The most important aspect of a successful negotiation is the planning that takes place prior to the bargaining session. Skilled negotiators think in terms of contingency planning. They consider many options and explore many alternatives in advance of the negotiating session. Plan for contingencies by taking the following four steps:

1. List all alternatives open to you.
2. List all alternatives open to your opponent.
3. Identify your opponent's most likely response to each of your alternatives.
4. Decide on your response to each of your opponent's alternatives.

For example, the buyer of a piece of commercial real estate wanted the seller to take back a second mortgage at below market interest rates. The seller had already considered this potential option and had researched the tax laws. He mentioned that this was unacceptable, in that it might require him in the future to list additional income on his tax return. The buyer dropped this demand and it was not brought up again in the negotiations.

Determine Your Approach

An important input to your planning is the basic negotiation stance you hope to take. Will your approach be soft, hard, or principled?

The soft approach focuses on preserving the relationship. The hard approach concentrates on winning and beating your adversary. The principled approach dwells on discovering a rightful solution to the problem.

Table 12-1 can help you decide which basic approach to use in your planning. Match your approach to the negotiation situation. If preservation of the relationship is a high priority, use the soft approach. If concerns such as ethical, legal, or safety issues are involved, the hard approach may be required. In most management cases, the principled approach is appropriate.

In addition, you may wish to match your style to that of your opponent. If you adopt a soft approach and your opponent takes a hard approach, you may lose big. In the reverse case, you may be viewed as a bully and damage a relationship. Figure 12-3 shows that the most

Table 12-1. *Three negotiation approaches.*

	Soft	*Hard*	*Principled*
Focus:	Relationship	Goals	Problem
Participants regarded as:	Friends	Adversaries	Problem solvers
Illustrative tactics:	Cultivate relationship	Threaten relationship	Focus on problem
	Make offers	Make threats	Explore interests
	Yield to pressure	Apply pressure	Yield to principle
Approach to: People Problem	Soft Soft	Hard Hard	Soft Hard
Style	Flexible	Intractable	Focus on interests
Losses/gains	Accept losses	Demand gains	Look for mutual gains
Emphasis	Agreement	Your position	Objective criteria
Contest of will:	Avoid it	Win it	Use standards independent of will

Source: Table adapted by the author from a chart in Roger Fisher and William Ury, *Getting to Yes* (New York: Houghton Mifflin Company, 1981), p. 13. Copyright © 1981 by Roger Fisher and William Ury. Reprinted by permission.

preferred cells are soft/soft (relationship emphasized) and principled/principled (searching for the win/win). Diagnose which approach your opponent is using, and then consciously match your style to the situation.

Manage Your Negotiation Team Carefully

Often, teams are brought into negotiating situations because they represent additional resources that can be focused on the problem.

Two issues are central in effective team bargaining: (1) team composition and (2) team leadership. Have you selected the best possible

Figure 12-3. How to match your negotiation approach to your opponent's.

YOU	Soft	Hard	Principled
Principled	OK	OK—at least you are protected.	Win/win
Hard	Possibly OK (but you may be perceived as a bully)	Major conflict	↑ Move up to principled
Soft	Friends	You lose	Possibly OK

OPPONENT

members for your team? Have you covered all the bases in terms of expertise? Once the team is selected, leadership roles must be carefully defined. Use the leadership model in Chapter 9 to make sure each member understands who is in charge of each area. Have clear signals concerning calls for caucus. Know precisely who will do the talking at the table and what his authority is.

For example, John Bulinsky, an inexperienced treasurer, blurted out at the negotiating table, "We've got tons of cash just now because of that pension plan conversion." The seller demanded full payment immediately instead of the five-year payout that the buyer had hoped for.

Focus on the Long Term

Often, in the heat of a fast-paced negotiation session, there is overemphasis on short-term problems. If you are in a situation where the long term is significant, make sure you address these issues adequately. Skilled negotiators tend to keep a long-term focus.

For example, an investor was about to settle at a good price for a commercial office building. However, the tenant's current lease had a confusing renewal clause that could have resulted in a reduction of rent in the first renewal period starting two and a half years after purchase. The investor had the lease clarified by both the seller and tenant before he settled on the purchase.

Search for Common Ground

Negotiation is a process of exchange: "I'll give you this if you give me that." It is important to identify the areas of common interest early on. Skilled negotiators are quite good at seeking out areas of common interest and agreement.

For example, a machine shop wanted to purchase two new lathes. The machinery dealer's daughter was becoming interested in aviation. The machine shop had an airplane it wanted to sell. The negotiators discovered this overlap and the settlement involved the trade of a Cessna 182 for two lathes.

Don't Be Irascible

Unskilled negotiators often unwittingly use words and approaches that annoy and irritate their opposition. Unless it is carefully planned, with a well-defined objective, raising the temper of your opposition is not likely to help you at the table. Skilled negotiators avoid saying things such as "It seems to me you haven't analyzed this situation very carefully," or "Why are you being so stubborn and inflexible?" Skilled negotiators avoid using emotion-laden words and insulting innuendos.

For example, a purchasing agent and vendor worked several days attempting to hammer out a deal, but they seemed to get nowhere. A skilled vice-president stepped in and settled with the vendor in an hour. The purchasing agent had been unwittingly raising the level of hostility at the table through his irritating style of interaction.

Use Positive Framing

A successful negotiation is a function of both form and content. Sometimes the way in which you package and present your proposal can be an important factor. Consider the following scenario:

You are the vice-president of manufacturing in a large corporation that has had a serious depression in one product line. As a consequence, you are being pressured to close four plants, each employing 1,000 workers. You have come up with the following alternatives. As vice-president, which alternative would you choose?

Solution Set A

A1. This solution has a 25 percent probability of saving all the plants, but a 75 percent probability of saving no plants and no jobs.
A2. This solution will enable you to save one plant and 1,000 jobs.

Further research has brought the following alternatives to light. Again, which would you choose?

Solution Set B

B1. This alternative has a 25 percent probability of losing no plants and no jobs, but a 75 percent probability of losing all plants and all jobs.
B2. This alternative will involve losing three plants and 3,000 jobs.

Did you select A2 and then B1? Most managers would. Now look carefully at A1 and B1. They are exactly the same alternative, only worded differently. The same is true for A2 and B2. The solutions are identical. A1 is the same as B1; A2 is the same as B2. However, in laboratory tests it is not uncommon to have most subjects select A2 for problem A and B1 for problem B. Why?

Research in this area has demonstrated certain consistent behavior patterns. People tend to be generally conservative when you talk in terms of saving. And people tend to be more willing to take risks when you talk in terms of losing.[1] Therefore, in negotiations, it is not only what you say but the context and the manner in which you say it that can have a major impact. Structure your proposals and counterproposals in terms that accentuate the positive.

---

[1] Max H. Bazerman and Margaret A. Neale, "Heuristics in Negotiation: Limitations to Effective Dispute Resolution," in Max H. Bazerman and Roy J. Lewicki, eds., *Negotiating in Organizations* (Beverly Hills, Calif.: Sage Publications, 1983).

Avoid Conflict Spirals

There are two dynamics that have been identified in bargaining theory:

1. *Deterrence theory*—The more weapons available, the less likely their use.
2. *Conflict spiral*—The more weapons available, the more likely their use.

Deterrence theory implies that as you and your enemy get stronger, there is less likelihood of conflict. The conflict spiral implies just the opposite.

If you and your opponent are in a situation in which you are each able to punish the other in many ways, it is essential to determine the type of spiral you are enacting. If you find yourself not in a deterrence-theory environment but in a full-blown conflict spiral, terminate the negotiations as quickly as possible. The increased use of punishers is not likely to lead to a settlement.

If you find yourself in a short-lived conflict spiral in which you are trading blows at the table, take a break. Adjourn until the next day. Stop!

In family counseling, the term is "gunnysacking." An argument begins, and one of the participants opens his gunnysack of past grievances. The conflict spirals, and the result is more anger, little communication, and small chance of a peaceful or equitable settlement.

For example, your subordinate gives you incorrect information that makes you look like a fool at a budget meeting. He then arrives 10 minutes late for his meeting with you. Before you're finished, you've not only discussed the misinformation but also questioned his motivation, reliability, and basic common sense. You both become angry and hostile, and make little progress.

Be Flexible

Skilled negotiators are flexible. They have the ability to modify their positions and approaches as appropriate. They tend to think in terms of desirable ranges rather than absolutes. They consider and use more options. Their agenda for negotiations is flexible. There is no rigid sequence of items to be covered. Have you constructed a flexible agenda for your negotiations? If you have a rigid list of items that must be considered in an exact sequence, you are less likely to reach a settlement than if you are more open and flexible.

For example, a management negotiation team decided that a demonstration of their hard-line position would be important right from the start. In showing the labor negotiators that they would not be pushovers, they insisted on their agenda, on their time for meetings, and that they speak second. The result was an intractable labor team, responding in kind—unwilling to listen and ready to do full battle over every issue. They perceived the tone to be "give no quarter" and fought over even the most minute detail. The negotiations were long and the probability of a strike much increased.

Ask a Lot of Questions

The more you can find out about your opponent's needs and wants, the more successful you will be. Questions are usually a risk-free approach to discovering more about your opponent. Ask him what his goals are. Ask him what his assumptions are. Ask him what underlying model he is using in setting his price. The more you keep him talking in response to your questions, the more you learn.

The technique of reflective or active listening can also be quite useful. Your opponent makes a demand, and instead of responding directly, you say, "You feel that . . ." (restatement of demand). Often this can deflect a head-on confrontation and at the same time permit you to learn more about underlying issues.

For example, in talking to the plant manager, a negotiator discovered that the used equipment available for sale had been fully depreciated on the company's books. Therefore, the buyer understood that any money generated from a sale would go straight to profits. Consequently, he offered a much lower price on the piece of machinery than he would have if he had not known about the depreciation.

Choose Your Verbal Negotiating Tactics

As you can see from Table 12-2, a variety of verbal negotiating tactics are available. Before going into the negotiation, review this table and select those tactics you hope to use most frequently. Remember, each negotiation is different and you must be flexible in moving from one tactic to another.

Table 12-2. *Verbal negotiating tactics.*

Tactic	Description	Example
Promise	I will do something you want me to do if you do something I want you to do. (Conditional, positive)	I will lower the price by five dollars if you increase your order by 100 units.
Threat	I will do something you don't want me to do if you do something I don't want you to do. (Conditional, negative)	I'll walk out of the negotiation if you leak this story to the press.
Recommendation	If you do something I want you to do, a third party will do something you want. (Third party, positive)	If you lower your price, all of the teenagers will be able to buy your product.
Warning	If you do something I don't want you to do, a third party will do something you don't want. (Third party, negative)	If you don't settle, the press will spill this whole sordid story on the front page of every newspaper in the country.
Reward	I will give you something positive (something you want), now, on the spot. (Unconditional, positive)	Let's make it easier on you tomorrow and meet closer to your office. I have really appreciated your willingness to meet at my building.
Punishment	I will give you something negative (something you don't want) now, on the spot. (Unconditional, negative)	I refuse to listen to your screaming; I am leaving.
Normative appeal	Appealing to a societal norm.	Everybody else buys our product for five dollars per unit.

Source: From Nancy J. Adler, *International Dimensions of Organizational Behaviour* (Boston: PWS-KENT Publishing Co., 1986), pp. 177–178. © by Wadsworth, Inc. Used by permission of PWS-KENT Publishing Company, a division of Wadsworth, Inc.

Tactic	Description	Example
Commitment	I will do something you want. (Unconditional, positive)	I will deliver 100 units by June 15.
Self-disclosure	I tell you something about myself.	We have had to lay off 100 employees this month. We really need to sign a major contract by the end of the year.
Question	I ask you something about yourself.	Can you tell me more about your Brazilian operation?
Command	I order you to do something.	Lower your price. (or) We are going to talk about delivery now.

Use Consensus Testing

It is quite useful, at various points in the bargaining session, to take stock of where you stand. Summarize and test for consensus. Say to your opponent, "All right, let's make sure we know where we are. You want. . . ; we want . . . Do you agree that is where we stand?" Sometimes, when you test for consensus you discover that you are really a lot closer to agreement than the single-issue discussion had led you to believe. You can also use this as an opportunity to put a positive frame on the situation discussed earlier.

For example, negotiators spent an inordinate amount of time discussing motor size on a new piece of equipment. When they did consensus testing, they discovered that they were in agreement on all other issues, and this item represented less than 1 percent of the total purchase price. Agreement came shortly thereafter.

Create Alternatives

The more alternatives you can create in a negotiating situation, the more likely you are to succeed. This is a part of searching for common ground and striving for a win/win outcome. If you are deadlocked on issue A, perhaps a new issue B can generate positive worth for both sides. The more dimensions you have to work with, the more successful you can be. The price may be fixed, but what about financing, delivery dates, paint options, and so forth? Successful negotiators are creative. Part of this comes from advanced planning and part represents a problem-solving attitude. Be analytical and creative as you try to generate new alternatives.

For example, it seemed like a traditional real estate deal, but before it was over, the following issues had been generated and agreed upon: price, first mortgage amount, interest rate, second mortgage amount, interest rate on second mortgage, the fact that the second mortgage would be assumable by the next buyer, the start of the payments on the second mortgage, and real estate commissions. Each time the deal appeared to be hopelessly deadlocked, a new alternative was generated that enabled progress to occur.

Search for a Win/Win Outcome

One of the hardest things about negotiations is that they often are win/lose scenarios. "I must try my best to win, and that must be at your expense. Anything you get represents a loss to me" is the common belief. When a win/win approach can be identified, agreement is highly likely. Win/win solutions are generated through problem solving, which requires goodwill, creativity, openness, and mutual trust. Often a total win/win solution is impossible, but if you can do it, you are more likely to get a rewarding outcome.

For example, a vendor did not have the capacity to meet a customer's delivery requirements. The customer had unused building space. The vendor leased this building from the customer to provide additional subassembly capability, met the delivery schedule, and provided for long-term expansion.

PRACTICE PLANNING FOR NEGOTIATIONS

Ninety percent of your success in bargaining will depend on your preparation. Unless you do your homework, you will wind up like Harry Thorpe, pushed and pulled by everybody else according to their preferences rather than yours. But you can take charge if you plan. Now is the time to get practice in negotiation planning. Think of a hypothetical situation. Make it as specific and as relevant as possible. For example, negotiate with your boss for a raise, deny a subordinate's request, or reach an understanding with your spouse about something. With that in mind, do the following exercise.

1. *Set your objectives.* What are your objectives? What do you really want out of this bargaining session? Have you considered all aspects of potential settlements that might fulfill your basic objectives? Answer the following question: What would you hope to get, ideally? Write yourself a "fantasy contract" of what things would look like if everything went your way.

_____

_____

What is your cutoff point? What value would you minimally accept and still settle?

_____

_____

_____

2. *Anticipate your opponent's objectives.* Anticipate your opponent as best as you can. Remember, he is looking at the negotiation through his preferences, not yours. Try to move away from your own goals as you analyze his true objectives.

What are your opponent's objectives? What settlement would he ideally like?

_____

_____

What is his cutoff point? What is the least you think he would take?

_____

_____

_____

3. *Specify the negotiation space.* Now, visualize the negotiation space. On the line below, specify your target, your cutoff point, your opponent's target, and his cutoff point. Take a look at how large your negotiation space is and consider what you will do to try to: (1) discover his cutoff point with more accuracy, (2) move his cutoff point, and (3) conceal your own cutoff point.

_____

4. *Make contingency plans.* Before you sit down at the table, make a set of contingency plans. What is the most likely set of conceivable moves or offers that the other can make in bargaining? For each possible move, what will your response be? Consider role-playing the bargaining interaction in advance with an associate who assumes the position of your opponent.

   a. What is the most likely package you will be offered? Specify.

_____

_____

_____

   b. What will be your response to the above offer? Specify.

_____

_____

_____

    c. What other conceivable moves could your opponent make? Specify.

1. _____

2. _____

3. _____

    d. What would be your response to each of the above moves?

1. _____

2. _____

3. _____

5. *List the long- and short-term issues.* Focus on the long term as much as possible. List below the short-term issues, then brainstorm all the possible long-term aspects that might be a factor.

Short-Term Issues

1. _____   4. _____

2. _____   5. _____

3. _____   6. _____

Long-Term Issues

1. _____   4. _____

2. _____   5. _____

3. _____   6. _____

6. *Search for common ground.* What are the likely areas of mutual interest? The more common ground you identify at the outset, the more
likely you are to be successful. List below areas of common ground/
mutual interest.

_____

_____

_____

7. *Frame the offer.* Remember the importance of your opponent's perceptual set. Try to frame your offers in the best possible positive
light. Emphasize how your opponent is saving resources through
agreement, and minimize the discussion of losses. List below any
framing techniques you can use to put your proposals in the most
positive light.

_____

_____

_____

8. *Use flexibility.* Be flexible in your agenda setting and in your responses to proposals at the table. Don't respond too quickly with a

counterproposal. Think about it awhile first. Make sure your agenda can be adapted, if necessary, to address issues in a flexible manner.

Are you flexible in your agenda and approach? Have you established ranges as well as ideal outcomes? Where can flexibility be added to this negotiation?

_____

_____

_____

9. *Create alternatives.* The more alternatives you can create in the negotiation, the more successful it will be. List below additional alternatives that at least should be considered in the negotiation. Be creative and brainstorm.

_____

_____

_____

10. *Seek a win/win solution.* What are the circumstances under which both of you can win? Can you capitalize on or increase this area?

_____

_____

_____

11. *Determine who will negotiate for you.* Selecting the right person to negotiate can be a crucial variable in negotiation effectiveness. You

want someone who is levelheaded, who can think quickly, who is good in front of other people, and most important, who has been a successful negotiator in the past. Your negotiator should have positive self-esteem, high targets, tolerance for frustration, and a style that fits both his team and the opposition. Select your negotiators carefully. If you are using a negotiation team, make sure they understand the decision-making authority and responsibility of each member. You may wish to have a spokesman, an analytical specialist (good with numbers), and an interpersonally sensitive person who attempts to "read" the other side. If you are going to do the negotiating personally, make sure you are prepared and have the appropriate backup.

Who will negotiate?   ☐ Individual   ☐ Team

If it is a team, clearly specify the decision authority and role of each member.

Team leader _____   Leadership style _____

Member 1 _____   Role _____

Member 2 _____   Role _____

Member 3 _____   Role _____

12. *Decide what you will talk about.* Set the agenda for bargaining carefully, making sure you address all the issues you have identified. Are there any nonnegotiable issues? What order would you like to follow? Can you be flexible about the agenda? Are you going to hit the easy issues first or the hard ones? I recommend the easy ones. Will you separate the issues, or only agree on a total package? If you go for the package, you maximize the chances that the whole deal will be rejected because of one unacceptable point. Instead, separate the issues and have a number of packages that you can put together like building blocks. Write your agenda.

_____

_____

13. *Determine where you will negotiate.* Is there a home-court advantage in negotiating? You bet there is! Whenever possible, do your bargaining where you live—that is, in your own home, your office, car, or anywhere as long as it's yours. Don't be dismayed if your opponent refuses to come to your home court to bargain; he probably knows about home-court advantages, too. However, try hard not to go to his place. Insist on a neutral third site. Set up the bargaining environment to meet your goals; choose a square table to maximize the competitive aspects or a round table to emphasize unity. Where will you negotiate?

14. *Set when you will negotiate.* What time pressures are you operating under? Is your opponent operating under? What is your target date for a settlement? Do you face the likelihood of a strike, lost opportunities, and so on? If at all possible, arrange a situation in which your opposition faces a deadline you do not. If you don't have to catch a return flight tomorrow to the West Coast and he does, the time pressures on you will be much less than those on your opponent. When will you negotiate?

AT THE BARGAINING TABLE

Once you meet your opponent at the bargaining table, remember you are attempting to do three things:

1. Discover his cutoff point
2. Disguise your cutoff point
3. Move his cutoff point in your direction

15. *Discover your opponent's goals.* Where does your opponent stand? Try to get him to reveal his objectives first. For example, an acquisition team talked with the owner of the company for half a day before any numbers were exchanged. The owner finally came across and specified his asking price. The acquisition team immediately caucused with great delight, since the initial asking price was less than half of what their first offer would have been.

Ask your opponent to make the first offer. What will you do to get the ball rolling?

_____

_____

16. *Make the initial offer.* If you come in with a high target, you may do well, but you may also deadlock. If you come in with a low target, you may do less well, but settlement is more likely. Suppose that you place your house up for sale and find happily that it clears the first week at your full asking price. Your emotions are mixed, however, because you wonder if you set your target too low.

What will your initial offer be?

_____

_____

17. *Make your concessions work for you.* Use a hard or soft concession rate as appropriate to the situation. Hard bargainers make only small concessions when the other side makes a concession. Soft bargainers make a large concession when the other side makes a concession. Research indicates about the same success rate for each strategy. Therefore, decide whether you'll be hard or soft based on your analysis of your opponent. My own preference is to give small concessions in different areas to give your opponent a perception

of cooperation and flexibility. The concession style for this negotiation will be:

_____

_____

18. *Use time pressure to your advantage.* Under high time pressures, the probability of a deadlock increases. However, you may get quick settlement, which may be quite favorable. For example, one side realizes that its opponents are concerned about the tax consequences of the deal and want to close before December 31. Consequently, it extracts significant concessions as the deadline approaches.
    What is the time pressure in your negotiation?

_____

_____

19. *Define your verbal negotiating tactics.* Consciously choose your primary verbal negotiating tactics. They are listed and described in Table 12–2, but you must decide the extent to which you use promises, threats, recommendations, warnings, rewards, punishments, normative appeals, commitments, self-disclosures, questions, and commands. List below the primary tactics that you plan to use.

_____

_____

20. *Caucus for unity.* Make sure your team understands that you can privately caucus to analyze and discuss your opposition's offer and your counteroffer at any time. Talk offers over privately before giving a counteroffer.

THE AGREEMENT PHASE

Only two things can happen as a result of bargaining: You reach an agreement or you don't. This statement is often treated as trivial by practicing managers, because it seems so obvious. However, this is not always the case. Critical issues remain whether you reach agreement or decide that agreement is impossible.

If You Can Agree

If you can agree, the critical issues left for negotiation are:

1. The amount of ambiguity in the contract
2. The formality of the negotiated settlement
3. The duration of the agreement

Ambiguity

Mismanaging the degree of ambiguity in negotiated settlements has caused losses of uncounted millions of dollars to countless organizations in America. For example, when interest rates started their steep climb several years ago, banks were caught holding many mortgages at interest rates as low as 4½ to 5 percent. These "old" mortgages did not contain interest-rate ambiguity. When inflation struck, banks took losses. The remedy for this? Most banks now use variable-interest mortgages; ambiguity is built into the contract. Tying the mortgage interest rate to the prevailing market protects the bank from rising interest rates and enables the homeowner to take advantage of declining interest rates. The ambiguous settlement is more favorable to both.

Formality

How formal should your agreement be? Do you need a red carpet, lawyers, and contracts, or will a handshake do? Each type of settlement has its advantages and disadvantages. The informal contract, of course, is unreliable from the legal standpoint. It does, however, constitute a firmer bond than the more formal contract. It puts the personal good-will and faith of the parties on the line for enforcement.

The formal contract, with its multiple clauses and tricky provisions, may be more easily enforceable. However, it also may lock you into a situation where clauses of the contract are unenforceable owing to changes in the environment. Or small parts of the contract, every bit as legal as the larger base agreement, may make the remainder of the agreement undesirable.

Duration

Ordinarily, longer term agreements favor borrowers, management, and those in power positions. This is because it is "money in the bank" to lock a supplier or lender into a long-term agreement when you anticipate continuing inflation. A three-year labor-management contract with a 7 percent increase may be much more valuable to management expecting inflation than a one-year contract with a 5 percent increase.

Putting It All Together

There is a tendency to let down during the agreement phase. Make sure you and your team stay alert and nail down all the details. Sometimes it's frustrating, but getting the details settled at this point can save you much trouble in the future.

If You Can't Agree

If parties can't agree, you need to know something about the general topic of third-party intervention. Basically, this process involves the use of a neutral third party in the bargaining to arrange a settlement when there would otherwise be a deadlock. You act as a third-party interventionist when you intervene between two of your subordinates.

There are three kinds of third-party interventions: mediation, arbitration, and final offer arbitration.

Mediation

Mediation occurs when the parties to bargaining consult and agree on one or a set of persons who will serve as advice givers. For example, a federal mediator may be requested in deadlocked labor-management negotiations. The mediator is called in not to legislate or argue for either position but to listen to both sides and to evolve a compromise position.

Arbitration

Arbitration is ordinarily reported in the press as either "regular arbitration" or "compulsory arbitration." Actually, there is only one kind of arbitration and it is always compulsory. Arbitrators can force solutions on the deadlocked participants.

In many disputed labor-management cases, a three-member arbitration team is brought in: one person sympathetic to labor, one sympathetic to management, and the third supposedly objective. The arbitrators then listen to both sides of the grievance and vote on "who is right." The vote of the arbitrators has the force of an imposed settlement, and the issue is considered closed at that point.

Final Offer Arbitration

This form of arbitration, which has been used in government organizations, works exactly like regular arbitration. However, the arbitrator is also charged with "giving the entire game to one or the other side." The arbitrator listens to the total package proposals of both sides and then puts in force one of the total packages. This type of settlement threatens the losing side with total defeat in the negotiations, since the loser may have to live with a set of propositions it finds totally unfair and economically unfeasible. It is generally regarded as a threatening tactic used by outside intervention agencies, such as government, to prevent deadlock.

CONCLUSION

If you apply all the rules in this chapter, you will improve your negotiating effectiveness. The techniques are time tested. A majority of them are also backed by a good deal of empirical research. Here is how you should go about implementing them.

The Negotiation Checklist (Form 12-1) lists things you should do before you enter any negotiation of consequence. Treat it as if you were a pilot and it were a preflight checklist. Don't trust your luck that the plane will fly without checking it out first. Do this and you will be better able to implement the principles of negotiation effectiveness.

NEGOTIATION CHECKLIST

Prenegotiation Planning

1. IS IT A NEGOTIATION?   *Yes*   *No*
   Are there two or more parties?   ☐   ☐
   Do the parties have incompatible goals?   ☐   ☐
   Can each of the parties block the other from obtaining its
   goals?   ☐   ☐
   Is there an absence of restraints, such as geography, time,
   legal considerations, or competitive information, that pre-
   vent you from bargaining?   ☐   ☐
   Are the parties relatively equal in power?   ☐   ☐
   Is there something to trade?   ☐   ☐

2. WHAT ARE YOUR OBJECTIVES?
   What is your target? Specify it in terms of dollars, quantities, payment
   terms, and the like.

   _____

   What is your cutoff point? (What is the most you will pay?) _____

3. WHAT ARE YOUR OPPONENTS' OBJECTIVES?
   What is their target? Remember to try to view the world as they see it.

   _____

   What is their cutoff point? _____

4. SPECIFY THE NEGOTIATION SPACE
   On the line below specify your target, your cutoff point, your opponents'
   target, and their cutoff point. Take a look at how large your negotiation
   space is and consider what you will do to try to:

   1. Discover their cutoff point with more accuracy
   2. Move their cutoff point
   3. Conceal your own cutoff point

   |____|____|____|____|____|____|____|____|____|____|

5. CONTINGENCY PLAN
   What is the most likely package you will be offered? Specify.

   _____

   _____

What will be your response to the above offer? Specify.

_____

_____

_____

What other conceivable moves could your opponents make? Specify.

1. _____

2. _____

3. _____

What would be your response to each of the above moves?

1. _____

2. _____

3. _____

6. SHORT-TERM/LONG-TERM ISSUES

Short-Term Issues	Long-Term Issues
1. _____	1. _____
2. _____	2. _____
3. _____	3. _____

7. COMMON GROUND

List below any areas of common ground/mutual interest.

_____

_____

_____

8. FRAMING

What can you do to put this negotiation in a positive frame?

_____

_____

_____

9. FLEXIBILITY
   Do you have a flexible agenda?   Yes ☐   No ☐
   What can you do to make it more flexible?

   _____

   _____

10. CREATE ALTERNATIVES
    What new alternatives can you brainstorm that might be brought to the table?

    1. _____   4. _____

    2. _____   5. _____

    3. _____   6. _____

11. WIN/WIN
    List below any win/win areas:

    _____

    _____

    _____

12. WHO WILL NEGOTIATE?
    Individual ☐   Team ☐
    If it is a team, clearly specify the decision-making authority role of each member.

    Team leader: _____ Leadership style (Ch. 9): _____

    Member 1: _____ Role: _____

    Member 2: _____ Role: _____

    Member 3: _____ Role: _____

    Member 4: _____ Role: _____

13. WHAT WILL YOU TALK ABOUT?
    Specify your agenda for bargaining below. Indicate the items that you will
    discuss and the order in which you will discuss them.

    1. _____

    2. _____

    3. _____

    4. _____

    5. _____

14. WHERE WILL YOU NEGOTIATE?

    Your territory ☐   Their territory ☐   Neutral territory ☐

    _____

    _____

15. WHEN WILL YOU NEGOTIATE?

    Specify below your negotiation times:

    _____

    _____

    Specify any deadlines you or your opponents face:

    _____

    _____

At the Table

16. DISCOVERY
    What will you do to try to find out as early as possible where your oppo-
    nents stand?

    _____

    _____

    _____

17. INITIAL OFFER
    What will your initial offer be?

    _____

    _____

    What do you consider this?
    High ball ☐   Low ball ☐

18. CONCESSION RATES
    What kind of bargainer will you be?
    Hard bargainer ☐   Soft bargainer ☐

19. TIME PRESSURE
    Specify any time pressures that will be operating.

    _____

    _____

20. VERBAL NEGOTIATION TACTICS
    Choose which of the following you will use:
    ☐ Promises   ☐ Normative appeals
    ☐ Threats   ☐ Commitments
    ☐ Recommendations   ☐ Self-disclosures
    ☐ Warnings   ☐ Questions
    ☐ Rewards   ☐ Commands
    ☐ Punishments

The Agreement Phase

21. IF YOU AGREE
    What is the degree of ambiguity in the settlement?
    High ☐   Moderate ☐   Low ☐

    What is the degree of formality in the settlement?
    High ☐   Moderate ☐   Low ☐

    What is the duration of the contract?

    _____

    Are there renewable options?

    _____

22. IF YOU DISAGREE
    What is your action plan?

_____

_____

_____

Will you use any of the following?
Mediation ☐   Arbitration ☐   Final offer arbitration ☐
Specify who.

_____

_____

Other Issues

_____

_____

_____

_____

_____

_____

_____

_____

_____

Chapter 13

Staffing

4:05 P.M.   Harry's secretary buzzes him. "Mr. Thorpe, the candidate for administrative assistant is here for her interview."

"Send her in," says Harry. He digs through the piles of paper on his desk, muttering, "Now where did I put that resume?"

An energetic-looking woman in her mid-thirties enters the office. "Hello, Mr. Thorpe, I'm Pat Buckingham."

"I'm pleased to meet you, Pat," says Harry. "Please have a seat. I must apologize. Things are mass confusion today, but that is why I am looking for an administrative assistant. Tell me something about yourself. What is your philosophy concerning administrative organization?"

"Well," begins Pat, "I like to see a well-organized office. . . ."

Harry Thorpe is making a big mistake. He is conducting the selection interview in a way that is often done: unprepared, ad hoc, and unstructured. Harry is asking for continued staffing problems because he has not realized a number of important things.

STAFFING IS IMPORTANT

The S in POSDCORB (Chapter 2) is the most important letter. Choosing the best people for the available positions is a pivotal aspect of the manager's job. If you staff well, surround yourself with good people, and match people and jobs judiciously, the rest of management tends to fall into place.

Staffing Is Difficult

Matching people with organizational positions, fitting them into functional departments, and integrating them into the culture of the organization are demanding exercises. Each staff opening requires a special combination of skills. Attracting the ideal person is difficult; selecting that person is sometimes even harder.

Selection Interview Does Not Work Well

In 1915, a Carnegie Tech researcher asked six personnel managers to interview thirty-six applicants for sales positions. For twenty-eight of these applicants, the personnel managers disagreed on whether the applicant belonged in the top or bottom half of the sample. One candidate was ranked first by one interviewer and thirty-sixth by another. The selection interview often has tremendous reliability and validity problems.

A lengthy discussion of why the interview doesn't work is possible, but, in short, the following seven factors come into play:

1. Material is not consistently covered.
2. Decisions are made quickly (often in the first 4 minutes).
3. Managers respond to irrelevant cues—for example, a smile, firmness of handshake, clothing choice, interpersonal attractiveness.
4. The interviewer often shapes the behavior of the interviewee.
5. The same data are interpreted differently by different interviewers (see perception discussion, Chapter 8).
6. A description of the ideal candidate does not exist.
7. Job responsibilities and applicant competencies are not clearly defined.

The list could go on and on. Some studies have even indicated that the interview adds nothing to the accuracy of the selection decision. But there is hope! In this chapter, you will become familiar with the essentials of staffing success.

TEN STEPS TO STAFFING SUCCESS

How often have you seen staffing decisions handled the way Harry is handling his? Managers often do not recruit carefully for a position, they fail to define the job requirements specifically, and they conduct casual and imprecise interviews. But the interview process can work for you, if you follow these ten steps.

1. Write the job description.
2. Conduct the job analysis.
3. Select the behavioral dimensions.
4. Construct an interview form.
5. Recruit qualified candidates.
6. Study the resumes or applications.
7. Interview the applicants, record the data, defer judgment.
8. Score the interviews.
9. Use multiple interview consensus.
10. Make the hiring decision.

Writing the Job Description

Before you recruit and hire someone, you must know what you want that person to do. Before the applicant accepts the job, he must know what you expect of him. A good job description accomplishes these purposes. The description should be clear, concise, to the point, as specific as possible. It should indicate not only duties and responsibilities but also how the individual's time will be allocated across various activities. A typical job description is included in Figure 13-1. Each job description is different, but the basic objective is to have a clear communication of duties, responsibilities, and objectives. You may wish to review Chapter 7 for the characteristics of good objectives.

Conducting the Job Analysis

The job description provides some basic input into a more careful review of the activities necessary for the successful performance of the

Figure 13-1. Typical job description.

Sales Manager, Leasing

Generally responsible for managing the effort of a sales team to maximize profits from leasing sales. Individual must be well organized, energetic, and creative in directing corporate resources toward sales objectives.

Specific Responsibilities

30% organize/direct sales force: Dispatch, allocate, and review sales resources. Assist in planning sales calls and structuring proposals. Teach and coach salesmen concerning the technical aspects of capital equipment leasing and effective sales approaches. Perform a quality check (math, projected profits, risk exposure, etc.) on all proposals before they are presented. Review salesmen's performance and make bonus recommendations. Hire new salesmen as needed.

30% customer contact: The sales manager is expected to have his own customer contacts and to spend a significant amount of time in the field, either on his own or with individual salesmen.

20% broker relations: Interface with, screen, and "work" brokers to effect optimal return from the corporation's resources. Oversee the first credit decision (go or no go) and then assign a salesman or upstream broker to complete the proposal.

20% direct mail and public relations: Keep flow of information to customers through direct mail campaigns, brochures, mass mailings, and other promotional activities. Ensure that banks, brokers, aircraft salesmen, capital equipment salesmen, and others are aware of the corporation's capabilities in the leasing area.

Background

Experience in technical aspects of capital equipment leasing or related areas. Three-plus years of managing salesmen. MBA preferred. Individual must have strong planning and organizing skills.

Compensation

Excellent salary, fringes, and incentive pay. Negotiable based on capabilities and experience.

---

job. The job analysis is basically a commonsense listing of the specific behaviors necessary for success in the particular job. Look at Figure 13-1. The portion entitled "organize/direct sales force" lists a number of specific behaviors the manager must effect in order to be successful. These specific behaviors are as follows:

- Schedule the sales calls
- Coach sales personnel
- Mathematically analyze proposals
- Review performance of salesmen
- Recruit and hire salesmen

Thus, the job analysis essentially looks in detail at the daily behaviors required of a successful incumbent. These details require certain backgrounds, skills, and managerial competencies of the successful candidate. The job analysis may be done very informally, as in the case of hiring one individual to work for you personally, or may be done in a very formal fashion by the personnel department when a number of jobs are involved. Whether formal or informal, it is a necessary and essential step for successful staffing.

Selecting the Behavioral Dimensions

The job analysis provides the manager with the basic input for selecting appropriate dimensions of behavior. These dimensions are taken from the assessment-center literature and are here provided in the Behavioral Dimensions Checklist (Form 13-1). From this universe of thirty-two dimensions, the manager must select ten or so that are relevant to success on this job.

It is advisable to have other individuals (three or so) who understand the job in question complete the Behavioral Dimensions Checklist as well as doing it yourself. The dimensions selected will help you focus on appropriate behaviors during the interview. From a brief review of the hypothetical sales manager job description (Figure 13-1), you can see, for example, that oral communication skills, planning and organizing skills, initiative, energy, and the like would be appropriate dimensions. After you and the others have filled out the Behavioral Dimensions Checklist, total the scores and select the dimensions you will explore in the interview.

One of the key factors that lead to failure in the selection interview is its typically unstructured nature. The purpose of an interview is to collect facts. Unstructured interviews can take curious paths that lead to interesting conversations but reveal few hard facts. The successful interviewer disciplines himself to make sure that a variety of areas are covered and that the emphasis is on facts, not opinions, on history, not amateur psychological interpretations of motive.

To keep the interview structured, an interview form is essential. An Interview Report (Form 13-2) has been included for our hypothetical sales manager position. It is nothing more than a listing of the dimensions that have been selected as keys to success in the job, with some tentative questions for each dimension. This interview form is intended only as a guide; you do not have to slavishly ask the questions in the order presented, or even discuss the dimensions specifically. However, as the candidate talks, make sure you search out information that will help you assess the candidate on the various dimensions.

The following three points might help you focus on facts in the interview:

1. *Ask "What?" not "Why?"* Responses to "why" questions can easily be altered by the candidate to fulfill his perception of what is desired by the interviewer. In addition, these responses are often difficult to interpret, and the "why" question itself may be threatening and generate defensiveness. "What" questions tend to result in factual responses, which are easier to interpret.

2. *Explore the past.* Remember that the best predictor of future human behavior is past human behavior. Ask what past experience or education gives the applicant the capabilities necessary to do the job you have for him in the future.

3. *Take notes.* Don't be afraid to write while the candidate is talking. Just delay your note taking by a few seconds so that it is not obvious what triggers your data collection. It is unwise to think that you can rely on your memory when you're interviewing several applicants. You may also be required to justify your decision; this is easier to do if you have kept adequate documentation.

Recruiting Qualified Candidates

The selection interview helps you choose the best candidate from those available. If you do not attract qualified candidates, even the most carefully conducted, insightful interview will not help. You must generate a pool of candidates to choose from. This is effective recruitment. Use whatever techniques are appropriate to your particular situation for recruiting. Many approaches work: newspaper ads, technical journal ads, contact with employment agencies, trade school and university placement services, contacts with past and present employees.

It is important to remember that there is a funneling effect in recruitment. It is not inappropriate, in an important staffing decision, to have fifty applicants, to conduct ten interviews, and to offer the position to one person. Your recruiting efforts, therefore, should be sufficient to generate many more applications than the number of positions available. This, of course, becomes more difficult at higher level jobs, but the bottom line is, the more interest you generate through recruitment, the more likely you are to find first-rate people.

Studying the Resumes or Applications

Take a copy of the ten or so dimensions you have selected for your interview, and use them as the basis for scoring the individual resumes or applications. It is preferable to have others do this as well. This practice makes interviewers translate behavioral dimensions into practical, quantifiable characteristics that can be recorded on resumes or applications. You and the other interviewers will be talking the same language, using the same conceptual model, and being specific in the use of the quantitative assessment. This provides a good basis for selection of the final candidates, who will then be invited for interviews.

In addition, the resumes provide information on candidates' backgrounds and past accomplishments. Fundamentally, the interview process attempts to fill in any gaps in the resume or job application. Of course, the interviewer must be intimately familiar with the data to know where the gaps are.

Interviewing, Recording Data, Deferring Judgment

One of the problems of the selection interview is its interaction between the candidate and the interviewer. If the interviewer is not careful, he can easily shape the candidate's behavior, just as though he were a pigeon in a Skinner box. It is also easy to focus on irrelevant cues, flamboyant dress, excessive mannerisms, and peculiarities in speech pattern. The interview that becomes a conversation can easily wander into interesting but nonproductive areas.

A built-in problem is that the interview combines data gathering and data evaluation. It is difficult to handle both processes simultaneously. Some research has found that very successful interviews occur when one person interviews the candidate and records the data without any evaluative remarks, then another individual reviews the interviewer's notes and scores the interview. Although this process is not possible in many management situations, the principle is applicable. Defer judgment until well after the interview. The purpose of an interview is to gather facts! By delaying judgment until all the applicants have been interviewed, you will increase the likelihood of accurate assessment and selection.

Another important aspect of the selection process is permitting the applicant to out-select. Be as candid as possible concerning the problems with the job, challenges, difficulties, and so forth. Candidates know best their weaknesses and shortcomings. Sometimes the apparently outstanding candidate knows in his heart that he cannot handle the responsibility. He is also the best judge of whether he will fit into the organization's culture. The interview should be a two-way communication to make sure that the candidate knows as much as possible about the job, the organization, its culture, and your approach to management. If the candidate then turns down the job, don't be upset. Perhaps he knows best. You may have been saved a costly mistake by permitting the candidate to out-select.

Scoring the Interview

After you have collected data in written form under the various dimensions on your interview report, it is time to score it. Judge the candidate's score on each behavioral dimension and record it. I use a ten-point scale, but any form that suits you will do (e.g., one to five; a, b, c; etc.).

Using Multiple Interviewer Consensus

If you had the opportunity to have other individuals interview the candidate, now is the time to compare scores. Don't expect full agreement. Hold a consensus-testing session during which you discuss the differences that exist. Have each interviewer provide the data that caused him to make the assessment he did. This form of group interaction is often useful in improving the accuracy of the interview process. It is also an important method for increasing team acceptance of the new member.

Making the Hiring Decision

Finally, you're at the point where a decision must be made. Remember, human behavior is extraordinarily complex and difficult to predict. Even under the best of circumstances, you are going to make mistakes. Take into account all of the information you have generated and then offer the job to the best candidate. You won't always be successful, but if you follow an orderly process in your hiring decisions, you will eventually be able to surround yourself with outstanding people. This is a major secret to good management.

Remember, you achieved your present position not on the coattails of your superior but on the shoulders of your quality subordinates. Hire good people, nurture them, reward them, lead them, provide them with enthusiasm and energy, run an organization that has a cultural norm of integrity, and you are highly likely to succeed. Good luck!

BEHAVIORAL DIMENSIONS CHECKLIST

This master form is used to select the appropriate behavioral dimensions for a particular interview. Rate each dimension below on a 10-point scale for importance.

Dimension	Importance Rating (1–10)
Management	
1. Planning and Organizing—Establishing a course of action for self and/or others to accomplish a specific goal; planning proper assignments of personnel and appropriate allocation of resources.	_____
2. Delegation—Utilizing subordinates effectively. Allocating decision-making and other responsibilities to the appropriate subordinates.	_____
3. Control—Establishing procedures to monitor one's own job activities and responsibilities or to regulate the tasks and the activities of subordinates. Taking action to monitor the results of delegated assignments or projects.	_____
4. Development of Subordinates—Developing the skills and competencies of subordinates through the creation of insight and/or through training and development activities related to their current and future jobs.	_____
5. Technical/Professional Knowledge—Level of understanding of relevant technical/professional information.	_____

Source: William C. Byham, "Targeted Selection: A Behavioral Approach to Improved Hiring Decisions" (Pittsburgh: Development Dimensions International, Copyright 1979, revised 1981). Used with permission.

Dimension	Importance Rating (1–10)
6. Technical/Professional Proficiency—Level of performance in technical/professional area.	

Communications

7. Oral Communication—Effective expression in individual or group situations (includes organization, gestures, and nonverbal communication).	_____
8. Oral Presentation—Effective expression in presenting ideas or tasks to an individual or to a group when given time for preparation (includes organization, gestures, and nonverbal communication).	_____
9. Listening—Use of information extracted from oral communication. The ability to pick out the essence of what is being said.	_____
10. Written Communication—Clear expression of ideas in writing in good grammatical form; includes the plan or format of the communication.	_____

Interpersonal Dimensions

11. Sensitivity—Actions that indicate a consideration for the feelings and needs of others. Awareness of the impact of one's own behavior on others.	_____
12. Individual Leadership—Utilization of appropriate interpersonal styles and methods in guiding individuals (subordinates, peers, superiors) toward task accomplishment.	_____

Dimension	Impor- tance Rating (1–10)

13. Group Leadership—Utilization of appropriate interpersonal styles and methods in guiding a group with a common task or goal toward task accomplishment, maintenance of group cohesiveness, and cooperation. Facilitation of group process.

_____

14. Negotiation Skills—Communication of data, arguments, or positions in a manner that produces an agreement with one who is in direct conflict/disagreement. Ability to bargain and reach compromise.

Motivation

15. Job Motivation—The extent to which activities and responsibilities available in the job overlap with activities and responsibilities that result in personal satisfaction; the degree to which the work itself is personally satisfying.

_____

16. Willingness to Lead/Willingness to Manage—Another way of looking at motivation. Focuses on the power element of leadership or management.

Decision-Making Dimensions

17. Analysis—Identifying issues and problems, securing relevant information, relating and comparing data from different sources, and identifying cause-and-effect relationships.

_____

18. Judgment—Developing alternative courses of action and making decisions that reflect factual information, are based on logical assumptions, and take organizational resources into consideration.

_____

19. Risk Taking—Initiating action that involves a deliberate gamble in order to achieve a recognized benefit or advantage.

_____

Dimension	Impor-tance Rating (1–10)
20. Decisiveness—Readiness to make decisions, render judgments, take action, or commit oneself.	_____
21. Innovativeness—Generating and/or recognizing imaginative, creative solutions to work-related situations.	_____

Personal

22. Initiative—Originating action and maintaining active attempts to achieve goals; self-starting rather than passively accepting. Taking action to achieve goals beyond what is necessarily called for.	_____
23. Ability to Learn—Quickly assimilating and applying new job-related information which may vary in complexity.	_____
24. Energy—Maintaining a high activity level.	_____
25. Tolerance for Stress—Stability of performance under pressure or opposition.	_____
26. Work Standards—Actions that indicate high goals or standards of performance for self, subordinates, others, and the organi-zation. Dissatisfied with average performance.	_____
27. Tenacity—Staying with a position or plan of action until the de-sired objective is achieved or is no longer attainable.	_____

Dimension	Impor-tance Rating (1–10)
28. Adaptability—Maintaining effectiveness in varying environments, tasks, responsibilities.	_____
29. Range of Interests—Breadth and diversity of general and position-related knowledge; well informed.	_____
30. Impact—Creating a good first impression, commanding attention and respect, showing an air of confidence.	_____
31. Career Ambition—The expressed desire to advance to higher job levels with active efforts toward self-development for advancement.	_____
32. Integrity—Maintaining social, ethical, organizational norms in job-related activities.	_____

INTERVIEW REPORT

Behavioral Dimensions for Sales Manager

Candidate _____ Assessor _____ Date _____

Dimension	Rating (1–10)

1. Planning and Organizing—Establishing a course of action for self and/or others to accomplish a specific goal; planning proper assignments of personnel and appropriate allocations of resources.   _____
    1. Can you describe a detailed plan that you have made?
    2. How do you go about setting your basic priorities?
    3. What do you think of Management by Objectives?

2. Delegation—Utilizing subordinates effectively. Allocating decision-making and other responsibilities to the appropriate subordinates.   _____
    1. Can you give some examples of when you have successfully delegated work to others?
    2. How do you maintain quality control when you delegate?
    3. Can you describe how many subordinates you have had in the past and what your working relationship with them has been?

3. Control—Establishing procedures to monitor one's own job activities and responsibilities or to regulate the tasks and the activities of subordinates. Taking action to monitor the results of delegated assignments or projects.   _____
    1. Do you ever use a tickler file?
    2. What sort of control mechanisms have you used in projects in the past?
    3. Can you give an example of what has happened when a control system has failed?

Dimension	Rating (1–10)

4. Oral Communication—Effective expression in individual or group situations (includes organization, gestures, and nonverbal communication).   _____
   1. Did you communicate much in a face-to-face manner in your previous jobs? Describe.
   2. Describe a successful sales presentation you've made.
   3. What sorts of communications norms do you have with your subordinates?

5. Listening—Use of information extracted from oral communication. The ability to pick out the essence of what is being said.   _____
   1. How do you solicit feedback from your subordinates?
   2. Have you ever discovered something surprising by listening carefully on a sales call?
   3. How do you determine precisely the customer's needs?

6. Job Motivation—The extent to which activities and responsibilities available in the job overlap with activities and responsibilities that result in personal satisfaction; the degree to which the work itself is personally satisfying.   _____
   1. What time do you usually arrive for work?
   2. How important is your job in your overall life pattern?
   3. Can you give an example of success that you have attained through hard work in the past?

7. Analysis—Identifying issues and problems, securing relevant information, relating and comparing data from different sources, and identifying cause-and-effect relationships.   _____
   1. How do you determine whether a lease prospect is a good one?
   2. Can you give me some examples of experience that you have had with the mathematics of leasing?
   3. How will you check the work of your salesmen?

	Rating (1–10)
Dimension	

8. Decisiveness—Readiness to make decisions, render judgments, take action, or commit oneself.   _____
    1. How do you make decisions?
    2. Have you ever taken too long to make a decision?
    3. Once you've made a decision, how do you determine whether or not it was correct?

9. Tolerance for Stress—Stability of performance under pressure or opposition.   _____
    1. Describe a time in the past when your work world became very stressful. What happened?
    2. What are your stress-coping techniques?
    3. What are particularly stressful activities for you?

10. Other (define) _____   _____

OVERALL EVALUATION (1–10) _____

Comments on strengths and weaknesses: _____

Chapter 14

Project Management

4:32 P.M. Russ McKinley, a production supervisor, stops by Harry's office. Ralph Kingsley, his boss, has assigned him the role of project manager for the new system of quality and cost control that Harry has wanted for some time. Harry has asked for this meeting to make sure that Russ understands the project mission and objectives, and to size him up concerning how well he will do on his first project.

"Harry, Ralph wanted me to stop by to brief you on my plan of attack for our quality-cost program," says Russ.

"Great," replies Harry. "You know, Russ, this has been an important issue for me for some time, but we have just never seemed to be successful in implementing it. Ralph seems to have a lot of confidence in you and thinks that you can pull it off. Give this project a ten-plus priority rating, and you can be assured of my wholehearted support.

This chapter reflects the results of an ongoing research collaboration with Professor Jeffrey K. Pinto of the University of Maine. I am indebted to him in the area of theory development and the empirical testing of relevant theories. I am also highly indebted to Professor Randall L. Schultz of the University of Iowa for many years of ongoing collaboration in implementation research.

But I am curious; how do you plan to manage this project? What is your plan for the next six months?''

"Well," says Russ enthusiastically, "I've got my team selected, and with your approval, we can get started next week. And to make sure we hit all of the important areas, I plan to use the Project Implementation Profile."

"The Project Implementation Profile?" queries Harry with a frown.

"Yes," responds Russ, "it has been developed by a couple of professors of business administration to make sure that things don't fall through the cracks during implementation of a complex project. They also have data that indicate it is useful for keeping score on how a project is going. It also helps make sure that the project manager attends to all of the dimensions for project success. Here, let me show you," says Russ as he pulls a document out of his folder. "You see, there are ten basic dimensions for project success."

"Interesting," muses Harry . . . and they review the profile together.

Harry Thorpe is getting his first briefing on the Project Implementation Profile—and by a subordinate, no less! The Project Implementation Profile was developed to assist practicing managers in the implementation of complex projects. This chapter has two functions that help you use this device in your project management:

1. It describes the ten-factor model.
2. It provides you with the specific Project Implementation Profile items.

PROJECT IMPLEMENTATION PROFILE MODEL

The Project Implementation Profile (PIP) is based on a model of successful project implementation to help the project manager understand how the process works. Figure 14-1 shows the ten key factors that need to be considered in managing the implementation of a project. Seven of these factors lie on a critical time path. The sequence indicates which factors are most important in the beginning of a project and which become important as the project moves forward. For example, the project manager needs to be aware of the importance of receiving top management support and of developing the project schedule before even considering the selection and training of personnel.

Figure 14-1. Ten key factors of the Project Implementation Profile.

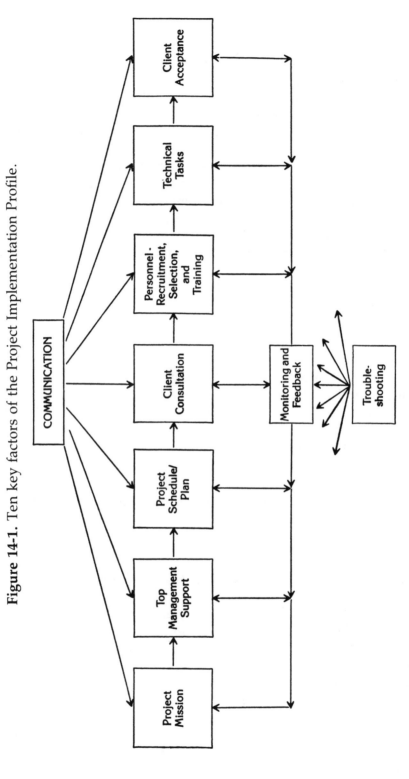

Three other factors in the model are shown as occurring at all steps in the implementation process. For example, communication and feedback are vital at every stage of the project to determine whether information is being traded and if complaints or errors are being acted upon.

In order for you to improve your project manager skills, you should (1) understand the ten key factors and (2) be able to use the Project Implementation Profile.

Factor 1: Project Mission

The initial step of the implementation process is to clarify the goals of the project. Implementation of any new project is an expensive use of organizational time, money, and energy. Are the project's mission and goals clearly defined, so that you know exactly where it is going and how it can help the organization? Your considerations should be:

1. Is the mission clear?
2. Do I understand why the project is being considered?
3. Is it necessary?
4. Do I think it can succeed?
5. Are the goals specific and operational?

Factor 2: Top Management Support

After you get a clear idea of what the mission and benefits of the project are, it is crucial to gain the support of top management. Without their vocal and visible support, the project may be seen as unnecessary, pointless, or unimportant by the rest of the organization. Early in a new project's life, no single factor is as predictive of its success as the support of top management. Your considerations should be:

1. Is top management convinced the project is necessary?
2. Are they convinced it will succeed?
3. Have they made their support clear to everyone affected by the project?
4. Do top management and I understand my role in the implementation process?
5. Do I have their confidence?
6. Will they support me, even in a crisis?

Factor 3: Project Schedule or Plan

For a project to get off the ground, it needs a well-thought-out, work-able plan. All activities necessary for successful implementation need to be scheduled. Furthermore, all necessary people, money, time, and other resources to complete the project must be allocated. Finally, there must be a way of measuring the progress of the implementation against schedule projections. Your considerations should be:

1. Does the plan make sense? Is it workable?
2. Is the allocation of time, money, and people acceptable?
3. Am I satisfied that I had enough input in the planning?
4. Will the organization follow through on the plan?
5. Do I need to worry about funds being cut or schedules being al-tered without consultation?
6. Does the plan have enough slack to allow for cost or time over-runs?

Factor 4: Client Consultation

"Client" here refers to whoever will ultimately be using the result of the project. It could be a customer or a department within the company. Because this project is for the client's benefit, close and frequent con-sultation with the client are imperative to make sure the effort is and stays in line with his needs.

Outside client considerations are:

1. Do I understand the client?
2. Do I know what he wants? (Or is it what I want him to want?)
3. Have I scheduled regular meetings with the client to keep him up to date on the project's progress?

Inside client considerations are:

1. Who are the key people who must support this project?
2. Is political activity needed to get client acceptance?
3. Is the client accepting or resisting?

Factor 5: Personnel—Recruitment, Selection, Training

As often occurs when implementing a new and unfamiliar project, we cannot always be sure that we have the necessary people for the project team. As a result, pay attention to selecting and training key personnel who can help make this a successful project. Neglecting this factor can force you to use personnel of convenience (simply because they are there), whether they will be helpful or destructive to the project. Your considerations should be:

1. Do I have the opportunity to pick and train my project team personnel? Or must I use personnel already in place?
2. Do I get along with them? Have I worked with them before?
3. Can I trust my key subordinates?
4. Does the organization have the kinds of personnel I need? Will I need to recruit them from outside?
5. Am I satisfied with the team's technical training and skills?

Factor 6: Technical Tasks

It is important that the implementation be well managed, by people who understand it. In addition, you must have adequate technology available to support the project (i.e., equipment, training, and the like). For a project to be successfully implemented, skilled people and proper technology are equally significant. Your considerations should be:

1. Have I assigned the correct technical problems to the right people?
2. Have I adequately documented and detailed the required technology?
3. Does the technology work well?
4. Does my team understand all aspects of the technology necessary for success?
5. Have I made provisions to update technology as minor changes in the project occur?

Factor 7: Client Acceptance

The obvious bottom line, in determining whether a project has been successfully implemented, is "Has the client bought it?" This question must be asked whether the client is internal or external to the organization. Too often managers make the mistake of believing that, if they handle all the other steps well, the client will automatically accept the resulting project. The truth is that client acceptance is a stage in project implementation that must be managed like any other. Your considerations should be:

1. Have I considered in advance a strategy to sell this project to the client?
2. Do I have leeway to negotiate with the client?
3. In the event of problems in the "teething" period of the project, do I have troubleshooters in place to help the client?
4. Will the project team be allowed to assist in follow-up? Or will it be disbanded immediately upon completion?
5. Does the organization view this as a one-shot deal? Or are organization members helping us identify other potential clients?

Factor 8: Monitoring and Feedback

It is important that, at each step of the implementation process, key personnel receive feedback on how the project is going. Monitoring and feedback mechanisms allow the project manager to be on top of any problems, to oversee any corrective measures, to prevent deficiencies from being overlooked. They ensure a quality project along the way. Your considerations should be:

1. Do I regularly ask team members for feedback on how the project is going?
2. Do I regularly assess the performance of the team members?
3. Is the project ahead, behind, or on time?
4. Are all project team members kept up to date regarding any snags in the schedule?
5. Have I established formal feedback channels? Or am I relying on informal methods?
6. Is the monitoring system working? Or are we being told what we want to hear?

Factor 9: Communication

As can be seen from the model, communication is a key component in every factor of the implementation process and must be all-pervading. Communication is essential within the project team, between the team and the rest of the organization, and with the client. Project implementation cannot take place in a vacuum; there must be constant communication. Your considerations should be:

1. Have I clearly communicated to the project team the goals and objectives of the project?
2. Do team members have formal channels for communicating with me? Or must they hope to catch me at my desk?
3. Do I regularly provide the team with written status reports?
4. Am I using the team to keep communication channels open within the organization as well as to the client?
5. Is this project viewed as open or secret by the rest of the organization?
6. Have I attempted to control rumors about this project?

Factor 10: Troubleshooting

No project operates without a few hitches. Constant fine-tuning, adjusting, and troubleshooting are required at each step of the implementation process. It is important to realize that each project team member is capable of functioning as a "lookout" for problems. Actually, each team should contain technically competent people with the specific assignment of dealing with problems when and wherever they arise. Your considerations should be:

1. Do I encourage all team members to monitor the project, to be alert to problem areas?
2. Does the team have the capabilities required to answer problems as they arise? Or must I go outside for needed expert help?
3. If problems arise, can we solve them quickly?
4. Are there any potential problems that could kill the project?
5. Do I take immediate corrective action? Or do I let problems slide?
6. Do we have sufficient troubleshooting capability?

PROJECT LIFE CYCLE

The concept of a project life cycle[1] provides a useful framework for looking at project dynamics over time. The idea is familiar to most managers; it is used to conceptualize work stages and the budgetary and

---

[1] Much of the following discussion is reprinted from "Balancing Strategy and Tactics in Project Implementation," by Dennis P. Slevin and Jeffrey K. Pinto, *Sloan Management Review*, Fall 1987, pp. 33–41, by permission of the publisher. Copyright © 1987 by the Sloan Management Review Association. All rights reserved.

organizational resource requirements of each stage.[2] As Figure 14-2 shows, this frame of reference divides projects into four distinct phases of activity:

1. *Conceptualization.* The initial project stage. Top managers determine that a project is necessary. Preliminary goals and alternative project approaches are specified, as are the possible ways to accomplish these goals.
2. *Planning.* The establishment of formal plans to accomplish the project's goals. Activities include scheduling, budgeting, and allocation of other specific tasks and resources.
3. *Execution.* The actual "work" of the project. Materials and resources are procured, the project is produced, and performance capabilities are verified.
4. *Termination.* Final activities that must be performed once the project is completed. These include releasing resources, transferring the project to clients, and if necessary, reassigning project team members to other duties.

As Figure 14-2 shows, the project life cycle is useful for project managers because it helps define the level of effort needed to perform the tasks associated with each stage. During the early stages, requirements are minimal. They increase rapidly during late planning and execution, and they diminish during termination. Project life cycles are also helpful because they provide a method for tracking the status of a project in terms of its development.

Take another look at Figure 14-1. In theory, the factors are sequenced logically rather than randomly. For example, it is important to set goals or define the mission and benefits of the problem before seeking top management support. Similarly, unless consultation with clients occurs early in the process, chances of subsequent client acceptance will be lowered. In actual practice, however, considerable overlap can occur among the various factors and their sequencing is not absolute. The arrows in the model represent information flows and sequences, not causal or correlational relationships.

In addition to the seven factors that can be laid out on a sequential, critical path, three factors are hypothesized to play a more overriding role in the project implementation. These factors—monitoring and feed-

---

[2]The four-stage project life cycle is based on J. Adams and S. Barndt, "Behavioral Implications of the Project Life Cycle," in David I. Cleland and William R. King, eds., *Project Management Handbook* (New York: Van Nostrand Reinhold, 1988), p. 211.

Figure 14-2. Stages in the project life cycle.

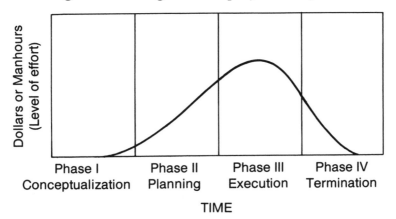

Phase I | Phase II | Phase III | Phase IV
Conceptualization | Planning | Execution | Termination

TIME

Source: J. Adams and S. Barndt, "Behavioral Implications of the Project Life Cycle," in David I. Cleland and William R. King, eds., *Project Management Handbook* (New York: Van Nostrand Reinhold, 1988). Reprinted by permission.

back, communication, and troubleshooting—must all necessarily be present at each point in the implementation process. Further, a good argument could be made that these three factors are essentially different facets of the same general concern (i.e., project communication). Communication is vital for project control, for problem solving, and for maintaining beneficial contacts with both clients and the rest of the organization.

Strategy and Tactics

As one moves through the ten-factor model, it becomes clear that the general characteristics of the factors change. The first three—mission, top management support, and schedule—are related to the "planning" phase of project implementation. The other seven are concerned with the actual implementation, or "execution," of the project. These planning and execution elements, respectively, can usefully be considered strategic—the process of establishing overall goals and of planning how to achieve those goals—and tactical—using human, technical, and financial resources to achieve strategic ends. Briefly, the critical success factors of project implementation fit into a strategic-tactical breakout in the following way:

- Strategic—mission, top management support, project schedule or plans
- Tactical—client consultation, personnel, technical tasks, client acceptance, monitoring and feedback, communication, troubleshooting

Strategy and Tactics Over Time

While both strategy and tactics are essential for successful project implementation, their importance shifts as the project moves through its life cycle. Strategic issues are most important at the beginning; tactical issues gain in importance toward the end. There should be continuous interaction and testing between the two: Strategy often changes in a dynamic corporation, so regular monitoring is essential. Nevertheless, a successful project manager must make the transition between strategic and tactical considerations as the project moves forward.

Our research in studying over 400 projects shows that the importance of strategy lessens over the project life cycle but *strategy never becomes unimportant*.[3] Similarly, the importance of tactics starts out low and grows as the project moves through its life cycle.

These changes have important implications. A project manager who is a brilliant strategist but an ineffective tactician has a strong potential for committing certain types of errors as the project moves forward. These errors may occur after substantial resources have been expended. In contrast, the project manager who is excellent at tactical execution but weak in strategic thinking has a potential for committing different kinds of errors. These will more likely occur early in the process, but may remain undiscovered because of the manager's effective execution.

STRATEGIC AND TACTICAL PERFORMANCE[4]

Figure 14-3 shows the four possible combinations of strategic and tactical performance, and the kinds of problems likely to occur in each sce-

---

[3]Jeffrey K. Pinto, "Project Implementation: A Determination of Its Critical Success Factors, Moderators, and Their Relative Importance Across Stages in the Project Life Cycle," unpublished doctoral dissertation, University of Pittsburgh, December 1986.

[4]Much of this section is based on Randall L. Schultz, Dennis P. Slevin, and Jeffrey K. Pinto, "Strategy and Tactics in a Process Model of Product Implementation," *Interfaces*, Vol. 17, No. 3, May–June 1987, pp. 34–46. Copyright 1987, The Institute of Management Sciences, 290 Westminster Street, Providence, Rhode Island 02903.

Figure 14-3. Strategy-tactics effectiveness matrix.

High	Potential for Type II and Type III errors High acceptance: misuse 2	High potential for implementation success 1
EFFECTIVENESS OF TACTICS	3	4
Low	High potential for implementation failure	Potential for Type I and Type IV errors Low acceptance: low use

Low   EFFECTIVENESS   High
OF
STRATEGY

Type I error: not taking an action when one should be taken
Type II error: taking an action when none should be taken
Type III error: taking the wrong action (solving the wrong problem)
Type IV error: addressing the right problem, but solution is not used

Source: Randall L. Schultz, Dennis P. Slevin, and Jeffrey K. Pinto, "Strategy and Tactics in a Process Model of Implementation," *Interfaces*, May–June 1987, p. 43.

nario. The values "High" and "Low" represent strategic and tactical quality—that is, effectiveness of operations performed.

A Type I error occurs when an action that should have been taken was not. Consider a situation in which strategic actions are adequate and suggest development and implementation of a project. A Type I error has occurred if tactical activities are inadequate, little action is subsequently taken, and the project is not developed.

A Type II error happens if an action is taken when it should not have been. In practical terms, a Type II error is likely to occur if the project strategy is ineffective or inaccurate, but goals and schedules are implemented during the tactical stage of the project anyway.

A Type III error can be defined as solving the wrong problem, or "effectively" taking the wrong action. In this scenario, a problem is identified or a project is desired, but because of a badly performed strategic sequence, the wrong problem is isolated so the implemented project has little value—it does not address the intended target. Such situations often involve large expenditures of human and budgetary resources (tactics), for which there is inadequate initial planning and problem recognition (strategy).

Type IV is the final kind of error common to project implementation: The action taken does solve the right problem, but the solution is not used. That is, if project management correctly identifies a problem, proposes an effective solution, and implements the solution using appropriate tactics—but the project is not used by the client for whom it was intended—then a Type IV error has occurred.

As Figure 14-3 suggests, each of these errors is most likely to occur given a particular set of circumstances:

Cell 1: high strategy/high tactics. Cell 1 is the setting for projects rated effective in carrying out both strategy and tactics. Not surprisingly, most projects in this situation are successful.

Cell 3: low strategy/low tactics. The reciprocal of the first is the third cell, where both strategic and tactical functions are inadequately performed. Projects in this cell have a high likelihood of failure.

The results of projects in the first two cells are intuitively obvious. Perhaps a more intriguing question concerns the likely outcomes for projects found in the "off diagonal" of Figure 14-3, namely, high strategy/low tactics and low strategy/high tactics.

Cell 4: high strategy/low tactics. In Cell 4, the project strategy is effectively developed but subsequent tactics are ineffective. We would expect projects in this cell to have a strong tendency toward "errors of inaction," such as low acceptance and low use by organization members or clients for whom the project was intended. Once a suitable strategy has been determined, little is done in the way of tactical follow-up to operationalize the goals of the project or to "sell" the project to its prospective clients.

Cell 2: low strategy/high tactics. The final cell reverses the preceding one. Here, project strategy is poorly conceived or planning is inadequate, but tactical implementation is well managed. Projects in this cell often suffer from "errors of action." Because of poor strategy, a project may be pushed into implementation even though its purpose has not been clearly defined. In fact, the project may not even be needed. However, tactical follow-up is so good that the inadequate or unnecessary project is implemented. The managerial attitude is to "go ahead and do it"; not enough time is spent early in the project's life assessing whether the project is needed and developing the strategy.

Case Studies

The four examples shown in Figure 14-4 are based on actual experiences of project managers or those involved in projects. The figure shows how the PIP (Form 14-1) can be used in real-world situations.[6]

High Strategy/High Tactics: The New-Alloy Development

One department of a large corporation was responsible for co-ordinating the development and production of new stainless-steel alloys for the automotive-exhaust market. This task meant overseeing the efforts of the metallurgy, research, and operations departments. The project grew out of exhaust-component manufacturers' demands for more formable alloys.

As Figure 14-4(1) demonstrates, the scores for this project, as assessed by the project team member, were uniformly high across the ten critical success factors. The project's high priority was communicated to all personnel, and this led to a strong sense of project mission and top management support. The strategy was clear and was conveyed to all concerned parties, including the project team, which was actively involved in early planning meetings. Because the project team would include personnel from the research, metallurgy, operations, production, and commercial departments, great care was taken in its selection and coordination.

In the new-alloy development project, a strong, well-conceived strategy was combined with highly competent tactical follow-up. The seeds of project success were planted during the conceptual and planning stages and were allowed to grow to their potential through rigorous project execution. Success in this project can be measured in terms of technical excellence and client use, as well as

---

[6]Used with permission of Project Management Institute. Jeffrey K. Pinto and Dennis P. Slevin, "The Project Implementation Profile: New Tool for Project Managers," *Project Management Journal*, September 1986, Vol. 17, No. 4, pp. 57–70.

Figure 14-4. Examples of PIP uses in real world.

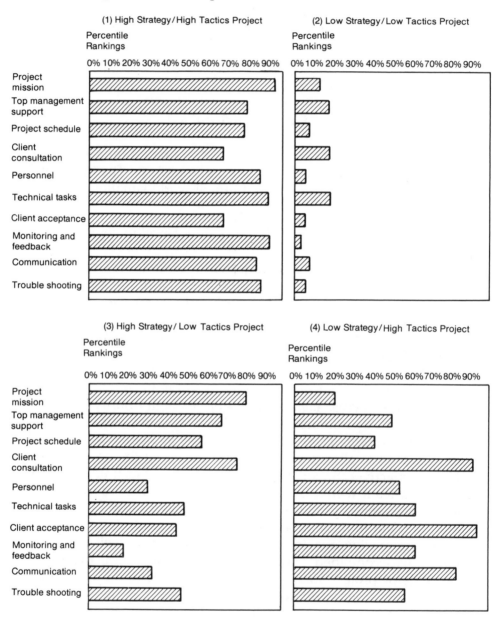

project team satisfaction and commercial profitability. In a recent follow-up interview, a member of a major competitor admitted that the project was so successful that the company still has a virtual lock on the automotive-exhaust market.

Low Strategy/Low Tactics: The Automated Office

A small, privately owned company was attempting to move from a nonautomated paper system to a fully integrated, automated office that would include purchasing, material control, sales order, and accounting systems. The owner's son, who had no previous experience with computers, was hired as MIS director. His duties consisted of selecting hardware and software, directing installation, and learning enough about the company to protect the family's interests. Figure 14-4(2) shows a breakdown of the ten critical success factors, as viewed by a project team member.

Several problems emerged immediately. Inadequate ''buy-in'' on the part of organization members, perceived nepotism, and lack of interaction with other top managers in purchasing decisions were seen as problems while the project was still in its strategy phase. A total lack of a formal schedule or implementation plan emphasized other strategic inadequacies destined to lead to tactical problems as well.

Tactically, the project was handled no better. Other departments that were expected to use the system were not consulted about their specific needs; the system was simply forced upon them. Little effort was made to develop project control and troubleshooting mechanisms, perhaps as a direct result of inadequate scheduling.

Project results were easy to predict. As the team members indicated and Figure 14-4(2) reinforces, the project was over budget, behind schedule, and coolly received—all in all, an expensive failure. The owner's son left the company, the manager of the computer department was demoted, the mainframe computers were found to be wholly inadequate and were sold, and upper management forfeited a considerable amount of employee goodwill.

High Strategy/Low Tactics: The New Bank Loan Setup

The purpose of this project was to restructure the loan procedures at a major bank. The project was intended to eliminate duplicate work done by branches and the servicing department and to streamline loan processes. These goals were developed and strongly supported by upper management, which had clearly conveyed them to all concerned parties. The project was kicked off with a great deal of fanfare; there was a high expectation of speedy and successful completion. Trouble started when the project was turned over to a small team that had not been privy to the initial planning, goal-setting, and scheduling meetings. In fact, the project team leader was handed the project after only three months with the company.

Project tactics were inadequate from the beginning. The team was set up without any formal feedback channels and with few communication links with either the rest of the organization or top management. The project was staffed on an ad hoc basis, often with nonessential personnel from other departments. This staffing method resulted in a diverse team with conflicting loyalties. The project leader was never able to pull the team together. As the project leader put it, "Although this project hasn't totally failed, it is in deep trouble." Figure 14-4(3) illustrates the breakdowns for the project as reported by two team members. Almost from the start of its tactical phase, the project suffered from the team's inability to operationalize the initial goals. Whether or not it achieves its final performance goals, this project will be remembered with little affection by the rest of the organization.

Low Strategy/High Tactics: The New Appliance Development

A large manufacturing company initiated the development of a new kitchen appliance to satisfy what upper management felt would be a consumer need in the near future. The project was perceived as the pet idea of a divisional president and was rushed along without adequate market research or technical input from the R & D department.

Figure 14-4(4) shows the breakdowns of the ten critical success factors for this project. Organizational and project team commitment was low. Other members of upper management felt the project was being pushed along too fast and refused to get behind it. Initial planning and scheduling developed by the divisional president and staff were totally unrealistic.

What happened next was interesting. It was turned over to an experienced, capable manager who succeeded in taking the project, which had gotten off to such a shaky start, and successfully implementing it. He reopened channels of communication within the organization, bringing R & D and marketing on board. He met his revised schedule and budget, using troubleshooting and control mechanisms. Finally, he succeeded in getting the product to the market in a reasonable time frame.

In spite of the project manager's effective tactics, the product did not do well in the market. As it turned out, there was little need for it at the time, and second-generation technology would make it obsolete within a year. This project was highly frustrating to project team members who felt, quite correctly, that they had done everything possible to achieve success. Through no fault of their own, this project was doomed by the poor strategic planning. All the tactical competence in the world could not offset the fact that the project was poorly conceived and indifferently supported, resulting in an "error of action."

IMPLICATIONS FOR MANAGERS

These cases, and the strategy-tactics effectiveness matrix, suggest practical implications for managers wishing to better control project implementation.

Use a Multiple-Factor Model

Project management is a complex task requiring attention to many variables. The more specific a manager can be regarding the definition and monitoring of those variables, the greater the likelihood of a successful project outcome. It is important to use a multiple-factor model to do this, first to understand the variety of factors affecting project success, then to be aware of their relative importance across project implementation stages. This chapter offers such a model: Ten critical success factors that fit into a process framework of project implementation; within the framework, different factors become more critical to project success at different points in the project life cycle.

Additionally, both the project team and clients need to perform regular assessments to determine the health of the project. The time for accurate feedback is when the project is beginning to develop difficulties that can be corrected, not down the road when the troubles have become insurmountable. Getting the project team as well as the clients to perform status checks has the benefit of giving insights from a variety of viewpoints, not just from that of the project manager. Furthermore, it reinforces the goals the clients have in mind, as well as their perceptions of whether the project satisfies their expectations.

Think Strategically Early in the Project Life Cycle

It is important to consider strategic factors early in the project life cycle, during conceptualization and planning. As a practical suggestion, organizations implementing a project should bring the manager and his or her team on board very soon. Many managers make the mistake of not involving team members in early planning and conceptual meetings, perhaps assuming that the team members should only concern themselves with their specific jobs. In fact, it is very important that both the manager and the team members "buy in" to the goals of the project and the means to achieve those goals. The more team members are aware of the goals, the greater the likelihood of their taking an active part in monitoring and troubleshooting.

Think More Tactically

In the later project stages, strategy and tactics are of almost equal importance to project implementation success. Consequently, it is important that the project manager shift the team's emphasis from "What do we do?" to "How do we want to do it?" The specific critical success factors associated with project tactics tend to reemphasize the importance of focusing on the "how" instead of the "what." Factors such as personnel, communication, and monitoring are concerned with better managing specific action steps in the implementation process. While it is important to bring the project team on board during the initial strategy phase, it is equally important to manage their shift into a tactical, action mode in which their specific duties help move the project toward completion.

Consciously Plan for and Communicate the Transition from Strategy to Tactics

Project monitoring will include an open, thorough assessment of progress at several stages of implementation. The assessment must acknowledge that the transition from a strategic to a tactical focus introduces an additional set of critical success factors.

Project managers should regularly communicate with team members about the shifting status or focus of the project. Communication reemphasizes the importance of a joint effort, and it reinforces the status of the project relative to its life cycle. The team is kept aware of the degree of strategic versus tactical activity necessary to move the project to the next life-cycle stage. Finally, communication helps the manager track the various activities performed by the project team, making it easier to verify that strategic vision is not lost in the later phases of tactical operationalization.

Make Strategy and Tactics Work

Neither strong strategy nor strong tactics by themselves ensure project success. When strategy is strong and tactics are weak, there is a potential for creating projects that never get off the ground. Cost and schedule overruns, along with general frustration, are often the side effects of projects that encounter "errors of inaction." On the other hand, a project that starts off with a weak or poorly conceived strategy and receives strong subsequent tactical operationalization is likely to be successfully implemented but address the wrong problem. New York advertising agencies can tell horror stories of advertising campaigns that were poorly conceived but still implemented, sometimes costing millions of dollars, and that were ultimately judged disastrous and scrapped.

In addition to having project strategy and tactics working together, it is important to remember (again following Figure 14-3) that strategy should be used to drive tactics. Strategy and tactics are not independent of each other. At no point do strategic factors become unimportant to project success; instead, they must be continually assessed and reassessed over the life of the project in light of new project developments and changes in the external environment.

PROJECT IMPLEMENTATION PROFILE

Now that you understand the general factors in the model, it is time to get some experience with the Project Implementation Profile (Form 14-1). Try the profile now on a current or past project. Each time you use it, you will improve your project management skills. For current projects you may wish to complete the profile once a month or so to track the results.

PROJECT IMPLEMENTATION PROFILE

Project name: _____

Project manager: _____

Profile completed by: _____

Date: _____

Briefly describe your project, giving its title and specific goals:

_____

_____

_____

_____

Think of the project implementation you have just named. Consider the statements on the following pages. Using the scale provided, please circle the number that indicates the *extent* to which you agree or disagree with the following statements as they relate to activities occurring in the project about which you are reporting.

FACTOR 1—PROJECT MISSION

	Strongly Disagree		Neutral			Strongly Agree	
1. The goals of the project are in line with the general goals of the organization	1	2	3	4	5	6	7
2. The basic goals of the project were made clear to the project team	1	2	3	4	5	6	7
3. The results of the project will benefit the parent organization...........................	1	2	3	4	5	6	7
4. I am enthusiastic about the chances for success of this project	1	2	3	4	5	6	7
5. I am aware of and can identify the beneficial consequences to the organization of the success of this project	1	2	3	4	5	6	7

Factor 1—Project Mission Total	

FACTOR 2—TOP MANAGEMENT SUPPORT

	Strongly Disagree		Neutral			Strongly Agree	
1. Upper management will be responsive to our requests for additional resources, if the need arises	1	2	3	4	5	6	7
2. Upper management shares responsibility with the project team for ensuring the project's success	1	2	3	4	5	6	7
3. I agree with upper management on the degree of my authority and responsibility for the project	1	2	3	4	5	6	7
4. Upper management will support me in a crisis	1	2	3	4	5	6	7
5. Upper management has granted us the necessary authority and will support our decisions concerning the project	1	2	3	4	5	6	7

Factor 2—Top Management Support Total	

FACTOR 3—PROJECT SCHEDULE/PLAN

	Strongly Disagree		Neutral			Strongly Agree	
1. We know which activities contain slack time or slack resources that can be utilized in other areas during emergencies	1	2	3	4	5	6	7
2. There is a detailed plan (including time schedules, milestones, manpower requirements, etc.) for the completion of the project	1	2	3	4	5	6	7
3. There is a detailed budget for the project	1	2	3	4	5	6	7
4. Key personnel needs (who, when) are specified in the project plan	1	2	3	4	5	6	7
5. There are contingency plans in case the project is off schedule or off budget	1	2	3	4	5	6	7

Factor 3—Project Schedule/Plan Total	

FACTOR 4—CLIENT CONSULTATION

	Strongly Disagree		Neutral			Strongly Agree	
1. The clients were given the opportunity to provide input early in the project development stage	1	2	3	4	5	6	7
2. The clients (intended users) are kept informed of the project's progress	1	2	3	4	5	6	7
3. The value of the project has been discussed with the eventual clients	1	2	3	4	5	6	7
4. The limitations of the project have been discussed with the clients (what the project is *not* designed to do)	1	2	3	4	5	6	7
5. The clients were told whether or not their input was assimilated into the project plan	1	2	3	4	5	6	7

Factor 4—Client Consultation Total	

FACTOR 5—PERSONNEL

	Strongly Disagree		Neutral			Strongly Agree	
1. Project team personnel understand their role on the project team........................	1	2	3	4	5	6	7
2. There is sufficient manpower to complete the project	1	2	3	4	5	6	7
3. The personnel on the project team understand how their performance will be evaluated	1	2	3	4	5	6	7
4. Job descriptions for team members have been written and distributed and are understood...	1	2	3	4	5	6	7
5. Adequate technical and/or managerial training (and time for training) are available for members of the project team....................	1	2	3	4	5	6	7

Factor 5—Personnel Total	

FACTOR 6—TECHNICAL TASKS

	Strongly Disagree		Neutral			Strongly Agree	
1. Specific project tasks are well managed.......	1	2	3	4	5	6	7
2. The project engineers and other technical people are competent	1	2	3	4	5	6	7
3. The technology that is being used to support the project works well	1	2	3	4	5	6	7
4. The appropriate technology (equipment, training programs, etc.) has been selected for project success.................................	1	2	3	4	5	6	7
5. The people implementing this project understand it..................................	1	2	3	4	5	6	7

Factor 6—Technical Tasks Total	

FACTOR 7—CLIENT ACCEPTANCE

	Strongly Disagree		Neutral			Strongly Agree	
1. There is adequate documentation of the project to permit easy use by the clients (instructions, etc.)	1	2	3	4	5	6	7
2. Potential clients have been contacted about the usefulness of the project	1	2	3	4	5	6	7
3. An adequate presentation of the project has been developed for clients	1	2	3	4	5	6	7
4. Clients know who to contact when problems or questions arise	1	2	3	4	5	6	7
5. Adequate advance preparation has been done to determine how best to "sell" the project to clients.	1	2	3	4	5	6	7

Factor 7—Client Acceptance Total	

FACTOR 8—MONITORING AND FEEDBACK

	Strongly Disagree		Neutral			Strongly Agree	
1. All important aspects of the project are monitored, including measures that will provide a complete picture of the project's progress (adherence to budget and schedule, manpower and equipment utilization, team morale, etc.)	1	2	3	4	5	6	7
2. Regular meetings to monitor project progress and improve the feedback to the project team are conducted.	1	2	3	4	5	6	7
3. Actual progress is regularly compared with the project schedule	1	2	3	4	5	6	7
4. The results of project reviews are regularly shared with all project personnel who have impact upon budget and schedule	1	2	3	4	5	6	7
5. When the budget or schedule requires revision, input is solicited from the project team. .	1	2	3	4	5	6	7

Factor 8—Monitoring and Feedback Total	

FACTOR 9—COMMUNICATION

	Strongly Disagree		Neutral		Strongly Agree		

1. The results (decisions made, information received and needed, etc.) of planning meetings are published and distributed to applicable personnel 1 2 3 4 5 6 7

2. Individuals/groups supplying input have received feedback on the acceptance or rejection of their input 1 2 3 4 5 6 7

3. When the budget or schedule is revised, the changes *and* the reasons for the changes are communicated to all members of the project team 1 2 3 4 5 6 7

4. The reasons for the changes to existing policies/procedures are explained to members of the project team, other groups affected by the changes, and upper management 1 2 3 4 5 6 7

5. All groups affected by the project know how to make problems known to the project team 1 2 3 4 5 6 7

Factor 9—Communication Total	

FACTOR 10—TROUBLESHOOTING

	Strongly Disagree		Neutral		Strongly Agree		

1. The project leader is not hesitant to enlist the aid of personnel not involved in the project in the event of problems 1 2 3 4 5 6 7

2. Brainstorming sessions are held to determine where problems are most likely to occur...... 1 2 3 4 5 6 7

3. In case of project difficulties, project team members know exactly where to go for assistance 1 2 3 4 5 6 7

4. I am confident that problems that arise can be solved completely 1 2 3 4 5 6 7

5. Immediate action is taken when problems come to the project team's attention 1 2 3 4 5 6 7

Factor 10—Troubleshooting Total	

Project Performance

		Strongly Disagree		Neutral		Strongly Agree		
1. This project has/will come in on schedule ...	1	2	3	4	5	6	7
2. This project has/will come in on budget	1	2	3	4	5	6	7
3. The project that has been developed works (or, if still being developed, looks as if it will work)	1	2	3	4	5	6	7
4. The project will be/is used by its intended clients...................................	1	2	3	4	5	6	7
5. This project has directly benefited/will directly benefit the intended users, through either increasing efficiency or employee effectiveness	1	2	3	4	5	6	7
6. Given the problem for which it was developed, this project seems to do the best job of solving that problem—i.e., it was the best choice among the set of alternatives.........	1	2	3	4	5	6	7
7. Important clients, directly affected by this project, will make use of it	1	2	3	4	5	6	7
8. I am/was satisfied with the process by which this project is being/was completed	1	2	3	4	5	6	7
9. We are confident that nontechnical start-up problems will be minimal, because the project will be readily accepted by its intended users....................................	1	2	3	4	5	6	7
10. Use of this project has led/will lead directly to improved or more effective decision making or performance for the clients...........	1	2	3	4	5	6	7
11. This project will have a positive impact on those who make use of it	1	2	3	4	5	6	7
12. The results of this project represent a definite improvement in performance over the way clients used to perform these activities	1	2	3	4	5	6	7

PROJECT PERFORMANCE TOTAL	

Percentile Scores

Now see how your project scored in comparison to a data base of 409 projects. If you are below the 50th percentile on any factor, you may wish to devote extra attention to that factor.

Percentile Score	*Raw Score*				
% of Individuals Scoring Lower	Factor 1 Project Mission	Factor 2 Top Management Support	Factor 3 Project Schedule/ Plan	Factor 4 Client Consultation	Factor 5 Personnel— Recruitment, Selection, Training
100	35	35	35	35	35
90	34	34	33	34	32
80	33	32	31	33	30
70	32	30	30	32	28
60	31	28	28	31	27
50	30	27	27	30	24
40	29	25	26	29	22
30	28	23	24	27	20
20	26	20	21	25	18
10	25	17	16	22	14
0	7	6	5	7	5

Percentile Score	*Raw Score*					
% of Individuals Scoring Lower	Factor 6 Technical Tasks	Factor 7 Client Acceptance	Factor 8 Monitoring and Feedback	Factor 9 Commu- nication	Factor 10 Trouble- shooting	Project Performance
100	35	35	35	35	35	84
90	34	34	34	34	33	79
80	32	33	33	32	31	76
70	30	32	31	30	29	73
60	29	31	30	29	28	71
50	28	30	2	28	26	69
40	27	29	27	26	24	66
30	26	27	24	24	23	63
20	24	24	21	21	21	59
10	21	20	17	16	17	53
0	8	8	5	5	5	21

Tracking Critical Success Factors Grid

After you have compared your scores, you can plot them below and mark any factors that need special effort.

Percentile Rankings

	0%	10%	20%	30%	40%	50%	60%	70%	80%	90%	100%
1. Project mission											
2. Top management support											
3. Project schedule											
4. Client consultation											
5. Personnel											
6. Technical tasks											
7. Client acceptance											
8. Monitoring and feedback											
9. Communication											
10. Troubleshooting											
Project performance											

Chapter 15

Effective Meetings, Teams, and Task Forces

4:50 P.M. Harry rushes down the corridor to the conference room, arriving 5 minutes late for the biweekly "quality enhancement" meeting. Harry dreads these meetings. A task force of engineers and production people has been assembled to "do something" about quality. Harry has never really been sure what that something is, and since the meeting is not his responsibility, he hasn't spent any time in trying to define the charge.

Joe Smallman, the chairman, has already called the meeting to order, and as usual they are rambling, talking about one small issue concerning quality of maintenance supplies provided by an outside vendor. The participants are bored. Nothing is getting done. Comments are made that at worst stimulate conflict in the group and at best pontificate and lead to no action. Harry says to himself, "Why do I have to spend so much time in ineffective meetings when there is real work to be done out there?"

Harry is wasting time, isn't he? Probably it is just in the nature of groups that they're gross time wasters, right? Wrong!

In my time-management seminars with practitioners, meetings inevitably fall into two categories: most effective activities and most ineffective activities. Meetings are places where things get done, but meetings are also great time wasters. They are not inherently bad; they are necessary and important to any successful organization, but there are some fundamental things that Harry Thorpe needs to know about small groups and the conduct of effective meetings to enhance his managerial performance.

WHEN TO USE A GROUP

The first question any manager should ask concerning groups and meetings is "Should I use a group in the solution to this problem?" Some organizations develop cultures that emphasize the use of groups whether or not they are warranted. Other organizations emphasize just the opposite: numerous manager-with-one-subordinate meetings and very little group activity. The small group can be a very potent tool for the manager, but you should consciously address the question of whether a group is appropriate for the particular problem you are trying to solve. A number of issues impact upon the desirability of group process.

Conformity Pressures

Decades of behavioral research have indicated that conformity pressures in groups can be quite strong. As a classroom exercise with management students I have often "salted" a group of five or six individuals with one "deviant" (a person who holds an extreme position). In roughly one out of four cases, the deviant does not hold and maintain his position, even for the short 15 minutes that the exercise lasts. The conformity pressures are obvious and quite strong. Conformity drives out creativity, and this is often a potential liability of the group process.

Time Pressures

We all know that it takes a group longer to solve a set of problems than it does a collection of individual efforts. If time pressures are severe, it may not be possible to involve a group. However, in many cases this is a justification for taking action that perhaps warranted input from a problem-solving group.

Cooperation and Acceptance

One of the strongest principles emerging from research over the past several decades is that individuals and groups tend to cooperate in the implementation of decisions that they have participated in making. If you need the group to assist in implementation, if acceptance is important, if cooperation is essential, then the small-group process may be warranted, even if it is time-consuming and less efficient.

Greater Resources

One of the major benefits of small groups is the greater resources offered by individual members. Heterogeneous groups contain people with diverse backgrounds and different experiences, approaches, and problem-solving skills. In an effective group process these resources are combined to generate a truly superior outcome.

Motivational Issues

Social psychologists call it "social facilitation." Individuals often work at a higher level of motivation when they are either working with another person or in front of some audience. Group cohesion is a powerful force for the organization. You may wish to use a group because of the positive motivational impact it may have on the members.

Specialization

Related to the resources issue just mentioned, groups permit individuals to specialize in different aspects of a problem. It is possible to assign different members of your task force specific portions of a complex problem. This specialization permits a higher level of problem recognition and solving.

Decision Quality

Do you have confidence that the group can produce a quality decision? The answer to this question is a function of a number of issues, such as the quality of the group members, their preparation, their motivation, the quality of the group process, and so forth. However, you must at least be optimistic that the outcome of the group can be something superior to just an average of individual opinions.

Political Issues

Never underestimate the power of a group to help you form coalitions and get people on board from a political standpoint. Anthropologists have suggested that small tribal bands of ten or so individuals have been around for millennia. Perhaps there is something fundamental and inescapable in the utility of a small group to help with political problems. Each member of your problem-solving group is a potential emissary to the rest of the organization for the solution that evolves from the group process.

You may wish to use the Group Appropriateness Audit (Form 15-1) as a tool to address some of the "when-to-use-a-group issues" just discussed. Use the seven-point scale for each of the key issues to provide some general guidance concerning whether a group is appropriate to the problem you are trying to solve. If a group is appropriate, then by all means use it; it is a powerful tool for the manager. If it is not appropriate, then save yourself and others the time and energy required by group meetings.

EFFECTIVE MEETINGS

There are a number of steps that a practicing manager can take to improve meeting effectiveness. Make sure you address all of the following in order to get maximum performance from your team.

Objectives

It is of obvious and crucial importance that you understand *why* you are meeting. There are a myriad of potential reasons. You may have received a mandate from above. If this is the case, do you understand it? The group may be called together for the solution of specific problems. The primary objective of the meeting may be to sort out some power realities across the organization. A team or task force may be solution oriented rather than problem oriented. Quality circles, as implemented in some organizations, represent a solution in search of a problem. Finally, the objectives may be to provide a good CYA exercise for the various departments involved. Nonetheless, make sure that you understand your objectives and the organization's objectives in the expenditure of meeting time.

Participants

Select the participants for your meeting based on the criteria of information, power, and coordination needs:

1. *Information* implies that you invite people who are experts or in possession of key information for solving the problem at hand. Many task forces deal with highly complex problems that require differentiated specialists.
2. *Power* implies that the participants in the meeting have the authority to act. If you want to achieve improvement and change as the result of your meeting, ensure that the participants have the power to take the action that is decided upon.
3. *Coordination needs* refers to the concept of organizational integration (see Chapter 11). If you have different departments or subgroups involved in the solution of the problem, make sure they are invited early on in the development of the task force.

Place

Often this variable is predetermined because of limited availability of conference rooms and other issues, but the place of a meeting can be significant. I have attended meetings at a number of top management retreats, which worked particularly well because the ambience was conducive to creativity and cooperation. If you are meeting off-site, select your conference facility with care.

Agenda

Prepare your agenda well in advance along with accompanying relevant materials. Distribute these to your team members so they have an opportunity to read and reflect upon them prior to the meeting. On the agenda itself, make sure you specifically address the objectives of the meeting and set the basic ground rules for operating the group.

Visual Aids

When it comes to group meetings, a picture is worth even more than a thousand words. Flip charts, felt-tip markers, masking tape, overhead projectors, and so forth are not just trivial ancillary items. Use drawings, diagrams, lists, tables, and so forth to effect group problem solving. Don't hesitate to use flowcharts and a variety of other graphics to put complex conceptual material into a more understandable format.

Handouts

If you provide people with relevant material to use during the meeting and to take away with them, they are more likely to attend to your problem while off-line and not in the actual meeting. Prepare the handouts in a careful fashion for use both in the meeting and on the outside.

Leadership Issues

Research on small groups has indicated that two types of leaders or leadership functions emerge during meetings. Both types must be attended to have group effectiveness.

- *Task leadership* means that the leader keeps the group focused on the task at hand, provides the resources necessary to resolve the problem, and is instrumental in helping the group arrive at a careful problem definition and resolution. A variety of task leadership functions must be accomplished. Ask yourself who will be the task leader in your group. Will it be you? Can some of the task leadership functions be shared with others?

- *Socioemotional leadership* refers to the maintenance side of small-group functioning. It is the lubrication that enables the wheels to run a little more smoothly. It's the humor, the compassion, the camaraderie, and other positive affective phenomena that make people enjoy the small-group process. Maintenance needs are significant and important, especially if the team is going to spend much time together. Ask yourself who will handle the socioemotional leadership needs. Will it be you? Can this function be shared throughout the group?

As the group evolves in its decision making, it is up to you to see that both task and socioemotional leadership are provided. At key points,

Figure 15-1. Task/maintenance progress in the small group.

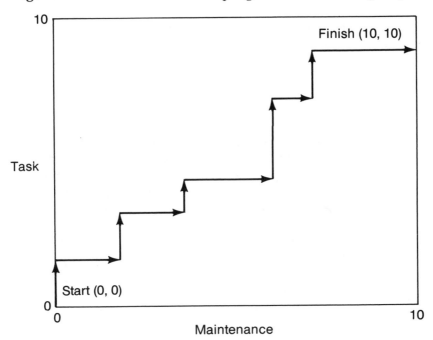

you must intervene with the appropriate action. You may do this directly, or merely ensure that it occurs.

As shown in Figure 15-1, the group typically begins the meeting at the (0, 0) point: zero progress on task; zero progress on maintenance issues. Your job is to make sure the group moves to the (10, 10) position (high task and high maintenance) through a sequence of key interventions.

Ask yourself two key questions:

1. What sort of leadership is needed here? ☐ Task ☐ Socioemotional

2. How will I get it done? ☐ Myself ☐ Others

Try to keep your group progressing in both task and maintenance dimensions.

Group Process

Be prepared to observe your group move through three fundamental phases as it attempts to solve the problem.

1. *Orientation.* This reflects the up-front time: The group members discuss who they are, why they are there, what their objectives are, how they will operate (e.g., consensus versus majority rule versus leader makes the final decision), and so forth. Most groups spend insufficient time in orientation. Rather, they jump immediately into the problem-solution phase and consequently waste time rechecking assumptions and revisiting orientation issues.

2. *Evaluation.* This reflects the problem-solution phase of the small-group process. As mentioned earlier, most groups move naturally into this phase, and in fact, as a leader one of your major concerns may be to restrain the enthusiasm for problem solution until you've handled the orientation setup issues. Nonetheless, most of your time likely will be spent in the evaluation phase.

3. *Control.* This represents the assignment of tasks, milestones, control devices, and other tools to make sure the action gets accomplished. Many meetings break up with a high level of enthusiasm, the group having shared lots of problem-solving ideas, but no action is accomplished because the control phase is ignored. Make sure you know who is going to do what, and by when, before you conclude each meeting.[1]

Group-Process Checklist

Use the following checklist to make sure you are taking an active role in managing all the elements of your meeting. Remember, the group functions differently as it moves through the different phases of the group process.

---

[1] Robert F. Bales and Fred L. Strodtbeck, "Phases in Group Problem-Solving," *Journal of Abnormal and Social Psychology*, Vol. 46 (1951), pp. 485–495.

Orientation (Make sure you spend enough time in this phase)

☐ Why are we here?

☐ What are our objectives?

☐ Do we have a leader?

☐ How will we function? (majority, consensus, leader decides)

☐ Should we be taking any basic approaches to this problem? I.e., any specific methodologies for solution?

☐ What is our accountability?

☐ What power do we have?

☐ What coordinative responsibilities do we have?

Evaluation (Try to maintain an open brainstorming, productive, problem-solving climate)

☐ What is the problem?

☐ What are the alternatives?

☐ What are the benefits and costs of each alternative?

☐ Have we explored all aspects of the problem?

☐ Are there any particular risks involved?

☐ Are task leadership functions adequate in this group?

☐ Are socioemotional leadership functions adequate in this group?

☐ What is our recommended solution?

☐ Does everyone agree (consensus testing)?

☐ Have we left anything out?

Control (Make sure that something actually happens after the meeting)

☐ Where do we go from here?

☐ Who does it?

☐ By when?

☐ Will we have interim progress reports?

☐ Minutes?

☐ When do we meet again?

Minutes

While compiling meeting minutes may seem a bureaucratic approach, it can often be quite helpful as a management tool. Ask yourself who will keep minutes of what occurs. Perhaps you wish to do this yourself, since it is an obvious leadership issue. Perhaps you wish to delegate this to others so that you can focus more on the task at hand and on socioemotional issues. Minutes also help keep the attention of your task force on the key issues when you are not meeting. Just the availability of a document that they can review may help to hold their attention on key issues.

Follow-Up

Managers are busy; consequently, if you don't follow up with your group members on a regular basis, the tasks associated with the meetings may not get done. Make sure you touch base with key members on a weekly basis, at a minimum. Keep the channels of communication open and make sure you are tracking positive progress to the solution of the problem.

CONCLUSION

Meetings are a lot of work. It takes a good deal of energy in advance of the meeting and after it, too, in order to enhance group effectiveness. There are tremendous pressures on all managers, who often arrive late and unprepared because they are so busy attending to the multifaceted roles of a management job. However, there is an orderly process you can follow to make sure you get the maximum out of your teams and task forces. Management in the future is going to be accomplished more and more through teams and task forces. Tom Peters, in *Thriving on Chaos*, says, "Involve everybody in everything."[2] While this is ob-

---

[2] Thomas J. Peters, *Thriving on Chaos: Handbook for a Management Revolution* (New York: Random House, 1987).

viously a strong statement, it reflects the reality that, as the environment becomes more complex and dynamic, more and more people have to be involved in problem solving. The mechanism for that involvement is effective management of small groups. If you follow the tools suggested in this chapter, your meetings are likely to be more effective, and your managerial effectiveness should increase as well. Use the following checklist to ensure successful meetings.

- [ ] Objectives
- [ ] Participants
- [ ] Place
- [ ] Agenda
- [ ] Visual aids
- [ ] Handouts
- [ ] Task leadership
- [ ] Socioemotional leadership
- [ ] Orientation
- [ ] Evaluation
- [ ] Control
- [ ] Minutes
- [ ] Follow-up

GROUP APPROPRIATENESS AUDIT

This form is intended to help you answer the question "Should I use a group?" If your responses to the items below are primarily to the left (lower numerical scores), then you probably should not use a group for the problem at hand. If your responses are primarily to the right (higher numerical scores), then perhaps a group is an appropriate vehicle to solve the problem at hand.

Do Not Use a Group if:		**Use a Group if:**
Conformity pressures may be a problem. Creativity and open exploration of alternatives may be constrained.	1 2 3 4 5 6 7	Conformity pressures may actually be desirable. The group may work more effectively than the sum of the individuals. Constraint of creativity is not a problem.
Time pressures are severe; there is little time for group process.	1 2 3 4 5 6 7	Time pressure is not an issue; there are no immediate time deadlines.
Cooperation of the group is not necessary for the implementation of the solution. Group acceptance is not an issue.	1 2 3 4 5 6 7	Cooperation of the group is essential for a successful resolution of this problem. Group acceptance of the solution is very important.
Greater resources represented by a group are not necessary to solve this problem. I basically have all the information and expertise necessary.	1 2 3 4 5 6 7	Greater resources represented by group members are essential for an effective solution to this problem. I do not possess sufficient information and expertise to solve this without the group.
Motivational issues are not a concern. Group cohesion is not relevant to the solution of the problem.	1 2 3 4 5 6 7	Motivational issues are an important aspect in this case. A cohesive group would help in its solution.
Specialization on the part of group members in solving this problem is not essential.	1 2 3 4 5 6 7	Specialization by various group members to solve components of the problem is essential.

342

I lack confidence that the group will resolve this issue with a quality decision.	<u>1 2 3 4 5 6 7</u>	I am confident that the group process will lead to a higher quality decision.
Political issues are not significant; there is no political reason for assembling the group.	<u>1 2 3 4 5 6 7</u>	Political issues are an important aspect of the solution of this problem; getting the group on board is essential for political or power reasons.

Chapter 16

Entrepreneurship/ Intrapreneurship

5:45 P.M. Harry sits at his desk. "Thank God that's over," he mutters to himself. "One of these days I'm going to have to take a seminar on how to run effective group meetings."

He picks up a piece of reading material that has been on his desk for a week. At the top is noted "HMT, FYI" with Sarah Freeman's initials and "Re our desire to get more entrepreneurial." Harry begins to read. It's an article from a professional journal: "A review of the entrepreneurial literature suggests that firms can control their behavior in the entrepreneurial dimension: risk taking, proactivity, and innovation. Hence, entrepreneurship can be *learned* by managers and consequently it should be *taught* by the firm." Harry mutters to himself. "Wonder what all this means—sure wish we could entrepreneur more. What's happened to the good old entrepreneurial spirit that we had in the old days? I just don't understand. . . ."

This chapter reflects an ongoing research collaboration with Professor Jeffrey G. Covin of Georgia Institute of Technology. I am indebted to him for contributions in the area of theory development and the empirical testing of relevant theories.

Harry just doesn't understand, does he? He wants to be entrepreneurial because it sounds good and everybody seems to be doing it, but he doesn't really understand what this means. Although the terms "entrepreneurship" and "intrapreneurship" are widely known and used in the field, this chapter will develop and explain a specific perspective that I and my colleagues have used to better understand these issues. It is essential for Harry's well-being that he understand entrepreneurship and where it fits into a high-performance organization. Harry needs to understand the concept of entrepreneurship, for both *security* and *success*.

- *Security*, because job creation in our economy occurs primarily in small organizations rather than in large corporations. A 1988 survey suggests that now, of managers who leave their jobs, one in six starts his own firm, compared to one in fourteen in 1985. If Harry ever needs to find another job, it may be essential that he understand how a small entrepreneurial firm or subunit of a larger firm operates.

- *Success*, because entrepreneurial management can lead to great corporate advancement if done correctly. If Harry can diagnose where he is and take the appropriate entrepreneurial steps at the right time, then his career may be enhanced whether he is operating a successful subunit or a smaller company.

ENTREPRENEURSHIP VS. INTRAPRENEURSHIP

There are few words that have a more positive connotation for top managers than "entrepreneurship" (see Chapter 8). The dictionary definition of the word describes an owner-manager who takes responsibility for a business and is willing to pay the price for risks that don't work out. It sounds good to have a collection of dynamic, proactive risk-takers who will make an organization work in these hostile and turbulent times. In fact, the word "intrapreneur" has been coined to represent the manager who acts as an entrepreneur within the confines of a larger organization.

This sounds like a great idea. What chief executive wouldn't want hundreds of successful intrapreneurs rattling about his corporation, making quick, decisive moves that result in growth and profits? Consequently many, if not most, of the *Fortune* 500 firms have engaged in some level of intrapreneurial activity, or what is commonly called "corporate venturing." The track record has not always been good, however. The fit between the new venture and the established corporation often is not a good one. As one pundit said, "Once the corporation integrates the new venture into its ongoing systems and processes, it's death by a thousand cuts." One multinational company reports eighteen failures in new ventures and no successes to date. That does not mean that they have given up; they still are optimistic. An entrepreneurial venture must be understood and fostered in order to work.

Whether you are an entrepreneur—establishing or thinking about establishing your own business—or an intrapreneur—running a dynamic and aggressive small venture within a larger firm—this chapter is relevant for you. It lays out a variety of principles that will help you better understand this whole area. In addition, it provides a tested model for diagnosing where your subunit stands on entrepreneurship and related variables. Then it looks at possible action plans for improved entrepreneurial behavior.

ENTREPRENEURSHIP DEFINED

First, let's talk about what entrepreneurship is not! I agree with Howard Stevenson and his colleagues at Harvard when they say, "The search for a single psychological profile of the entrepreneur—the conventional approach to the subject—is bound to fail."[1] There are so many different situations, different personalities, different factors—chance, timing, good or bad luck, and so forth—that it is extraordinarily difficult to isolate the personality characteristics of the "typical" entrepreneur. The problem is that there just isn't a typical individual to study. Each case is different. However, do not be discouraged by this; the construct of entrepreneurship may have relevance if we view it in terms of *firm behavior*.[2]

> *Entrepreneurship represents organizational behavior. It includes risk taking, proactivity, and innovation on the part of the organization.*

---

[1]Howard H. Stevenson, Michael J. Roberts, and H. Irving Grousbeck, *New Business Ventures and the Entrepreneur* (Homewood, Ill.: Richard D. Irwin, 1985).

[2]Based on the work of our colleagues D. Miller and P. H. Friesen, "Innovation in Conservative and Entrepreneurial Firms: Two Models of Strategic Momentum," *Strategic Management Journal,* Vol. 3 (1982), pp. 1–25. Copyright © 1982 John Wiley & Sons, Ltd. Reprinted by permission of John Wiley & Sons, Ltd. And based on the work of Pradip N. Khandwalla, *The Design of Organizations* (New York: Harcourt Brace Jovanovich, 1977). Professor Jeffrey G. Covin of Georgia Institute of Technology and I have adapted an entrepreneurship scale consisting of three major components.

I believe that while entrepreneurship is tenuous and fleeting as a personality trait, it can be studied, measured, diagnosed, and enhanced as a *firm behavior*. Let's look at the three subcomponents more closely.

1. *Risk taking*. The willingness to take on high-risk projects with chance of very high returns. The willingness to be bold and aggressive in pursuing opportunities.

2. *Proactivity*. The willingness to initiate actions that competitors then respond to. Attempts to be first in introducing new products, services, and administrative technologies, rather than merely responding to competitors.

3. *Innovation*. The willingness to place strong emphasis on research and development, new products, new services, improved product lines, and general technological improvement in the industry.

THE SOLUTION: BE ENTREPRENEURIAL

Now that we understand the characteristics of entrepreneurship, the solution is simple. Just encourage key managers in the organization to take risks, be proactive, and innovate and the firm will automatically perform better. Right? Wrong! Unfortunately, the world is complex and simple solutions often end up with simple outcomes, or failure. While you hate to ever discourage anyone from being entrepreneurial, you must understand that there are other key elements that enter into the picture. The research that Professor Covin and I have conducted involving substantial numbers of firms indicates that the organization's external environment and internal structure must be taken into account in any entrepreneurship decision.

Environmental Hostility

The tardigrade, also known as a water bear, is a small but robust organism less than one millimeter long. Under normal conditions it contains 85 percent water by weight. However, it can survive environmental extremes, even when water accounts for less than 2 percent of its body weight.

The concept of an appropriate "fit" between the organization and its environment is not a new one, but it still makes perfect sense. The environment often indicates what strategies are feasible, what risks make sense, and what organizational approaches are appropriate. A benign environment may encourage conservatism and maybe this is not all wrong! In one of our studies including 161 smaller firms with average sales of approximately $8 million per year, we found that organizations with entrepreneurial approaches generally performed best in *hostile* environments while firms with more conservative approaches generally performed best in more *benign* environments.

It can be argued that high risk taking and proactivity are less needed in benign environments. Rather, the firm should focus on issues such as efficiency, productivity, and control. This more or less typified much of American manufacturing in the 1960s and 1970s.[3]

In a similar vein, we discovered in the same study that smaller firms with high *organicity indices* (i.e., organic structures) generally performed best in hostile environments while firms with more *mechanistic structures* generally performed best in more benign environments. The concept of organic versus mechanistic structures is shown in Table 16-1.

Organic vs. Mechanistic Structures

Companies can be scored in terms of the degree to which they have an organic organizational structure. Table 16-1 indicates some of the key elements that define organic versus mechanistic structures. In general, an organic organization is more adaptable, more openly communicating, more consensual, and more loosely controlled. As the table shows, the mechanistic organization tends to be much more traditional, more tightly controlled, and more hierarchical.

There is a strong interaction between entrepreneurship and organizational structure.

A company cannot merely be entrepreneurial in order to be successful. Rather, it must also support its entrepreneurial efforts with an adaptive, innovative, quick-to-react *organic* organizational structure. As Figure 16-1 illustrates, high-performing firms are in cells 1 and 3.

Cell 1—Effective entrepreneurial companies. They have the desired combination of entrepreneurial behavior (risk taking, proactivity, and

---

[3]While this may be generally true, Michael E. Porter in *Competitive Strategy* (New York: Free Press, 1980) gives several excellent examples of firms that have innovated in mature, stable environments, sometimes revolutionizing the industry. However, these tend to be the exception to the rule.

Table 16-1. *Organic vs. mechanistic organizational structures.*

Organic	Mechanistic
Channels of communication are open with free flow of information throughout the organization.	Channels of communication are highly structured with highly restricted flow of information.
Operating styles are allowed to vary freely.	Operating styles must be uniform and restricted.
Authority for decisions is based on expertise of the individual.	Authority for decisions is based on formal line management position.
Free adaptation by the organization to changing circumstances.	Reluctant adaptation with insistence on holding fast to tried-and-true management principles despite changes in business conditions.
Emphasis on getting things done rather than on following formal procedures.	Emphasis on formal procedures; reliance on tried-and-true management principles.
Loose, informal control with emphasis on norm of cooperation.	Tight control through sophisticated control systems.
Flexible on-job behavior permitted to be shaped by the requirements of the situation and personality of the individual doing the job.	Constrained on-job behavior to conform to job descriptions.
Participation and group consensus used frequently.	Supervisors make decisions with minimum consultation and involvement of subordinates.

Source: Adapted from Pradip N. Khandwalla, *The Design of Organizations* (New York: Harcourt Brace Jovanovich, 1977), p. 411.

innovation) and an organic structure to support and nurture that behavior.

Cell 2—Pseudo-entrepreneurial companies. They take risks and act in an entrepreneurial fashion, but are stymied by a mechanistic, bureaucratic, rigid organizational structure.

Cell 3—Efficient bureaucratic companies. They won't take risks and don't want to. Their mechanistic structure helps them operate in an efficient fashion. Therefore, they are successful.

Figure 16-1. Organicity and entrepreneurship.

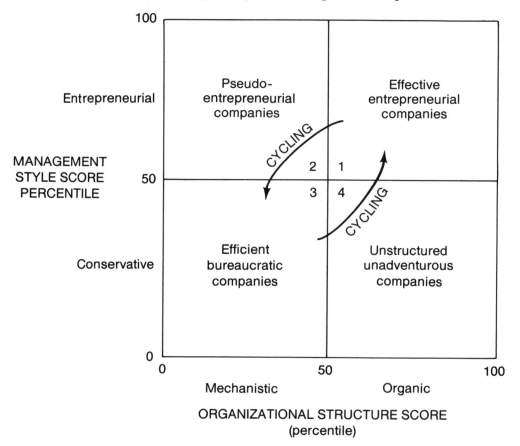

Source: Jeffrey G. Covin and Dennis P. Slevin, "The Influence of Organization Structure on the Utility of an Entrepreneurial Top Management Style," *Journal of Management Studies,* Vol. 25, no. 3 (May 1988), p. 223.

Cell 4—Unstructured unadventurous companies. They are quite organic and adaptable in their organizational structure, but also very conservative. They therefore do not get the full benefit of their adaptive, organic structures. They may be fun places to work because of the open communication channels, but they don't accomplish much.

How many times have you seen an efficient, bureaucratic organization forced to take action because of declining products or markets? And what does it do? It "tries" to act entrepreneurial. It takes risks. But often it finds it impossible to change its basic mechanistic culture to support such risk taking. Consequently, although top management may be behaving in an entrepreneurial fashion, the organization is just not prepared to support such a changed strategy and thus is a pseudo-entrepreneurial company.

Cycling

It becomes clear that successful organizations manage to cycle between cells 1 and 3. The entrepreneurial firm—say, one in the computer industry—is very proactive, is a high risk-taker, and is quite successful in its initial efforts. As it becomes more and more successful, it is forced to become more mechanistic in certain elements of its operations. Products must get out on time. Quality standards must be upheld, control systems must be in place, and so forth. Yet at the same time, research, new ideas, and innovation must be supported. A truly successful company manages to move back and forth between these key high-performing cells. An unsuccessful company gets caught in the transition of cell 2 or 4.

Important: In your personal career strategy, make sure you never take on an intrapreneurial venture in a highly mechanistic organizational culture. Make sure you have not only the support for your entrepreneurial decisions but also the backing of a flexible and adaptable organizational culture. Many corporate ventures fail because the large, heavily controlled corporation is unable to provide an organic nurturing environment for entrepreneurial decision making.

ARE YOU ENTREPRENEURIAL?

Related to the idea of the *fit* between an entrepreneurial venture and the organization in which it is lodged is the idea of a fit among you, your behaviors, and the leadership needs of an entrepreneurial venture. The word "entrepreneur" has such a positive connotation that most everyone wants to be one. But many people are not suited for this task. Ask yourself the question "Am I capable of engaging in entrepreneurial behavior?" Remember, entrepreneurship consists of risk taking, proactivity, and innovation. Look at Form 16-1 and ask yourself where you stand on each of these dimensions.

When you have completed Form 16-1, look at which side of the page your behaviors end up on. Ask yourself two questions:

1. Can I do it? Am I capable of being entrepreneurial?
2. Do I like to do it? Even though I may be capable, do I also get satisfaction from these activities?

Remember, not everyone is an entrepreneur. Not everyone is comfortable on the right side of the page. The next time you take a plane flight, think about whether you want the pilot to score at the far right on the form. You don't really want someone in the cockpit who is taking risks and being innovative. Rather, you want someone who is careful, methodical, predictable—not a risk-taker. Both sorts are needed in successful organizations. Don't feel that somehow you are a less successful manager just because you happen to be more predictable. Jokingly, I sometimes say that we have a name for a creative accountant—a felon.

The important issue is that you understand your basic capabilities and needs, and that you manage to engineer a fit between them and the requirements of your job.

VALUATION OF BUSINESS OPPORTUNITIES

One of the first questions the venture capitalist asks himself is "What is this company worth and how much am I paying for it?" Obviously, the venture capitalist makes his money by accurately valuing opportunities—that is, deciding how much the entrepreneurial effort is worth. This is a complex issue, and each venture capitalist you talk to has his own tricks and principles for this difficult trade. However, one of the more useful valuation approaches that I've seen was proposed by David Silver.[4]

Silver's equation is straightforward:

$$V = P \times S \times E$$

where

V = Valuation
P = Problem
S = Solution
E = Entrepreneurial team

---

[4]David A. Silver, *Venture Capital: The Complete Guide for Investors* (New York: John Wiley & Sons, 1985).

The independent variables are defined in more detail as follows:

- *Problem* is a surrogate for the total potential market represented by a solution to the problem at hand. Efficient disk storage capacity for personal computers is a problem of significant magnitude; the market is quite large. Power supplies for supercomputers may be a problem of much smaller market potential just because of the small market size.

- *Solution* indicates the quality of the solution for that given problem. A new videodisk storage technology offering several orders of magnitude improvement over previous approaches might be a high S score. Similarly, an excellent-quality power supply for supercomputers might also score high on the S variable.

- *Entrepreneurial team* represents the quality of the management team assembled for pursuit of the venture. Many venture capitalists and investors will tell you that they look at management quality first when they evaluate a business plan.

In one application of this model, each of the above was assigned a score from 0 to 3. Of course, this scaling is arbitrary, and you could use a 5- or 10-point scale if you wish. Since the function is multiplicative, if a score is 0, it is obviously a knockout score. You wouldn't want to engage in an entrepreneurial venture in which either P, S, or E scored 0. With a maximum score of 3 on each variable, the valuation algorithm can have a maximum possible score of 27—that is, $3 \times 3 \times 3$.

Some examples of how this model has been applied to real ventures are as follows:[5]

Venture A

Score: $V = P \times S \times E$
$0.0 = 3.0 \times 2.0 \times 0.0$

This company has developed proprietary software that does automatic translation of computer languages—for example, from Fortran to C, or Cobol to Ada.

Comment: This problem is an enormous one, since any user who wants to upgrade or change systems may be faced with these sorts of problems, hence we gave it a score of 3.0 for problem. The solution is fairly good, although it still requires additional development; human intervention is required in almost all cases, hence an

---

[5]L. Frank Demmler, personal communication, March 1988.

S score of 2.0. On the entrepreneurial side, a 0.0 was given, in that at the time it was reviewed, there was really no management. Obviously, if management could be brought to the party, the valuation would increase dramatically.

Company A was ultimately acquired by another firm that had existing management in place. It seems to be a logical and good fit between solution and entrepreneurial team.

Venture B

Score: $V = P \times S \times E$
$$3.375 = 1.5 \times 1.5 \times 1.5$$

This firm has developed a proprietary and patented system for prelubrication of internal combustion engines, such as those used for generators and off-road construction vehicles.

Comment: The problem is significant although not overwhelming, hence a *P* score of 1.5. The solution is patented and receives a 1.5 score. The entrepreneur seems to have the ability to build an entrepreneurial team, although it was not in place at the time of the valuation, hence a 1.5 score for *E*.

This company was ultimately funded by private investors at a relatively high valuation price.

Venture C

Score: $V = P \times S \times E$
$$4.5 = 2.0 \times 1.5 \times 1.5$$

This company has developed two in-home diagnostic tests: One is a new version of a glucose tester for diabetics, and the second is a beta strep tester for those people who are so afflicted.

Comment: The problems in both cases are fairly significant, hence an overall problem score of 2.0. The solution was reasonable, hence a 1.5 score. The entrepreneurial team was sound in that they had previous experience, hence a 1.5 score.

One major concern was that, if successful, the firm might be vulnerable to competition from larger, better-funded firms. As of the time of this valuation, the firm was seeking funding.

This is all fine if you are a venture capitalist, but how does the concept of valuation apply to Harry Thorpe, or to you? It's quite simple. If you are considering an entrepreneurial or intrapreneurial venture, one of the first questions you should ask is how it scores on its valuation. What is the likely career progression of the manager who takes on an intrapreneurial venture that scores all 1s on the valuation model? Would you like to be in his shoes? Successful managers pick their successes carefully. Before you take on responsibility, score it carefully to make sure you know what the likelihood is for success and what the payoff will be. After all, most entrepreneurial ventures fail—only one in ten succeeds—so why not be careful? The valuation model will help you get a general sense of the overall merits of an entrepreneurial idea.

THE TOTAL PICTURE

As Figure 16-2 indicates, the relationship between entrepreneurship and performance is not a simple one. It is moderated by the basic level of

Figure 16-2. Entrepreneurship and its moderators.

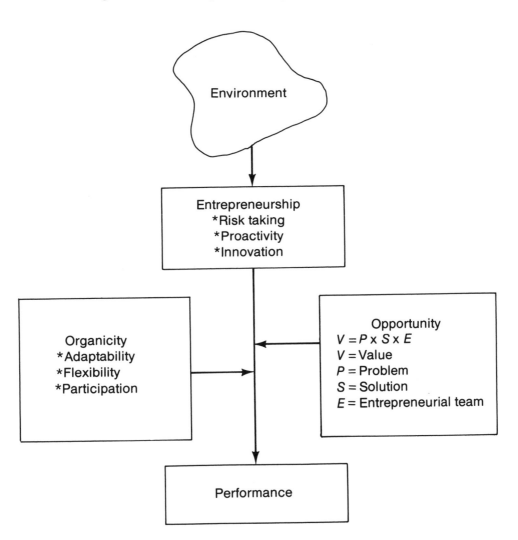

organicity in the organizational structure and by the basic level of opportunity in the venture itself, and it is impacted heavily by the environment—its hostility or its benignity. As you attempt to be entrepreneurial in your organizational setting, take all these variables into account.

Now that we have covered the theory, it is time to do an entrepreneurship/intrapreneurship audit of your job situation. Complete Form 16-2 for your firm or appropriate business subunit. Get a measure of where you stand on entrepreneurship and organicity and where you would like to go.

ENTREPRENEURIAL BEHAVIOR AUDIT

Rate your level of entrepreneurial behavior by circling the number to the left (lower numbers) or right (higher numbers) that best defines your stand on these issues.

RISK TAKING

Basically conservative; don't really enjoy taking risks.

1 2 3 4 5 6 7 8 9 10

High risk-taker; like a good calculated risk, enjoy an occasional gamble.

PROACTIVITY

Prefer a reactive stance—like to wait and see what's going to occur.

1 2 3 4 5 6 7 8 9 10

Enjoy taking charge and doing things before they are required.

INNOVATION

Have basically a non-innovative orientation to products and services.

1 2 3 4 5 6 7 8 9 10

Enjoy innovative products and services; like to be at the cutting edge of research and new product development.

ENTREPRENEURIAL STYLE/ORGANIZATIONAL STRUCTURE AUDIT

This analysis will assist you in diagnosing your organization on the key dimensions of entrepreneurial managerial and organic organization structure. Please answer the questions on the following pages in reference to the "business unit" that you would like to diagnose. A business unit can be defined as an organization or some part of an organization that has its own competitive strategy. If you are a member of an independently held, single-industry firm, the entire firm would be a business unit. However, large, diversified, multi-industry firms contain numerous business units (sometimes referred to as subsidiaries, divisions, strategic units, etc.). If you are a member of a multi–business unit firm, please answer the questions on the following pages in reference to your specific business unit rather than in reference to the overall firm.

There are *no correct or incorrect answers* to the items on this questionnaire, so please respond as openly and objectively as possible.

1. TARGET BUSINESS UNIT
Choose a business unit that you would like to diagnose. You may wish to choose the business unit in which you work. State the formal name and briefly describe the unit:

_____

_____

_____

2. BASIC OBJECTIVES
What are the business unit's basic objectives?

_____

_____

_____

_____

Source: Copyright © 1988 by Jeffrey G. Covin and Dennis P. Slevin. Entrepreneurship style item 7 and organizational structure items 1–7 are adapted from Pradip N. Khandwalla, *The Design of Organizations* (New York: Harcourt Brace Jovanovich, 1977). Entrepreneurship items 1, 2, 3, and 8 are adapted from D. Miller and P. H. Friesen, "innovation in Conservative and Entrepreneurial Firms: Two Models of Strategic Momentum." *Strategic Management Journal,* Vol. 3 (1982), pp. 1–25. Copyright © 1982 John Wiley & Sons, Ltd. Reprinted by permission of John Wiley & Sons, Ltd.

3. PERFORMANCE

How well has the business unit performed over the last year in comparison to its key competitors? Please circle the number that represents your best estimate for each item.

	Terrible	Poor	Fair	Good	Excellent	Not Applicable
Sales level ($)	1	2	3	4	5	N/A
Profitability	1	2	3	4	5	N/A
Product/service quality	1	2	3	4	5	N/A
Business unit's ability to reach critical goals	1	2	3	4	5	N/A
Overall business unit performance/success	1	2	3	4	5	N/A

Comments related to performance: _____

_____

_____

_____

4. ENTREPRENEURIAL STYLE SCALE

Please complete the following scale to diagnose the level of entrepreneurship that exists in your business unit.

Please circle the numbers in the following scales which best describe the business practices or operating management philosophy of the business unit you have chosen to analyze. Circle 1 if the statement on the left-hand side of the scale best describes your reaction to the item. Circle number 7 if the statement on the right-hand side of the scale best describes your reaction to the item. Circle numbers 2 through 6 depending upon your best estimate of an intermediate position.

In general, the top managers of my business unit favor:

1. A strong emphasis on the marketing of tried-and-true products or services.   1 2 3 4 5 6 7   A strong emphasis on R & D technological leadership, and innovations.

How many new lines of products or services has your business unit marketed in the past five years (or since its establishment)?

2. No new lines of products or services.   1 2 3 4 5 6 7   Very many new lines of products or services.

3. Changes in product or service lines have been mostly of a minor nature. 1 2 3 4 5 6 7 Changes in product or service lines have usually been quite dramatic.

In dealing with its competitors, my business unit:

4. Typically responds to action that competitors initiate. 1 2 3 4 5 6 7 Typically initiates actions that competitors then respond to.

5. Is very seldom the first business unit to introduce new products/services, administrative technologies, etc. 1 2 3 4 5 6 7 Is very often the first business unit to introduce new products/services, administrative technologies, etc.

6. Typically seeks to avoid competitive clashes, preferring a "live-and-let-live" posture. 1 2 3 4 5 6 7 Typically adopts a very competitive, "undo-the-competitors" posture.

In general, the top managers of my business unit exhibit:

7. A strong proclivity for low-risk projects (with normal and certain rates of return). 1 2 3 4 5 6 7 A strong proclivity for high-risk projects (with chances of very high returns).

In general, the top managers of my business unit believe that:

8. Owing to the nature of the environment, it is best to explore it gradually via timid, incremental behavior. 1 2 3 4 5 6 7 Owing to the nature of the environment, bold, wide-ranging acts are necessary to achieve the business unit's objectives.

When confronted with decision-making situations involving uncertainty, my business unit:

9. Typically adopts a cautious "wait-and-see" posture in order to minimize the probability of making costly decisions. 1 2 3 4 5 6 7 Typically adopts a bold, aggressive posture in order to maximize the probability of exploiting potential opportunities.

Now total your raw score for entrepreneurship style by adding together the numbers you have circled for the above nine items. Enter it in the box below.

ENTREPRENEURIAL STYLE RAW SCORE TOTAL (Items 1 through 9 above)	

5. ORGANIZATIONAL STRUCTURE SCALE (Mechanistic versus organic)
Please respond to the following items. It will help you diagnose the organization structure of your business unit on the mechanistic versus organic dimension.

In general, the operating management philosophy in my business unit favors:

1. Highly structured channels of communication and a highly restricted access to important financial and operating information.	1 2 3 4 5 6 7	Open channels of communication with important financial and operating information flowing quite freely throughout the organization.
2. A strong insistence on a uniform managerial style throughout the business unit.	1 2 3 4 5 6 7	Managers' operating styles being allowed to range freely from the very formal to the very informal.
3. A strong emphasis on giving the most say in decision making to formal line managers.	1 2 3 4 5 6 7	A strong tendency to let the expert in a given situation have the most say in decision making, even if this means temporary bypassing of formal line authority.
4. A strong emphasis on holding fast to tried-and-true management principles despite any changes in business conditions.	1 2 3 4 5 6 7	A strong emphasis on adapting freely to changing circumstances without too much concern for past practice.
5. A strong emphasis on always getting personnel to follow the formally laid down procedures.	1 2 3 4 5 6 7	A strong emphasis on getting things done even if it means disregarding formal procedures.
6. Tight formal control of most operations by means of sophisticated control and information systems.	1 2 3 4 5 6 7	Loose, informal control; heavy dependence on informal relationships and norms of cooperation for getting work done.
7. A strong emphasis on getting line and staff personnel to adhere to formal job descriptions.	1 2 3 4 5 6 7	A strong tendency to let the requirements of the situation and the individual's personality define proper on-job behavior.

Now total your raw score for organizational structure by adding together the numbers you have circled for the above items. Enter it in the box below.

ORGANIZATIONAL STRUCTURE RAW SCORE TOTAL (Items 1 through 7 above)	

Percentile Norms

Using the norms below based on a total of over 300 firms, convert your raw scores to percentile scores by circling the raw score on the chart below.

Percentile Score	Raw Score	
% of Firms Scoring Lower	Entrepreneurial Style	Organizational Structure
100	61	49
90	52	45
80	48	42
70	45	39
60	41	38
50	39	35
40	36	34
30	32	31
20	28	29
10	24	24
0	11	9

6. ORGANICITY AND ENTREPRENEURSHIP

See how your unit scored in comparison to other firms. Use your percentile scores to plot yourself in the following quadrant.

	100		
Entrepreneurial MANAGEMENT STYLE SCORE 50 (percentile) Conservative	Pseudo-entrepreneurial companies	Effective entrepreneurial companies
	Efficient bureaucratic companies	Unstructured unadventurous companies
	0		

```
        0            50           100
   Mechanistic      Organic
ORGANIZATIONAL STRUCTURE SCORE
        (percentile)
```

7. FIT ISSUES

The structures of some business units support and facilitate the management styles in those units. When this is true, there is a good fit between style and structure. In other cases the organizational structure is inappropriate for the prevailing style, in that the structure may inhibit or detract from its effectiveness. When this is true there is a poor fit between style and structure.

1. Estimate the degree of fit between your business unit's style and structure.

Terrible	Poor	Fair	Good	Excellent
1	2	3	4	5

2. On what basis do you give this evaluation? Be specific.

_____

_____

_____

_____

_____

_____

_____

_____

_____

_____

_____

_____

_____

_____

_____

8. ENTREPRENEURSHIP ACTION PLAN

1. Based on the structural and style characteristics just presented, where do you find your unit? Check the category that applies.

☐ Cell 1—effective entrepreneurial companies

☐ Cell 2—pseudo-entrepreneurial companies

☐ Cell 3—efficient bureaucratic companies

☐ Cell 4—unstructured unadventurous companies

2. Circle the category above that you would like to move toward. Indicate below where you would like to go.

| Entrepreneurial style: | ☐ Low | ☐ High |
| Organic structure: | ☐ Low | ☐ High |

9. ACTION PLAN

Review all the data (both numbers and comments) you have just developed. What actions can your business unit take to try to accomplish the transition indicated above?

_____

_____

_____

_____

_____

_____

_____

_____

_____

_____

_____

FORM 16-2.

_____

_____

_____

_____

_____

_____

_____

_____

_____

_____

_____

Chapter 17

Health and Life-Style

6:05 P.M.   Harry jumps into a cab, tells the driver he has a 7:15 flight, and asks him to step on it. He lights a cigarette. He is tense, perspiring, out of breath. "Boy, I'm out of shape," he thinks. He recalls the tennis match last Sunday with his neighbor, who is a couple of years older. Harry won the first set, but after that he just didn't have it.

"I ought to lose weight, quit smoking, get in shape," he thinks. "Wonder if I'm on my way to being a coronary case." His thoughts are rudely interrupted. "Son of a gun! I forgot to call Harrison back! Wish this cab had a phone. I'll try to reach him from the airport, if I'm not too late."

The management job is very taxing on a person's physical health, since it requires a lot of stamina and energy to keep going. The subject of fitness, however, is pleasant only to those who are already fit. The rest of us feel slightly guilty when we think about our weight, or the cigarettes we smoke, or our lack of exercise. However, think of it this way. How would you like to get a management aid that:

- Makes you more effective and capable as a manager
- Makes you feel more attractive and confident
- Makes you feel less tired, less anxious, and less stressed
- Lets you get more done more quickly

Fitness can do all these things for you, plus a number of others, such as reducing your chances of having a heart attack. What would you pay for this magic? More important, what will it cost you to go without it?

THE COMPONENTS OF LONGEVITY

You've probably read of certain people, the Vilcabambans in the mountains of Ecuador or the inhabitants of the Caucasus in Russia, who lead incredibly long lives; some claim to be 140 or even 160 years old. Even if they are off by several decades, it is still worth examining what accounts for such longevity. No doubt healthy genes have something to do with it, but scientists have also looked at other aspects of their environment. While it cannot be stated definitely that these factors guarantee long lives, it is noteworthy that their environments are characterized by:

1. Freedom from stress
2. Extremely low caloric consumption (often less than 1,800 calories per day)
3. Daily strenuous exercise (the people live a very physical existence, working virtually every day in the fields)

Contrast those characteristics with the elements of a typical manager's job:

1. High stress
2. High-calorie restaurant food
3. Little time for exercise

It's little wonder that so many executives feel tired, become overweight, and suffer any of a number of health problems that could be avoided. Obviously, you can't move to the mountains of Ecuador, but you can learn to manage stress and follow a sensible diet and exercise program that will add years to your life and make you feel and work better.

HARRY THORPE'S LIFE-STYLE[1]

Harry reaches into his briefcase and opens a nine-by-twelve-inch envelope marked "Confidential." Two weeks previously he had completed an in-depth questionnaire concerning his life-style. He begins the important process of attempting to assess where his life-style is taking him. Harry begins to read and take notes on some of the more interesting areas of his personal diagnosis. Figure 17-1 shows the Personal Life-Style Report Harry received.

FAT CITY

Most adults in our society have a weight problem. The reasons are simple. At the turn of the century, a typical "sedentary" man got up at 5:00 A.M., chopped wood for an hour, walked five miles to work, stood over an accounting table all day, walked five miles home, worked around the house, had supper, and went to bed. This was a "sedentary" occupation of that time. Most adults today do not use up nearly as many calories per day as their grandparents did. However, in the same period of time our eating habits haven't changed enough to compensate for our reduced level of physical activity.

There's another reason why most adults are overweight. After you reach age 25, your body's metabolism slows down and you need about 10 fewer calories per day per year—or 3,650 calories a year, which equals 1 pound of body weight. This means that if you eat the same amount this year as you did last year, and expend the same amount of energy, you will automatically gain 1 pound. Thus, if you are 45 years old and eat and exercise the same as you did when you were 25, you will probably be 20 pounds overweight. Awful, isn't it?

The problem of overweight, in theory, is very easy to understand. Imagine you ran a plant that had a very zealous purchasing agent who insisted on buying more raw materials each month than you could use in your production process. Over time, the raw materials would fill the warehouse, spill out onto the parking lot, and begin to occupy all us-

---

[1]Much of the material that follows is based on the Life Style Management System designed by Life Style Management Reports, Inc., 368 Congress Street, Boston, MA 02210. Their approach to life-style management includes a careful assessment involving a detailed questionnaire, a computer data base and software, and the generation of a report, segments of which are included in this chapter. We are grateful to them for permission to use these copyrighted materials to indicate how diagnosis and action planning can occur in the wellness area.

able space. As a manager, you would put a stop to this problem by telling the purchasing agent to buy less and to keep buying less until you had used up the excess. In much the same way, people become overweight by consuming more calories than they use in a day. The "overflow" is fat.

Figure 17-2 shows the portion of Harry's Personal Life-Style Report

Figure 17-1. Harry Thorpe's personal life-style report.

Age: 43 years   H. M. THORPE
Sex: male

April 5, 1992

Dear MR. THORPE:

Here is your Personal Life-style Report. It includes information about your current life-style patterns along with suggestions for ways to adjust them to improve your health and fitness.

Your Personal Life-style Report is divided into six sections:

   I. *You and your family:* Chronic illness and your family. Does it affect you? An overall look at your health. Are you taking care of yourself?
  II. *Disease prevention:* Important information about the causes and ways of preventing heart disease and cancer. What can you do?
 III. *Stress:* The stressors in your life and how to respond to them. What can you do to reduce stress?
  IV. *Nutrition:* Eating right. What in your nutrition pattern needs improvement?
   V. *Calorie balance:* Weight control. How can you balance your calories?
  VI. *Exercise:* Your present exercise routine. Should you plan changes?

As you read your report, you will note what a vital part your personal habits play in your health. You will also come to realize, we hope, that *you* can do many things to better your health and fitness and to increase your sense of well-being.

We wish you good health.

*   *   *   *   *   *   *   *
(*continued*)
Source: Life Style Management Reports, Inc., Boston, Mass.

Figure 17-1. Continued.

H. THORPE   PROFILE DATA SUMMARY-SERIES 85-LR   232-42-7313

April 5, 1992				
	Age	43	Sex	m
	Ht.	70 in.	Wt.	192 lbs.

REPORTED HISTORIES

FAMILY HISTORY OF: high blood pressure
PERSONAL HISTORY OF: profound fatigue and nervous stomach

LIFE-STYLE PRACTICES EVALUATION

TOBACCO HABIT: cigarette smoker

STRESS:

Stress-related physical conditions: moderate   Stressors: moderate

NUTRITION:

Nutrition pattern: very good   Cancer-prevention diet: fair
Eating pattern: very good

Dietary Substances

Sugar: moderate intake   Salt: moderate intake
Fat: high intake   Caffeine: high intake
Alcohol: 30 drinks/week

CALORIE BALANCE:

Reported weight: 192 lbs.
Stated best weight: 172 lbs.
Weight control desire: lose

EXERCISE:

	Frequency		Intensity	Time		Value
Flexibility	0	/week	-?- secs	-?-	min/sess	Very poor
Muscle S/E	0	/week	-?- effort	-?-	min/sess	Poor
Aerobic	1	/week	Moderate pace	41-60	min/sess	Fair

BIOMETRIC PROFILE

DISEASE PREVENTION

	v.good	good	fair	poor	v.poor
Smoking (heart)	████	████	████	████	
Tobacco use (cancer)	████	████	████	████	

	good	fair	poor
Cancer-prevention diet	████	██	

STRESS

	good	fair	poor
Stressors	████	██	
Physical conditions	████	██	

NUTRITION

	v.good	good	fair	poor	v.poor
Nutrition pattern	██				

	good	fair	poor
Eating pattern	██		
Dietary substances	████	████	

EXERCISE

	v.good	good	fair	poor	v.poor
Flexibility training	████	████	████	████	██
Muscle S/E training	████	████	████	██	
Aerobic training	████	████	██		

that is concerned with body weight. He wants to do something about his weight, and the information is helpful to him from a diagnostic and implementation perspective.

Figuring out How Much to Lose in How Much Time

The weight-loss problem is conceptually simple: Each pound of excess weight equals 3,500 calories. If you want to lose 20 pounds, you must "lose" $20 \times 3,500 = 70,000$ calories. You "lose" these calories by taking in less food than you burn up in work. All you need know is your current weight, your desired weight, and how many days you

(text continued on p. 375)

Figure 17-2. Portion of Harry Thorpe's report concerning weight.

Weight Control

Your reported height is *5'10"*.
You reported that your weight is *192* pounds.
You reported that your best weight is *172* pounds.
Pinch more than an inch: *yes.*

You said that your "best" weight is less than your present weight. You also indicated that you would like to lose weight.

The following weight control suggestions are based solely upon your stated preference to lose. It is important to consult your doctor prior to making any major change in your diet.

To lose weight, you should take in fewer calories than you put out. The best way to accomplish this is to increase your exercise/physical activity level and to decrease the amount of calories you eat. Research has shown that the pairing of exercise with diet results in a greater loss of fat tissue than diet alone or even exercise alone.

One pound of fat is approximately 3,500 calories. To lose 1 pound a week, you need a daily caloric loss of 500 calories. This means that your caloric output (activity level) needs to be 500 calories greater each day than your caloric intake.

Based on your reported weight, we recommend an approximate caloric output of 2,880–3,456 calories each day. You should adjust your caloric intake to be 500–1,000 fewer calories than your output. This will enable you to lose 1–2 pounds per week. Caution: We do not recommend a diet of less than 1,000 calories/day unless you are under the direct supervision of a doctor. Remember to eat nutritious food. Choose lower calorie foods (especially if you snack) and food preparations (baking, boiling rather than frying). Limit sweets and other "empty," non-nutritive calories.

Waist-to-Hip Ratio

You measured your waist to be *38.00* inches.
You measured your hips to be *38.00* inches.
Your waist-to-hip ratio is *1.00.*

It has been known for a long time that obesity is a contributing factor to heart disease. Recently, there have been indications that the distribution of fat on

Source: Life Style Management Reports, Inc., Boston, Mass.

the body may even be more important than the overall amount of fat with regard to cardiovascular disease. Waist-to-hip ratios larger than 1.0 in men and larger than 0.8 in women reflect a fat distribution that seems to be a contributing factor in heart disease. Ratios can be reduced by losing weight through a program of exercise and diet.

Body Weight and Composition

When you get on a scale, the weight that you read is the sum of all the materials that make up your body: muscles, bones, organs, chemicals, vessels, fluids, and fat. The first six of these represent your lean body weight: the amount the scale would read if you had no fat. However, fat is a part of you, and you need to have some fat for protection, insulation, and energy supply.

Too little fat or too much fat is unhealthy. With too little fat, the nervous system suffers and there is loss of energy. With too much fat, there is increased risk of coronary heart disease and diabetes, and movement becomes inefficient.

The recommended weight given in weight charts reflects the weight at which people of your age, sex, and height seem to live the longest. To be overweight means that you weigh more than the charts say is "ideal." Obesity is defined as weighing more than 20 percent over your recommended weight. Overweight may be due to too much fat, but it may also be due to extreme muscularity or a very large bone structure. There is a difference between being overweight and overfat.

The proportion of fat to lean tissue varies with changes in exercise/activity levels and/or dietary habits. To be overfat means that you have too much fat in proportion to your lean body weight. A good percent of fat for the adult male ranges between 8 percent and 20 percent of total body composition; the range for adult females is between 12 percent and 26 percent.

To be underfat means that you have too little fat tissue in proportion to your lean body weight. Researchers have suggested that a certain amount of body fat is essential for optimal health. This level is 12 percent for women and about 8 percent for men. Many men and women athletes train so intensively that their percent fat is below these critical levels. While this may be required for good performance in the short term, athletes should be aware of possible long-range negative consequences to their health.

Weight Control

Your body uses the food you eat to supply energy (calories) for your daily activities. If you eat more than you need for your activity level, your body will store the rest of the food as fat. This results in weight (fat) gain. If you eat less

(continued)

Figure 17-2. Continued.

food than you need for your activity level, your body will take some of the fat from storage and use it for energy. This will result in weight (fat) loss.

Therefore, there are two ways to lose or gain weight: (1) adjust the amount of food you eat, and (2) adjust your activity level. The best way to gain weight is to eat a greater quantity of nutritious food, and to build some muscle mass through exercise. The best way to lose weight is to limit caloric intake and increase activity level, especially aerobic activity. Always check with your doctor before starting a new exercise or diet program.

If you need to lose weight, consider the following general guidelines.
1. A gradual, steady weight loss of 1 to 2 pounds a week is the preferred rate.
2. Be prepared to experience a more rapid loss of weight in the beginning of your program and a slower rate of weight loss later.
3. Do not be alarmed by day-to-day fluctuations in weight. It is the long-term trend that is important.
4. Develop good eating habits that help control extra calories.
   • Plan for low-calorie items in your menus.
   • Eat slowly and chew your food thoroughly.
   • Learn to eat just enough food to satisfy hunger.
   • Do not leave serving platters on the table.
   • Establish goals with a system of rewards that does not include food.
   • Drink six to eight glasses of water a day.
5. Choose a diet plan that:
   • Does not eliminate or severely restrict any specific nutrient or general food group
   • Establishes proper eating patterns that you can easily sustain

Calorie Expenditure Chart

Body weight: (in lbs.)	105–115	116–126	127–137	138–148	149–159	160–170
CALORIES BURNED PER HOUR						
Light Intensity Activity						
Reading	70	75	80	85	90	95
Sleeping	50	55	60	65	70	75
Piano playing	95	100	110	115	120	130
Watching TV	60	65	70	75	80	80
Moderate Activity						
Aerobic (low)	215	230	245	260	275	290
Bicycling 5½ MPH	190	205	215	230	245	255
Walking 2 MPH	145	155	165	175	185	195
Bicycling 10 MPH	325	365	395	415	440	460
Tennis—singles	335	355	375	405	425	450
Walking 3 MPH	235	250	270	285	300	315

Vigorous Activity

Basketball	435	465	495	525	555	585
Skiing downhill	465	500	530	560	595	625
Tennis—singles						
competitive	470	500	535	565	600	630
Touch football	470	500	535	565	600	630
Walking 5 MPH	435	465	495	525	555	585

Extremely Vigorous Activity

Bicycling 13 MPH	515	550	585	620	655	690
Aerobic (high)	515	550	585	620	655	690
Jogging 5.5 MPH	515	550	585	620	655	690
Running 7.2 MPH	550	575	625	660	700	735
Running 8 MPH	625	670	715	755	800	845
Running 8.7 MPH	705	755	755	850	900	950
Running 11.4 MPH	955	1,025	1,090	1,155	1,220	1,285
Skiing cross-						
country 5 MPH	550	585	625	660	700	735

Adapted from: Charles Kuntzleman, *Maximum Personal Energy* (Emmaus, Penn.: Rodale Press, Inc., 1981).

have to meet your target. This checklist will aid you in these computations:

1. Current weight: ————

2. Desired weight: ————

3. Number of pounds to lose (item 1 minus item 2): ————

4. Number of calories to lose (item 3 times 3,500): ————

5. Number of days to target weight (give yourself enough time—no more than 1 to 2 pounds per week): ————

6. Number of calories per day to lose (item 4 divided by item 5): ————

7. Number of calories you need to eat each day to maintain your desired weight (see Table 17-1): ————

8. Number of calories you can eat each day on your diet (item 7 minus item 6): ————

Table 17-1. *Calorie allowance for adults of average physical activity: a quick guide to daily caloric intake, based on typical caloric expenditures.*

Desirable Weight	25 Years	45 Years	65 Years
MEN			
110	2,300	2,050	1,750
120	2,400	2,200	1,850
130	2,550	2,300	1,950
140	2,700	2,450	2,050
150	2,850	2,550	2,150
160	3,000	2,700	2,250
170	3,100	2,800	2,350
180	3,250	2,950	2,450
190	3,400	3,050	2,600
WOMEN			
90	1,600	1,500	1,250
100	1,750	1,600	1,350
110	1,900	1,700	1,450
120	2,000	1,800	1,500
130	2,100	1,900	1,600
140	2,250	2,050	1,700
150	2,350	2,150	1,800
160	2,500	2,250	1,900

Source: U.S. Department of Agriculture.

Exercise and Weight Loss

Don't try to "run off" overindulgences in food and drink. The 150-pound man uses up only about 120 calories per mile, no matter how fast he runs. For example, he'd have to run:

- 1+ mile to burn off a glass of wine
- 1 mile to burn off one piece of fudge
- 1.5 miles to burn off one beer
- 1.5 miles to burn off one martini
- 3 miles to burn off one slice of pie

Nevertheless, over a long period of time exercise can help you lose weight. If you are interested in integrating exercise into a weight-loss program, the Calorie Expenditure Chart may be of interest. It shows the number of calories you use per hour in various exercises. Exercise has a lot of other benefits, too, which are described in Figure 17-3.

HOW TO EASE INTO EXERCISE

Figure 17-3 is a nicely balanced approach to the whole issue of exercise. Your own exercise program should be individualized to your needs. Make sure you engage in the type of exercise that is suitable for you, and most important, in an exercise that you will continue over the long term. Here are four important principles to be aware of before you start:

1. *Get your doctor's permission.* Ask to take a treadmill or "stress" electrocardiogram. Regardless of the results of the test, you can still exercise, but it will let you know how much and of what intensity. Don't exercise if you have heart disease, had a recent heart attack, have uncontrolled diabetes, or have high blood pressure; neither should you exercise if you are 35 or more pounds heavier than you should be, or if you have an infectious disease. Take it easy if you have lung disease, anemia, arthritis, or any other chronic problem.

2. *Take it slow.* Most executives are Type A personalities. Consequently, they tend to attack an exercise program with aggressiveness, a need for achievement, ambition, and enthusiasm. They last on average about one week before fatigue sets in, muscles get sore, and interest wanes. For any exercise program to be effective, it will take at least three months to reach the peak of activity, perhaps even five or six months. Take it slow and steady.

3. *Know when to stop.* Nausea, dizziness, or chest pains are *not* signs you are really exercising your body. They're signs you've overdone it. STOP. Take it easier. See your doctor. Try to find a doctor who understands exercise.

4. *Keep a log of your progress.* Include the date, minutes of exercise, type of exercise, your weight, and any other comments. The log will help in two ways. It will encourage you to keep up your progress; and if you use it wisely, it will keep you from overdoing it.

(text continued on p. 380)

Figure 17-3. Portion of Harry Thorpe's report concerning exercise and fitness.

The human body is kept in good condition through sound dietary habits and exercise patterns. Muscles and organs become less efficient through disuse. Therefore, a regular program of exercise is necessary to function efficiently. Occasional exercise does not do much to improve health or fitness and, indeed, may even result in muscle or joint injury. There are guidelines to follow when establishing an exercise program to improve fitness levels. These are given on the following page of your report. The guidelines offered will develop and maintain good general fitness levels. Athletes may wish to increase the frequency, intensity, and/or time of their exercise program.

It is important for all fitness programs to include exercise for flexibility, muscle strength and endurance, and aerobic fitness. However, if your time is limited, aerobic activity should be the exercise of choice because of the overall health benefits of this type of activity.

Developing Flexibility

Flexibility means that your joints are able to move freely throughout their entire range of motion. This is important because a flexible person moves with greater ease, and is less likely to suffer injuries.

Your flexibility program should be done often enough to keep the muscles lengthened and the joints moving freely. You should do flexibility exercise almost daily if you sit a lot (driving, desk work, TV watching), if you are exposed to the possibility of joint injury (frequent lifting, bending, pulling), or if you usually "feel stiff." Stretching should also be done before and after vigorous exercise.

- Warm up your muscles before stretching by doing an easy exercise such as jogging in place for a few minutes.
- Stretch the various muscle groups slowly, holding the stretched position for about twenty seconds. (Do not "bounce"—this can tear muscles.)
- Move *all* joints through the entire range of motion.

Developing Muscle Strength and Endurance

After a reasonable amount of strength is acquired, muscle endurance is more important to most individuals because many daily tasks do not require a great deal of strength. Muscle endurance refers to the lasting quality of the muscle; that is, how many times a muscle group can repeat a movement or how long

Source: Life Style Management Reports, Inc., Boston, Mass.

it can hold a position. Muscle endurance can be acquired through any activity requiring repetitive movement such as weight training, calisthenics, or swimming. It is important that beginners allow at least a day's rest between exercise sessions (no more than three times a week is best). Working too hard, especially with weights, can cause injury.

Strength and endurance gains are achieved with two sessions per week. However, changes in body composition (increase in lean weight and decrease in fat weight) seem to occur only when the strength and endurance training is done at least three times a week.

- Warm up your muscles and stretch before your exercise session.
- Be sure to include all muscle groups in your exercise program.
- Aerobic activities also improve muscle strength and endurance. However, many of these activities (brisk walk, jog, cycling) primarily use the muscles of the lower body. You should supplement these activities with upper body strength and endurance exercise.

Developing Aerobic Fitness

Any consistent, rhythmical exercise is considered to be aerobic. There are many different kinds of aerobic activities including walking, jogging, cycling, skiing, dancing, swimming, and racquet sports. A good level of aerobic fitness will enable you to have increased energy and a normal appetite, and to burn calories more efficiently.

Aerobic exercise is important for the health of the heart. It can also be used as a means of weight control, because body fat is used to supply energy for this type of activity. The minimal frequency of aerobic activity required varies with the type of benefit you want to achieve. You can get cardiovascular benefits by exercising aerobically a minimum of twice a week. If you want to lose fat, you must exercise aerobically at least three times a week. In both cases, it is best to allow at least one day's rest between exercise sessions to allow the body to recover.

- Choose aerobic activities that you enjoy.
- Warm up and cool down before and after each exercise session with stretching and low-intensity activity (about 10–15 minutes before and after exercise).
- Start slowly and progress slowly and steadily. It is better to increase the length of time of exercise at first, then increase the pace after several weeks.
- Remember that it takes time to become fit. Don't overdo; it may lead to an injury.

A reminder: Check with your doctor before beginning or upgrading an exercise program.

CONCLUSION

Health maintenance can be viewed as a two-variable equation:

$$\text{Health maintenance} = \text{Weight control} + \text{exercise}$$

Obviously, there are many other aspects and components that affect your health-maintenance program. Books have been written exclusively about weight control and exercise. I cannot do justice to the topic in one short chapter. However, if you control your food consumption and begin a sensible exercise program, you will be more effective as a manager and more effective as a person.

You *can* do it. You can lower your weight to reach a target. You can be physically fit. Try one, try both, but *try*. Do it now. Get your spouse to go on a diet with you. Get your kids to encourage you. Go slowly, but get going. Make this a high-priority item, and you'll have the time as well as the ability to deal with other high-priority items for a good long time.

Chapter 18

Career Management

7:02 P.M.   Harry meets the president going through the security check at the airport. They are both late and have to make a mad dash for the gate. They make the plane with only 5 minutes to spare.

7:24 P.M.   Flight 98 makes an uneventful takeoff and turns westward toward San Francisco. Harry and the president are sitting in the smoking section of the first-class cabin. Before the "Fasten Seat Belt" sign is turned off, the president catches the flight attendant's attention and persuades her to bring them each a martini. Harry notices that the president is unusually silent and has a strained look on his face.

8:02 P.M.   After gulping his first martini and half of a second, the president turns to Harry and says, "Harry, I'm sorry for not being my usual self tonight, but I'm not feeling very cheerful. I don't want to cry on anybody's shoulder, but I suppose you know Martha and I have been having our troubles at home. She claims that the job takes too much of my life and that I don't have time for her and the kids. I know she's right but, dammit, our work's gotta come first, doesn't it? I guess tonight did it. My sudden departure blew the lid off things. When I left, she told me she was taking the kids and going to her sister's for a while to think things over. She said she wasn't sure she was coming back."

"Gee, Ron," says Harry, "I didn't know it was that bad. I guess these things happen in our line of work. I guess you could call it an occupational hazard; our work is time-consuming. Actually, my situation at home has been getting a little tense itself lately."

Neither knows what else to say and they both fall silent.

8:21 P.M.   The president has ordered and consumed most of his third martini. Because of the altitude and the alcohol, he is a bit drunk and quite sleepy. He says, half to himself, "Harry, you can't plan for a damn thing anymore."

8:30 P.M.   Harry is staring unseeingly at the quality-assurance proposal he had hoped to bring up to the president later during the flight. He is not feeling sorry for Ron as much as he is worrying about his own situation. He thinks to himself, "Ron and I are not so different. Ellen and the kids are great. They try to be understanding, but we have our troubles, too. It's hard to meet the demands of my job and my family, not to mention the community activities that are expected of me. I don't seem to have time for any of the things I might like to do for myself.

As a diversion, he put on the earphones and listens to music. The lyrics question the purpose of life. "What is it all about?" Harry wonders to himself. "Is it really rushing, running, scrambling, eating cold sandwiches, and drinking? What about home, family, and peace? What about me? I've got to get things sorted out. What do I really want to do?"

The awakening begins . . .

What Harry is trying to do at 36,000 feet in a 767 is called planning for career and personal satisfaction. Harry needs it. But he's not sure exactly how to proceed. The awakening can also begin for you as you initiate career planning. Where are you going? When? At what price? What goals would you trade off for other goals? Better yet, what are your job goals, your goals for your family, and your goals for personal development? What is it you want from your life and how are you going to get it?

What follows is an orderly attempt to help you answer these and related questions in a programmatic fashion.

SOME RUDE FACTS ABOUT LIFE

There are two unpleasant but true facts about life that I must remind you of:

- There is not enough time to go around. You just cannot do everything you want to do.
- Life comes in pieces. In your life there is at least a work piece, a family piece, and a personal piece. Each of them competes with the others for your attention. Put simply, there just isn't enough of you to go around.

Therefore, we can say that career and personal satisfaction planning is time management on a grand scale. Right? Wrong! The basic problem is one of setting goals. Too many people simply do not know what they want. They get so caught up in the activities of living that they forget about their goals. They become almost like pigeons, so busy pecking the target that they don't stop to consider whether or not they like the pellet. Career and personal satisfaction planning is *not* super time management because time management assumes that you know what you want. In this chapter you start by finding out *what* you want—or at least, by reminding yourself that activities are not goals.

PELLETS AND BARS

List your seven most important goals, including work, family, and personal goals. This is extremely important, so take some time to consider your answers.

1. _____

2. _____

3. _____

4. _____

5. _____

6. _____

7. _____

Difficult? When I've given this task to practicing managers or students the results are amazing. When I ask people to list their goals, their first tendency is to rattle off a list of activities: "I want to work really hard and get the next promotion." Or "I want to do a lot of traveling." Or even "I want to live where I can ski all year." When they are reminded that they are talking about what they do and not what they want, they get frustrated. They don't want to admit that they have confused their goals with their activities, their pellets with their bars. They want to continue in the same old groove and believe and have others believe that "I'm doing this, so I must like it, it must be my goal." That's not a very good explanation, either for them or for you.

Go back and review the list you have just made. How many of the items are activities rather than goals? How many are bars rather than pellets? Circle those items that are bars.

BREAKING LOOSE: AN EXCURSION IN FANTASY

If you are still having trouble thinking of pellets instead of bars, here are two brief exercises in fantasy. "Fantasy" is, of course, a bad word for many executives. Practicing managers are concrete, pragmatic people and they know that daydreaming does not help them get results. However, fantasy can help you get a handle on your basic goal structure.

The Lottery Exercise

Assume that you have just won the state lottery and tomorrow will receive a check for $500,000. You are to receive half a million dollars every year for the next twenty years. List the first seven things you would do or buy in the next six months with this money.

1. _____

2. _____

3. _____

4. _____

5. _____

6. _____

7. _____

The Prison Exercise

Imagine that you will begin to serve a long prison term in six months. It all seems a ghastly mistake of justice, but no appeal is possible. You have no alternative but to serve your time. List below seven things you would like to accomplish in the next six months.

1. _____

2. _____

3. _____

4. _____

5. _____

6. _____

7. _____

Now go back and circle the items on each list that have nothing to do with money or time pressures. What goals can you accomplish now, even without the wealth? What goals can you accomplish in the *next six months* even without the urgency of time?

You may be amazed to discover that many of these goals can be accomplished with some straightforward modification of your current situation.

MANY DIFFERENT BARS CAN GET THAT PELLET

The first thing to know about planning for satisfaction is that a lot of us are unaware of what our goals are. The second thing to know is that, whatever your goals may be, many different activities can fulfill them. Look at Figure 18-1. This is an actual example from a manager's goals statement, in which he lists his major goal as "I want to control others; I want power."

Look at all the different activities that might lead to this manager's goal. These are by no means complete, but they were all he could think of in a short time. They include career activities such as getting a promotion, becoming president of his firm, changing his occupation, and going into politics. They include personal development activities such

Figure 18-1. Actual manager's goals statement.

Goal: "I want to control others; I want power."

Bars (Activities)	Category
1. Start a religion	Career/personal development
2. Go back to school and become a therapist	Personal development
3. Get a promotion; become president of my firm	Career
4. Go into politics	Career/personal development
5. Work harder at job (see number 3)	Career
6. Be a better husband—talk more with wife	Family
7. Be a better parent—take more time with kids	Family
8. Get my MBA	Personal development
9. Study writings of Machiavelli	Personal development
10. Have more kids	Family/personal development

Priorities

Career	Personal Development	Family
1. Work harder at job	1. Get my MBA	1. Talk more with wife
2. Get a promotion		2. Take more time with kids

as getting his MBA, having more children, and studying the writings of Machiavelli. And they include family activities such as being a better husband and parent. The point is that there is an amazing range of activities you can use to meet your goals. Just because the activities you are now engaged in do not seem to be leading you to the goal you want, at the speed you want, is no reason to close out your options on other activities. Just because what you are now doing is not working is no reason to think you can't do something else that will move you toward your goal. Everybody has at least three areas in which they can pursue their goals. These are career, family, and personal development.

SPLITTING UP YOUR LIFE

Which of these three areas—career, personal development, or family—is most important to you? What if you had to choose between your career and your family? Between career and personal development goals? Between personal goals and family goals? This is what we have to figure out before we can start putting the pieces back together.

Managers make these choices every day, even though they don't identify them as such. For example, how many busy managers do you know who have "missed" seeing their kids grow up? They just weren't around enough. The job got their attention; the children didn't. How can we say that people aren't making these choices? They make them all right, they just don't make them consciously. They don't want to admit that they make them.

Let's find out what is most important to you. On the following checklist, answer the first question. Imagine yourself in a situation in which you actually had to choose between maintaining your family goals, such as keeping your spouse and children, and pursuing your career. Think of a possible transfer to China to help you make this choice. Whatever the scenario you have to dream up, make this choice. Choose your family or your career!

1. If you had to choose between your career and your family goals, what would you choose?

   ☐ Family goals

   ☐ Career goals

Then go to question 2, which follows. If you had to choose between the satisfaction of your career goals and those of your own personal development not related to work, which would you take? Would you give up your sailing, your golf, your exercise, your personal reading time to assure reaching your career goals? Would you give up your career goals, or at least part of them, so that you could meet your personal development goals?

2. If you had to choose between pursuing your career goals and your personal goals, which would you choose?

   ☐ Career goals

   ☐ Personal goals

Now on to question 3. If you had to choose between your goals for your family and those for yourself, which would you take? Would you give up the family's Sunday outings, stop going to the symphony, not worry about being a good parent if you could be sure that some of your personal goals could be satisfied?

3. If you had to choose between your family goals and your personal goals, which would you choose?

☐ Personal goals

☐ Family goals

Don't worry about the complexity of the questions or their interdependence. Of course, you are a better person when you are a better parent and spouse. Of course, you are a better worker when you are a better person. And of course, succeeding at your career helps you meet your family goals. Try for now to choose between them so you can set priorities. Which is most important to you? What would you do if you had to choose only one goal area? Now answer question 4 to get a basic feel for your priorities.

4. What is your number-one goal area
   (career, personal, family)? _____

   Your number-two goal area? _____

   Your number-three goal area? _____

DECIDING WHAT YOU ARE GOING TO DO

Here is what we know so far:

1. Goals are not the same as activities.
2. Many activities satisfy the same goals.
3. You have three important areas in your life.
4. One of the three areas in your life is your number-one priority. The others have second and third priority.

Now you can work with these four pieces of information because many of the hard choices have already been made. You've done a lot of creative brainstorming and it is now time to get back to reality. The Career Status Audit (Form 18-1) enables you to make some pragmatic assessments concerning your current job and your current strengths and weaknesses. It then permits you to move on to additional brainstorming activities, helping you assess your ideal state and your expected state five years hence. It concludes with a pragmatic action plan. Using the goals and activities analysis that you have already completed as a basis, take the Career Status Audit now. It will provide you with a compass for choosing the best possible path through the forest of your career.

SURVIVING THE MERGER OR ACQUISITION

They've become dreaded words in the management community these days: takeover, merger, acquisition, liquidation, downsizing, and numerous other terms that strike fear in the hearts of practicing managers. It's a globally competitive world, and firms are experiencing rates of change unheard of in the past. This makes the job of the manager even more difficult. Career planning is more important now than ever, because your career may span several organizations and be characterized by greater turmoil.

This section is an attempt to help you survive a merger, acquisition, or related business event. If you are faced with a major organizational change, use this manual as you've never used it before. You must pull together all possible resources to cope with this traumatic experience.

Own Stock

This is somewhat tongue in cheek, but it makes sense. If you own stock in your company, at the least you can anticipate roughly a 50 percent appreciation in the value of your shares before the acquisition team descends upon you. In fact, if you work for a decent company, it makes sense to have some ownership as a motivational tool for you and your coworkers.

Network

Talk to people. Don't just concentrate on the rumors circulating in the company. Broaden your network. Revitalize contacts you haven't talked to recently. Use your network to determine what alternatives are available.

Review Your Agenda

We talked about your nine-cell agenda in Chapter 2, in relation to time management. Remember? This is your back-of-the-envelope MBO document. Make sure your agenda is set optimally. You may wish to focus a bit more on short-run issues during the transition so that the results of your efforts are more visible. Drop to the bottom row in your agenda and make sure the goals in that row are visible and important to upper management.

Increase Your Coping Skills

Mergers, acquisitions, and related events generate tremendous stress. You are not going to be able to reduce the demand very much because it is externally imposed. However, you may be able to increase your coping skills. Make sure the rest of your life is as supportive as possible so you can cope with the new levels of stress occurring at work.

Do a Power Audit

Mergers and acquisitions have a lot to do with power. You may find your positional power base eroded. How is your personal power base? Remember, your expertise and information are the things you take with you. Manage your image so that top management perceives that you have power. Likewise, you may have to use political tactics in new and different ways. Review the political tactics list in Chapter 5, and see if you can generate your own list of things you can do to stabilize and enhance your power position.

Get Your MBO Records

If you've been following an MBO system either corporatewide or personal, make sure that your file is up to date and that you have tangible proof of your accomplishments for the past five years. If you don't have a corporatewide MBO system, make sure you get access to your performance-appraisal records and you can at least have a personal MBO system that is a record of your accomplishments.

Communicate

Talk to everyone. Make sure you are plugged into the right people. Treat the new organization as a client and listen as effectively as possible to the things they are saying. Try to anticipate what their priorities are and where they want to move the new structure.

Diagnose the Leadership Style

The basic leadership style in an organization may change. Probably as the result of a merger or acquisition, you will find a movement southward and eastward on the Bonoma-Slevin model. Look at Chapter 9 and try to anticipate the styles that will be coming into the organization. Will they be more autocratic? What can you expect? If you can anticipate the change, you may not be as upset by sudden moves in leadership style.

Diagnose the New Organizational Design

What will the new differentiation needs be? Will the leadership be bringing in a team of specialists? Often someone with alternative differentiated skills can become quite valuable in these settings. Do you have particular specialties that may be needed in the new organization? At the same time, ask yourself, "What are the new integration needs?" Substantial coordination is always needed in any merger or acquisition scenario. However, be forewarned that the integrator role is often a high-risk position. You may move rapidly because you will be highly visible as an integrator, but be prepared to handle the risks involved.

Use Negotiation Skills

It's probably best to start with a soft, relationship-oriented approach, at least initially. Then it may be appropriate to move toward a more principled approach and try to solve the problems generated by the transition. The hard-bargaining approach will probably be reserved for the very end, if things have gotten so bad that you are talking in terms of lawyers and lawsuits rather than win/win solutions to negotiable problems.

Get a Key Project

Find a project that is essential to the organization, at least in the short run. Get appointed the project manager so you have access to the resources and people needed for success. Use the Project Implementation Profile in Chapter 14 to make sure you are handling all ten factors appropriately. Send out lots of correspondence documenting your progress on the project, where things stand, where you are going, and so forth.

Run Effective Meetings

If you have groups to work with, lead them like you've never led before. Make sure agendas are in place before the meetings; be certain the meetings run well; and use minutes as a follow-up. Let yourself be perceived as someone who can get things accomplished in an efficient way involving small groups.

Diagnose the Entrepreneurial Style of the New Owners

Often a merger or acquisition implies a change in managerial style with regard to entrepreneurship. Do they want the organization to become more risk taking, proactive, and innovative? Try to anticipate the direction that the basic managerial style will take. Get yourself perceived as someone who is at the forefront. If the new owners want risk-takers and proactive managers, then try to fill that role.

Career Plan

Finally, make sure your career plan is in order, so that you are able to evaluate new opportunities and problems as they arise. Where are you trying to go? What are your strengths? What are your weaknesses? Use the material in this chapter to diagnose and plan your career direction.

Use all of the above, and you may be able to survive the merger or acquisition in significantly better shape than if you had used just intuitive skills to handle these transitions.

CONCLUSION

You've had an opportunity to both brainstorm and pragmatically plan your career. Remember,

- Goals are not activities.
- Different goals have different priorities.
- Goals are only achieved through activities.

You now have a better idea of where you want to go and how you will get there. You have a better sense of the extent to which your current job situation satisfies your basic needs. You have a better feeling for your job-related strengths and weaknesses. You have a better idea of where you ideally would like to be five years hence, and where you actually expect to be five years from now. And finally, you have the beginnings of an action plan to assist you in getting the most from your career. Start your career plan today. It will be modified substantially, but it will give you a start in achieving what you want in life. Go ahead and take action. With a little bit of luck, it will lead to a more effective and more satisfied you. Good luck!

CAREER STATUS AUDIT

Indicate on the 10-point scale the extent to which you agree that your current job provides the optimal amount of each dimension.

	Strongly Disagree				Neutral				Strongly Agree		

MOTIVATIONAL NEEDS

1. Need for achievement (Ability to surmount obstacles and reach difficult targets)
   0 1 2 3 4 5 6 7 8 9 10

2. Need for affiliation (Ability to associate with people that you like)
   0 1 2 3 4 5 6 7 8 9 10

3. Need for power (Ability to exercise influence over the behavior of others)
   0 1 2 3 4 5 6 7 8 9 10

4. Need for self-actualization (Ability to grow, develop, and acquire new skills)
   0 1 2 3 4 5 6 7 8 9 10

STRESS ISSUES

5. Type A behavior (About the right pace in terms of incidents per day, time pressure, deadlines, etc.; if your job is either too stressful or too boring, you would disagree with this item)
   0 1 2 3 4 5 6 7 8 9 10

6. Job involvement (Extent to which your emotional and physical involvement in your job is about right)
   0 1 2 3 4 5 6 7 8 9 10

7. Frustration level (Inordinate frustration does not exist)
   0 1 2 3 4 5 6 7 8 9 10

INDUCEMENTS ISSUES

8. Compensation (Wages and fringes)
   0 1 2 3 4 5 6 7 8 9 10

9. Job freedom (Ability to set your own schedule)
   0 1 2 3 4 5 6 7 8 9 10

10. Travel (About the right amount to suit you)
    0 1 2 3 4 5 6 7 8 9 10

11. Leisure time
    0 1 2 3 4 5 6 7 8 9 10

12. Potential for advancement
    0 1 2 3 4 5 6 7 8 9 10

FORM 18-1.

JOB SATISFACTION
1. Aspects of my job with which I am most satisfied:

_____

_____

_____

_____

_____

_____

_____

2. Aspects of my job with which I am dissatisfied and would like to change:

_____

_____

_____

_____

_____

_____

_____

_____

_____

_____

FORM 18-1.

STRENGTHS/WEAKNESSES ASSESSMENT

1. List below your key job-related strengths:

_____

_____

_____

_____

_____

_____

_____

_____

_____

2. List below your key job-related weaknesses:

_____

_____

_____

_____

_____

_____

_____

_____

_____

THE IDEAL STATE—FIVE YEARS HENCE
1. Write a brief paragraph describing what your life would be like five years
from now if you managed to realize all of your goals.

_____

_____

_____

_____

_____

_____

_____

_____

_____

_____

_____

_____

_____

_____

_____

_____

_____

_____

_____

_____

_____

EXPECTED STATE—FIVE YEARS HENCE
2. Write a brief paragraph indicating what you expect your life will be like five years from now if the most likely pattern is followed.

_____

_____

_____

_____

_____

_____

_____

_____

_____

_____

_____

_____

_____

_____

_____

_____

3. Compare this paragraph with the previous paragraph to determine if any changes should be made now to try to increase your likelihood of reaching your goals.

ACTION PLAN

What action steps can you take over the next twelve months to reduce the difference between your "ideal state" and your "expected state"? Be as specific and complete as possible.

_____

_____

_____

_____

_____

_____

_____

_____

_____

_____

_____

_____

_____

_____

_____

_____

_____

_____

_____

_____

Chapter 19

Harry Thorpe— The Survivor

S IX MONTHS later. Some interesting things have occurred in Harry Thorpe's life. The changes have been small, and in many cases, quite subtle. However, in the aggregate, they represent a Harry Thorpe who is doing a much better job of surviving. He may even make it. Let's take a look.

6:30 A.M.   Alarm rings. Harry gets out of bed with the usual Monday morning difficulty. However, instead of showering, he puts on a pair of shorts and running shoes, which he does at least four days a week. He opens the front door, glances at his watch, and sets off at a slow but steady gait for the track a half-mile away. He usually runs about two miles: a half-mile to the track, one mile on the track, and a half-mile back. After about 2 minutes, he feels terrible and wonders why he's doing this. After about 8 minutes, he begins to develop a second wind and feels a lot better. During the run home he experiences almost a sense of exhilaration.

6:59 A.M.   He returns home, glances at his watch. "Twenty-two minutes," he says to himself. "Two eleven-minute miles—not bad." He sits

400

down to read the paper and drink a cup of coffee while his pulse returns to normal. Ten minutes after exercise it's below 100.

7:18 A.M. Having showered and shaved, Harry has a slice of toast, orange juice, and some vitamins while he and his son discuss the changed standings as a result of yesterday's pro football games. He briefly goes over the plans for his wife's most recent project, and tries to be as excited as she seems to be.

7:22 A.M. Kissing his family good-bye, he departs for work. The roads are still filled with potholes and the drivers still incompetent, but Harry is different; he doesn't let these things get to him like he used to.

8:00 A.M. He arrives at the office and begins working on correspondence while the other employees come trickling in.

8:25 A.M. Harry's new secretary arrives. Three months ago Harry decided to transfer his previous secretary and upgrade the position when he calculated he could save 30 minutes a day by delegating more to a more qualified person. It was a hard decision, but he felt he had to make it.

8:29 A.M. Harry goes over his correspondence with his secretary. She will write three of the letters herself. He reviews his calendar with her:

10:00 A.M. Staff meeting.
11:30 A.M. Meet executive VP and president—brief them on status of negotiations with union.
1:00 P.M. Meet vendor of word-processing equipment.
3:00 P.M. Union negotiations meeting.

8:45 A.M. Harry dismisses his secretary and finishes going through his "garbage" file, reviewing his junk mail and tossing most of it out. He then begins to return phone calls from Friday.

8:49 A.M. Phones Steve Johnson, chairman of the local chamber of commerce: Steve wants Harry to help in a fund-raising drive for Children's Hospital. Harry says, "No, Steve, I'm sorry but I can't do it this year. Perhaps next year. I'd like to stay on top of this labor-management situation until we finally get a contract." Although Steve isn't very happy, Harry congratulates himself that he's learning how to say no.

9:01 A.M. Phone call: Quentin Hill, personnel manager, wants approval to hire two new secretaries. "Let's wait until the new word-processing equipment is in and operating before we hire anybody," Harry says. "It should speed up our productivity, and maybe we can save those two slots." Quentin is disappointed but agrees. They plan to reconsider his request in sixty days.

9:07 A.M.   Returns phone call to Harrison in Texas. Harrison needs priority on the Conrad offer. The customer is desperate for it in two weeks and wants a small design change. "The person who can really help you with this is one of my production managers, Deborah Walters," Harry says. "Let me put her on. If she can't help you with it, then get back to me." Harry then calls Walters on the local and explains the problem. "See what you can do to help him," he says. "Try to be as accommodating as possible without throwing your production schedule too much out of line. Let me know at the staff meeting how things worked out."

9:11 A.M.   Phone call: Ralph Kingsley reports there is a rumor on the shop floor that there may be a slowdown if the contract is not settled by the end of the week. Harry thanks him for the information and tells him not to make any moves or say anything to antagonize anybody until he hears from Harry.

9:14 A.M.   Harry puts down the phone and chuckles to himself. "I wonder if 'Hard Nose Harry' can pull this one off."

The moniker "Hard Nose Harry" was coined three months ago, when top management was planning on putting in a new materials-handling system throughout all their locations. They called in Harry for technical advice on the matter. The meeting went something like this:

PRESIDENT: Harry, this new system should save us a lot of man-hours in all of our locations. If you think it will work, we will probably put it in.

HARRY: Sure, Ron, it will work. It's a technically sound system. I've worked at it from all angles. What are they asking for it?

PRESIDENT: $2.6 million.

HARRY: Offer them $2.1 million.

PRESIDENT: What! You know they'll never accept that.

HARRY: Ron, I've done a lot of homework on this problem. The system is technically sound, but it will be the first one they've ever installed. They're anxious to get one in and operational so they can bring other potential customers by to see it in operation. Also, they've had a bumper year for profits and their fiscal year will end in two months. They'd love to spend some money on developmental costs of this system in a hurry. What harm could there be in offering them $2.1 million?

PRESIDENT: I guess it's worth a try. All they can say is no. You've really done your homework on this one.

They offered the vendor $2.1 million, and two weeks later settled for the complete system for $2.2 million. In executive committee meetings Harry was jokingly called "Hard Nose Harry" for his tough negotiation capability. In fact, he even received a confidential handwritten note from the chairman of the board, which started out, "Dear Hard Nose," and complimented him for saving the company $400,000.

Harry only wished that he felt more confident about his new reputation. As a consequence of that incident, Harry had been appointed the leader of the management negotiating team for the labor-management negotiations. They had been negotiating for almost three months, and the workers had been going without a contract for the past four weeks. It is only due to management's good relations with the employees that they have been able to continue work so far, and Harry knows that he is living on borrowed time. He hopes to conclude the negotiations this afternoon, if possible.

9:17 A.M.   Dan Felder drops in. He is a bright young MBA whom Harry hired as his administrative assistant four months ago. His main responsibility has been as an information-flow analyst. "Harry," he says, "I'm having trouble with Smithers in accounting. He says that the computer can't give the cost information that we need on the P12 line."

After reviewing the problem, Harry suggests that Felder meet the top programmer in the computer group and determine precisely the cost of generating that report, then meet with Smithers and the top programmer. "See if Smithers will agree," Harry says. "You may be able to sweeten the deal by getting a special report for him at the same time." Harry asks Felder to report on the subject next Monday morning and Felder agrees.

9:35 A.M.   Harry closes his door and instructs his secretary to hold all calls. He reviews his negotiation situation for the afternoon. He's got to report to the president and executive vice-president at 11:30 and then have a negotiation meeting at 3:00 P.M. Last Friday, the union was pretty close to agreement, and Harry hopes that they both will sign on the dotted line this afternoon.

9:55 A.M.   Harry walks to the coffee station to pick up a cup to take with him to the staff meeting. He passes a mirror and sees a trimmer figure than he is used to. He returns to his office reflecting that maybe the fifteen pounds he lost was worth it after all.

10:00 A.M.   Staff meeting. Besides Harry, in attendance are his administrative assistant, Dan Felder; the two production managers, Ralph Kingsley and Deborah Walters; Henry Carothers, the sales manager; Sarah Freeman, the engineering manager; Quentin Hill, the personnel manager; and Spencer Bernham, finance and accounting manager.

Felder has prepared an agenda on a flip chart and has passed out the weekly report, which he initiated with Harry's guidance two months ago and which includes weekly updates on production output, quality problems, average delivery times, backlog of orders, and problem areas. The report has been a great help to Harry and everyone on his staff. It also gives a framework for discussion at their weekly staff meetings.

10:45 A.M.   The president calls Harry, interrupting the meeting, and says, "Harry, I'd like you to go with me to Chicago. I think we can close that million-dollar Wacker deal."

"I'd like to go," Harry says, "but I have that negotiating meeting this afternoon. Could we send Carothers?"

"Can he handle it?"

"I'm sure he can. And it will do him good to see you in action."

The president laughs. "OK, Harry. You're a good salesman. Have Carothers get in touch with my secretary concerning our travel arrangements."

10:51 A.M.   Harry returns to the staff meeting and asks Carothers if he can make it. Carothers is pleased. "Sure, Harry, I'll be glad to go."

11:00 A.M.   The staff meeting ends. Everyone departs with clear action plans for the following five days. Bernham comes up and says, "Harry, we really seem to be accomplishing things in our staff meetings these days. I really think that the new format is a good idea."

Harry says, "Thanks, Spencer. We'll keep trying to improve it."

11:10 A.M.   Quentin drops by. He says, "Harry, I didn't want to bother everyone with it in the staff meeting, but we really should get cracking on that training program for first-line supervisors."

"OK, Quentin, what shall we do?"

"I think we should send our supervisors to an off-site location and bring in a good training firm that has competence in this area."

Harry thinks a moment. "Well, I know of two or three reputable firms, but I haven't heard anything lately. I could check and see what their current status is."

Quentin says, "Good. Why don't you check and get back to me?" He rises to leave and starts out the door. Harry says, "Quentin, you son of a gun! Where's the monkey?"

"What monkey?"

"Remember our discussion about three months ago?" Harry says. "We talked about monkeys on people's backs. Right now, tell me, where is the supervisory training program monkey?"

Quentin looks sheepish. "It just executed a beautiful leap from my back to yours, didn't it?"

Harry grins. "Yes, it did, and let's get it back where it belongs."

Quentin says, "Sure, Harry. If you'd like, I'll do some checking on available training programs and get back to you on Friday. I'll get the names of those firms from your secretary."

11:25 A.M. Harry leaves for the president's office. He makes it a point to try to arrive at all of his meetings about 2 minutes in advance of the official starting time, in order to look on time, composed, and organized.

11:30 A.M. Harry quickly and confidently briefs the president and executive vice-president concerning the status of the labor-management negotiations. "We're pretty close on wages, and our real disagreement appears to be on the 'safety strike' clause. They want the ability to call a strike if they feel that working conditions are unsafe. Ron, you know that we've always worked hard on safety, and this is giving them an unnecessary clause. Once we give it to them, we'll never get it back, and they'll essentially have the ability to call a wildcat strike anytime they want it. I think we have to stand firm on this issue. It's my assessment that we have about a fifty-fifty chance of settling with them this week and still keeping the safety clause out. They know as well as I do that safety is not the real issue here but that wildcat strikes are."

"OK, Harry," the president says, "do it your way. Good luck this afternoon."

11:55 A.M. Harry returns to his office, where he finds Carothers. "All set on the trip, Chief. I'll brief you when I get back."

"Great," Harry says, "and keep your eye on Ron. He is the greatest salesman when he really gets wound up."

12:00 NOON. Harry closes his office door and sits down to lunch: a sandwich, a low-calorie soda, and an apple. He has decided to have no more lunches with subordinates. He found himself getting too friendly with them, making it difficult to provide leadership in tough situations.

Harry also found out, when he thought about it, that he really hated business lunches; they only gave him calories and indigestion. When he observed the process, he discovered that most "business" at business lunches occurred in the 10 minutes between the main course and the dessert. He found that he enjoyed his lunch a lot more if he didn't have to worry about business while eating.

His new pattern is that he eats in the office and then spends 30 minutes reading material for his own personal development. He makes it a point not to read his mail or work on day-to-day matters. During the past three months he has read everything from *A Portrait of the Artist as a Young Man* to *The Whole Manager*.

Harry feels a lot more relaxed than he did six months ago. He should. His new typical workday consists of twenty incidents with six interruptions in a morning—down from thirty-two and fourteen six months ago. He finds himself delegating more and having more time to make sure the important problems are handled properly.

Harry even did a career plan of sorts about two months ago. He didn't come up with any earthshaking revelations until one month ago, when he refused a general manager job in Dallas. It would have been nice—more money and more responsibility. However, he just couldn't see a move for the family at this time. Ellen's business could not be moved easily. He didn't want to uproot the kids in order to lead a life that would be even more hectic in Dallas than the one he already had. He had no regrets about that decision. In fact, he was glad that he had the presence of mind to make it.

The kids seem to be better behaved, too. He tried behavior modification on his 12-year-old son, with some success. His room is now regularly neat. Also, Harry persuaded him to go out for soccer, even though the boy wasn't terribly enthusiastic about the idea. Harry now goes to soccer games on weekends and watches with pride as his son plays a good solid game at left halfback. In the past three months his son seems to have lost that baby fat he was carrying, and he is in much better physical condition. His state of mind seems to have improved substantially, too.

Behavior modification didn't work so well on his 15-year-old daughter, though, so Harry used a more old-fashioned approach. "Look," he said, "if you want to have the car and be able to drive when you turn sixteen, you are going to have to maintain an A-minus or better average in school." After she overcame the initial shock, her grades pulled up from a B-minus to a B-plus, and she is predicting confidently that the A-minus target will be reached in the next grading period.

Things are going better with Ellen, too. Her business is continuing to grow and she seems to have the workload under better control. They've now made it a rule that they'll have dinner together alone at least once a week. He has started looking forward to these quiet interludes with his wife, and finds that she's just as charming and even better looking than she was when he married her eighteen years ago.

On the personal front, Harry has made some real progress. During the past six months he has:

- Quit smoking
- Lost fifteen pounds
- Started jogging and has gotten to the point where he runs about eight miles a week, in addition to occasional weekend tennis
- Lowered his blood pressure to 130/86
- Lowered his pulse to 72

In short, he is more relaxed and has a feeling of control over his life.

Of course, there are still areas Harry needs to work on. He still has a tendency to get overly excited about things he probably shouldn't be so concerned about. He occasionally has "Type A attacks." He needs to cut his alcohol consumption even more. He also wants to lose that last five pounds and get down to his real fighting weight. Finally, he worries about his leadership style, sometimes feeling he is too tough on his subordinates. However, they seem to be reasonably happy lately, and they are sure getting a lot done.

12:45 P.M. Harry takes a quick tour of the plant. He makes it a point to greet everyone by name if possible, and looks for signs of shoddy workmanship, poorly policed areas, and so on.

1:00 P.M. He meets with the vendor of word-processing equipment and Dan Felder, his administrative assistant. After defining the problem for the salesman and setting basic guidelines, Harry turns the meeting over to Dan and excuses himself so he can move on to other important matters. Dan will brief him next week with a comprehensive recommendation on the system.

1:20 P.M. He drops in on Spencer Bernham. "Spencer, how are we doing financially right now if we have to take a strike?"

"Not bad," Spencer says. "Our working capital situation is the best it's been in the last three years, and we are staying pretty well on top of our accounts receivable."

"Why don't you check with the bank and get an extra line of credit now, just in case we do have a strike. Of course, I hope we won't need it, but we're in a lot better negotiating situation with the bank now than we might be in a couple of months."

"Good idea, Harry. How much do you think we should get?"

"Why don't you double our existing line."

"Great. I'll do it this week and let you know by Friday where we stand."

1:55 P.M. Phone call: Ralph Kingsley says in a trembling voice, "Boss, one of the loads shifted on a fork truck down here, and Jimmy Stevenson is now pinned under five tons of steel. We've got things under control, and we're getting him out as quickly as possible."

"How bad is he?" Harry asks.

"I don't know."

1:58 P.M. Harry tells his secretary and leaves on a dead run for the plant floor.

2:01 P.M. Harry arrives at the accident site. A small crowd has gathered. Ralph's production foreman is supervising a crew of five who are attaching cables to the load. The fork truck is leaning over at a crazy angle. The steel is lying against a concrete column, keeping most of its weight off Stevenson. His crumpled form is lying unconscious under the load.

2:10 P.M. Stevenson is freed. He regains consciousness, but is not very lucid. His left foot hangs at a funny angle as they load him into the ambulance.

2:12 P.M. Harry calls Stevenson's wife and explains the situation. "How bad is he?" she asks.

Harry answers, "I don't know, Mrs. Stevenson, but he wanted you to meet him at the hospital."

She says, "How will I get there? My car's in the garage."

"How about if I pick you up? I can be there in about ten minutes," offers Harry.

"OK," says the worried wife.

2:25 P.M. Harry pulls into the Stevenson driveway, picks up an anxious Mrs. Stevenson, and departs for the hospital.

2:36 P.M. They arrive at the emergency room. Kingsley is there and says with a somewhat relieved look, "He's going to be OK."

Mrs. Stevenson exclaims, "Thank God! How is he?"

Kingsley says, "A broken leg and perhaps other injuries, but he's going to be all right. Why don't you go in and see him?"

3:00 P.M. Harry calls his secretary and asks her to postpone his negotiating meeting to 4:00.

3:20 P.M. Harry checks with the physician and finds out that Jimmy Stevenson has his left leg broken in two places and possible internal injuries. However, his condition is stable, and with no complications he should be back at work in ten weeks.

3:30 P.M. Harry meets Kingsley on the hospital steps. "How did it happen?" he asks.

"It was just one of those fluke things. Our men are always cautious about shifting loads on fork trucks. Everybody was following the appropriate procedure, but the driver hooked the load on the column and at the same time his foot slipped off the brake. Then one of the restraining chains broke. Jimmy just happened to be at the wrong place at the wrong time."

"Lucky for him and us that he wasn't more seriously injured," Harry says. "Ralph, I want you to follow up on this and make sure no safety procedures were violated. Meet with all your first-line supervisors and have them hold a meeting with the men to restress safety around these heavy loads. Also, let's do a stress test on all the chains that we're using and throw out any suspicious ones."

"Sure, Harry, I'll get it done this week."

3:50 P.M. Harry returns to the plant floor and inspects the fork truck. Everybody, including the first-line supervisor who was at the scene, seems to agree it really was a fluke.

4:03 P.M. Harry returns to his desk and grabs a folder that his secretary hands him concerning the union negotiations.

4:10 P.M. Harry arrives at the conference room and shakes hands for about the fiftieth time with Sam Clemens of the union team. They spend the first 10 minutes talking about the Stevenson incident, with the union grumbling about unsafe working conditions. Finally, Sam comes to the point. He says, "Harry, we don't want a strike any more than you do. We'll call this whole thing settled based on where we are now if you'll just add five cents an hour to the wages and give us our safety-strike clause."

"I'm sorry," Harry says. "I'll give you five cents an hour, but no safety-strike clause. You know how we feel on that matter."

"Harry, that's just not acceptable, especially in view of the accident today."

Harry grits his teeth. "Look, Sam, we both know that accident couldn't have been helped. How much more per hour do you need to settle without the safety-strike clause?"

Sam is somewhat surprised. "Double that five cents and we've got a deal."

Harry does a quick calculation ($20,000 a year) and stands up. "Done."

A feeling of satisfaction sweeps the room. Both sides are glad to get the settlement. Both initial the appropriate document and then head down to the president's office for a celebration. "Harry, it was good of you to take Mrs. Stevenson to the hospital today," says Sam.

Harry replies, "Sam, we have a great work force here, and we want to keep them that way. We hire only first-rate people, and we want to keep them identified with the goals of the company. I only did what I thought was right in that situation, but thanks for the feedback anyway."

"Great, Harry. Let's hope we can work together for a long time."

6:00 P.M. Harry leaves the office to drive home. He feels good. He is relaxed. He is in control. He is basically satisfied with his job, and most important, he feels that he is getting things done.

Harry is surviving in the executive environment. He has gained mastery over the difficult, frenetic job of a general manager, and he no longer feels that he is being driven by incidents that are out of his control. Of course, he is not perfect and never will be. However, he has managed to implement a number of the concepts we have discussed in this book.

The challenge is now up to you to do the same thing. You can do it. You can make the needed changes in your managerial and personal life to improve your effectiveness as a manager and your satisfaction as a person. You have gained insight through this manual. All you need now is the desire to make the change. Good luck!

Selected Readings

CHAPTER 2: TIME MANAGEMENT

Ashkenas, Ronald N., and Robert H. Schaffer. "Managers Can Avoid Wasting Time." *Harvard Business Review*, Vol. 60, no. 3 (1982), pp. 98–104.

Fielden, John S. "What Do You Mean You Don't Like My Style?" *Harvard Business Review*, Vol. 60, no. 3 (1982), pp. 128–138.

Love, Sydney F. *Mastery and Management of Time.* Englewood Cliffs, N.J.: Prentice-Hall, 1978.

Winston, Stephanie. *The Organized Executive.* New York: Warner, 1983.

CHAPTER 3: INTOLERANCE AS A RESPONSE TO NONCOMPLIANCE

Greenberg, Herbert M. *Coping with Job Stress.* Englewood Cliffs, N.J.: Prentice-Hall, 1980.

Keirsey, David, and Marilyn Bates. *Please Understand Me.* Del Mar, Calif.: Prometheus Nemesis Books (dist.), 1984.

McKay, Matthew, Martha Davis, and Patrick Fanning. *Thought and Feelings: The Art of Cognitive Stress Intervention.* Richmond, Calif.: New Harbinger Publications, 1981.

CHAPTER 4: STRESS

Adams, John D., ed. *Understanding and Managing Stress: A Book of Readings.* San Diego: University Associates, 1980.
————. *Understanding and Managing Stress: A Workbook in Changing Life Styles.* San Diego: University Associates, 1980.
Gherman, E. M. *Stress and the Bottom Line: A Guide to Personal Well-Being and Corporate Health.* New York: AMACOM, 1981.
Jackson, Susan E. "Participation in Decision Making as a Strategy for Reducing Job-Related Strain." *Journal of Applied Psychology,* Vol. 6B, no. 1 (1983), pp. 3–19.
Roskies, Ethel. *Stress Management for the Healthy Type A: Theory and Practice.* New York: Guilford Press, 1987.
Matteson, Michael T., and John M. Ivancevich. *Controlling Work Stress.* San Francisco: Jossey-Bass, 1987.

CHAPTER 5: POWER

Bachrach, Samuel B., and Edward J. Lawler. *Power and Politics in Organizations.* San Francisco: Jossey-Bass, 1980.
Bartolome, Fernando, and Andre Laurent. "The Manager: Master and Servant of Power." *Harvard Business Review,* Vol. 64 (1986), pp. 77–81.
Mintzberg, Henry. *Power in and Around Organizations.* Englewood Cliffs, N.J.: Prentice-Hall, 1983.

CHAPTER 6: BEHAVIOR MODIFICATION

Leitenberg, Harold, ed. *Handbook of Behavior Modification and Behavior Therapy.* Englewood Cliffs, N.J.: Prentice-Hall, 1976.
Luthans, Fred, and Robert Kreitner. *Organizational Behavior Modification.* Glenview, Ill.: Scott Foresman, 1975.
O'Brien, Richard M., Alyce M. Dickinson, and Michael P. Rosow. *Industrial Behavior Modification: A Management Handbook.* New York: Pergamon Press, 1982.

CHAPTER 7: MANAGEMENT BY OBJECTIVES

Mali, Paul. *MBO Updated: A Handbook of Practices and Techniques for Managing by Objectives.* New York: John Wiley & Sons, 1986.

Odiorne, George S. *MBO II.* Belmont, Calif.: David S. Lake Publishers, 1979.

CHAPTER 8: EFFECTIVE COMMUNICATIONS

Fielden, John S. "What Do You Mean You Don't Like My Style?" *Harvard Business Review,* Vol. 60, no. 3 (1982), pp. 128–138.

CHAPTER 9: LEADERSHIP

Kotter, John P. *The Leadership Factor.* New York: Macmillan, 1988.

Kouzes, James M., and Barry Z. Posner. *The Leadership Challenge.* San Francisco: Jossey-Bass, 1988.

Tichy, Noel. *The Transformational Leader.* New York: John Wiley & Sons, 1986.

CHAPTER 10: MOTIVATION

Campbell, John P., and Robert D. Pritchard. "Motivation Theory in Industrial and Organization Psychology." In *Handbook of Industrial and Organizational Psychology,* M. Dunnette, ed. New York: John Wiley & Sons, 1976.

Davis, Keith, and John W. Newstrom. *Human Behavior at Work.* 7th edition. New York: McGraw-Hill, 1985.

Lawler, Edward E. III. *Pay and Organization Development.* Reading, Mass.: Addison-Wesley, 1983.

Locke, Edward A., and D. Henne. "Work Motivation Theories." In *International Review of Industrial and Organizational Psychology,* C. L. Cooper and I. Robertson, eds. New York: John Wiley & Sons, 1986.

Miner, John B. *The Human Constraint.* Washington, D.C.: Bureau of National Affairs, Inc., 1974.

———. "The Real Crunch in Managerial Manpower." *Harvard Business Review,* Vol. 51, no. 6 (1973), pp. 146–158.

Taylor, Frederick W. *The Principles of Scientific Management.* New York: Harper & Bros., 1911.

CHAPTER 11: ORGANIZATIONAL DESIGN

Beer, Michael. *Organizational Change and Development: A Systems View.* Santa Monica, Calif.: Goodyear, 1980.

Drucker, Peter F. "The Coming of the New Organization." *Harvard Business Review*, Vol. 88, no. 1 (1988), pp. 45–53.

Hull, William K. "Survival Strategies in a Hostile Environment." *Harvard Business Review*, Vol. 58, no. 5 (1980), pp. 75–85.

Kilmann, Ralph H. *Beyond the Quick Fix: Managing Five Tracks to Organizational Success.* San Francisco: Jossey-Bass, 1984.

Lawrence, P. R., and J. W. Lorsch. *Organization and Environment.* Cambridge, Mass.: Harvard University Press, 1967.

Nienstedt, Paul, and Richard Wintermantel. "Restructuring Organizations for Improved Productivity: A Case in Point." *Personnel*, August 1985, pp. 34–40.

CHAPTER 12: NEGOTIATION SKILLS

Adler, Nancy J. *International Dimensions of Organizational Behavior.* Boston: Kent Publishing Co., 1986.

Brooks, Earl, and George S. Odiorne. *Managing by Negotiations.* New York: Van Nostrand Reinhold, 1984.

Fisher, R., and W. Ury. *Getting to Yes.* New York: Houghton Mifflin, 1981.

Harris, Charles E. *Business Negotiating Power—Optimizing Your Side of the Deal.* New York: Van Nostrand Reinhold, 1983.

Lewicki, Roy J., and Joseph A. Litterer. *Negotiation.* Homewood, Ill.: Richard D. Irwin, 1985.

Raiffa, Howard. *The Art and Science of Negotiation.* Cambridge, Mass.: Harvard University Press, 1982.

CHAPTER 13: STAFFING

Avery, R. D., and J. E. Campion. "The Employment Interview: A Summary and Review of Recent Research." *Personnel Psychology*, Vol. 35 (1982), pp. 281–322.

Guion, Robert M. "Recruiting, Selection, and Job Placement." In *Handbook of Industrial and Organizational Psychology*, M. Dunnette, ed. Chicago: Rand McNally, 1976.

Moses, Joseph L., and William C. Byham, eds. *Applying the Assessment Center Method.* New York: Pergamon Press, 1977.

Rosow, Jerome M., and Robert Zager. "Punch Out the Time Clocks." *Harvard Business Review,* Vol. 61, no. 2 (1983), pp. 12–31.

CHAPTER 14: PROJECT MANAGEMENT

Cleland, David I., and William R. King, eds. *Project Management Handbook.* New York: Van Nostrand Reinhold, 1983.

Graham, Robert J. *Project Management: Combining Technical and Behavioral Approaches for Effective Implementation.* New York: Van Nostrand Reinhold, 1985.

Roman, Daniel D. *Managing Projects: A Systems Approach.* New York: Elsevier Science Publishing Co., 1986.

CHAPTER 15: EFFECTIVE MEETINGS, TEAMS, AND TASK FORCES

Altier, William J. "SMR Forum: Task Forces—An Effective Management Tool." *Sloan Management Review,* Vol. 27, no. 3 (1986), pp. 69–76.

Huber, George P. *Managerial Decision Making.* Glenview, Ill.: Scott Foresman, 1980.

CHAPTER 16: ENTREPRENEURSHIP/INTRAPRENEURSHIP

Baumback, Clifford M., and Joseph R. Mancuso. *Entrepreneurship and Venture Management.* 2nd edition. Englewood Cliffs, N.J.: Prentice-Hall, 1987.

Covin, Jeffrey G., and Dennis P. Slevin. "The Influence of Organization Structure on the Utility of an Entrepreneurial Top Management Style." *Journal of Management Studies,* Vol. 25, no. 3 (May 1988).

———. "Strategic Management of Small Firms in Hostile and Benign Environments." *Strategic Management Journal,* forthcoming (1988–89).

Gartner, William B. "A Conceptual Framework for Describing the Phenomenon of New Venture Creation." *Academy of Management Review,* Vol. 10, no. 4 (1985), pp. 696–706.

Khandwalla, Pradip N. *The Design of Organizations.* New York: Harcourt Brace Jovanovich, 1977.

Miller, D., and P. H. Friesen. "Innovation in Conservative and Entrepreneurial Firms: Two Models of Strategic Momentum." *Strategic Management Journal*, Vol. 3 (1982), pp. 1–25.

Pinchot, G. *Intrapreneuring*. New York: Harper & Row, 1985.

Porter, Michael E. *Competitive Strategy*. New York: Free Press, 1980.

Welsh, John A., and Jerry F. White. *The Entrepreneur's Master Planning Guide*. Englewood Cliffs, N.J.: Prentice-Hall, 1983.

CHAPTER 17: HEALTH AND LIFE-STYLE

Benson, Herbert, and Robert L. Allen. "How Much Stress Is Too Much?" *Harvard Business Review*, Vol. 58, no. 5 (1980), pp. 86–92.

Cooper, K. H. *The New Aerobics*. New York: Bantam Books, 1970.

Gettings, Lisa, and I. Nick Maddox. "When Health Means Wealth." *Training and Development Journal*, Vol. 42, no. 4 (1988), pp. 81–85.

Sharkey, B. J. *Physiological Fitness and Weight Control*. Missoula, Mont.: Mountain Press Publishing Co., 1974.

CHAPTER 18: CAREER MANAGEMENT

Bardwick, Judith M. *The Plateauing Trap*. New York: AMACOM, 1986.

Bolles, Richard N. *What Color Is Your Parachute?* Berkeley, Calif.: Ten Speed Press, 1988.

Brockner, Joel, Jeanette Davy, and Carolyn Carter. "Layoffs, Self-Esteem, and Survivor Guilt: Motivational, Affective and Attitudinal Consequences." *Organizational Behavior and Human Decision Processes*, Vol. 36 (1985), pp. 229–244.

Hall, Douglas T., and Associates. *Career Development in Organizations*. San Francisco: Jossey-Bass, 1986.

Levinson, Harry. "A Second Career: The Possible Dream." *Harvard Business Review*, Vol. 61, no. 3 (1983), pp. 122–129.

Nielsen, John. "Management Layoffs Won't Quit." *Fortune*, 28 October 1985, pp. 46–49.

Index

accomplishment report, 142, 157–158
acquisitions, and career management,
   389–392
action plan
  behavior modification, 129
  communication, 182
  for management by objectives,
    148–151
  for motivation to manage, 219–220
  for organizational design, 240–242
  for power, 102
  for time management, 37–39
aerobic fitness, 379
agenda, 13–14, 335, 390
  hidden, 95
aggression, frustration and, 63
ambiguity, in contract, 276
arbitration, 277–278
assertive motivation, 204
assertive rights and behaviors, 205

assessment center, 144
authority, 20, 188
  power from, 91
autocrat, 185

bargaining, vs. negotiation, 252
Behavior Activity Profile, 70–74
behavioral dimensions, in job analysis, 289–290, 294–298
behavior modification, 41, 116–129,
  405
  action plan, 129
  applying, 126–128
  compliance vs. noncompliance, 42–
   43
  elements of, 122–124
  performance appraisal and, 125–
   126
Benson, Herbert, on relaxation response, 68

bureaucratic companies, 349
business opportunities, valuation of,
    352–355

calendar, personal, 25
calorie allowance, 376
career management, 381–399
    merger or acquisition and, 389–392
Career Status Audit, 394–395
cholesterol levels, 58
client-consultant problem-solving
    process, 171–173
coaching, 136
coercive power, 91
commitment, to management by ob-
    jectives, 139
communication, 161–182
    action plan for, 182
    Five Rs of reception in, 176
    Five Rs of transmission in, 173–176
    mergers and, 391
    message in, 177–179
    principles of, 170–171
    in project management, 308–309,
        321
communication effectiveness audit,
    179–181
compensation, management by objec-
    tives and, 142–143
complexity, of environment, 224
compliance, vs. noncompliance, 42–
    43
composite integration, 231–233, 235
conflict spiral, 262
conformity pressure, 332
consensus manager, 185
consultative autocrat, 185
contracts, 276–277
control, of group process, 338
cooperation, in group decision-mak-
    ing, 333
coping skills, 59, 390
Coping Skills Audit, 80–81
corporate venturing, 346

creativity, conformity pressure and,
    332
cycling, and entrepreneurship, 351

daily log, 16, 30–33
decision-making, authority for, 20
defensiveness, 134–135
delegation, 19–21, 67, 188–189, 401
Demand Audit, 78–79
deterrence theory, 262
dictation equipment, 25
differentiation, 222–224
    and environment, 224–225
dis-integration, 233
Drucker, Peter, 136
dynamism, 224

Emery Air Freight, 117
emotions, and perception, 165–166
Entrepreneurial Behavior Audit, 357
Entrepreneurial Style/Organizational
    Structure Audit, 358–365
entrepreneurship, 345
    characteristics of, 351–352
    cycling and, 351
    definition of, 346–347
    hostile environment and, 347–348
    organic vs. mechanistic structures
        in, 348–351
    vs. intrapreneurship, 345–346
environment
    changing, 67
    differentiation and, 224–225
    hostility in, 347–348
    personality and, 66–67
evaluation, in group process, 338
exercise, 377–379, 400
    and weight loss, 376–377
expert power, 90

family goals, 387
feedback, 123–124, 127–128
    in project management, 308
fight-or-flight response, 56–57

filters, and communication, 164
final offer arbitration, 278
first impression, 166–167
flexibility
    in negotiation, 262–263
    physical, 378
Friedman, Meyer, 45
frustration, 61–64

genetics, and stress, 55–58
goal orientation, 95–97
goals, 383–388
Group Appropriateness Audit, 334, 342–343
group pressure, and leadership style, 192
group process, 338–340
groups, *see* meetings

Halo Effect, 168
handouts, 336
health, 366–380
Herzberg, Frederick, 212
hidden agenda, 95
Hierarchy of Needs (Maslow), 85, 211–212
hiring decision, 293

information
    for decision-making, 198
    power from, 90
information exchange, 240
    and integration, 226
    meetings and, 335
innovation, 347
instantaneous integration, 229, 234
integration, 222–224, 226–232
    composite, 231–232, 235
    devices for, 238–239
    instantaneous, 229, 234
    model for, 235–238
    possible positions for, 233–235
    process, 229–230, 234
intelligence, theories of, 93–94

interruptions, 22–23
    in daily log, 17
interview
    in daily log, 17
    selection, 170, 286, 292, 299–301
intolerance for noncompliance, 43–44
    audit of, 53–54
    high level of, 51–52
    low level of, 52
    managing, 48–51
    setting level of, 49
intrapreneurship, entrepreneurship vs., 345–346

Jerrell/Slevin Management Instrument, 199–201
job analysis, 287, 289
job characteristics, motivation to manage and, 207–208
job description, 287, 288
    of manager, 10–13
job enrichment, 125, 214

leadership, 183–201
    checklist for, 193–194
    controlling style of, 196–197
    in meetings, 336–337
    after merger, 391
    and motivation, 214
    pressure and, 190–192
    styles of, 184–186
life change, and stress, 64–65
life-style, 368, 369–371
Lippmann, Walter, 167
listening, 25
log, daily, 16, 30–33
longevity, 367

Machiavellian Factor, 95
management, participative, 186–188
management activities summary, 17, 34–36
management by objectives, 130–160, 390

management by objectives (*cont.*)
  and compensation, 142–143
  learning, 140–142
  and motivation, 215
  setting objectives for, 137–139
manager, job description of, 10–13
Maslow, Abraham, 211
Maslow's hierarchy, 85, 211–212
May, Rollo, 85
McClelland, David, on managerial
  power, 85
mediation, 277
meetings, 331–343, 404
  agenda for, 335
  conformity pressures in, 332
  cooperation in, 333
  effectiveness of, 334–340
  handouts for, 336
  information for, 335
  leadership in, 336–337
  minutes of, 340
  and motivation, 333
  objectives of, 334–335
  politics of, 334
  specialization in, 333
  time pressures and, 332
  visual aids for, 336
mergers, and career management,
  389–392
Miner, John B., 204
minutes, of meetings, 340
model
  for integration, 235–238
  for project implementation profile,
  303–309
  for project management, 319–320
"monkeys," 21–22, 405
motivation, 202–217
  assertive, 204
  groups and, 333
  leadership and, 214
  management by objectives and, 215
  of others, 209–211
  rewards and, 215
motivational hygiene theory, 212–214

motivation to manage, 203–206
  action plan for, 219–220
  audit of, 218
  changing, 209
  and job characteristics, 207–208
  research on, 206–207

negotiation, 250–284, 402–403
  agreement phase of, 276–278
  alternatives in, 265–266
  approach to, 257–258
  at the bargaining table, 273–275
  checklist for, 279–284
  consensus testing in, 265
  flexibility in, 262–263
  after merger, 391
  objectives of, 267
  planning in, 257
  practice planning for, 266–273
  research on, 255–266
  and satisfaction, 256
  space for, 254–255, 268
  targets in, 256
  third-party intervention in, 277–278
  time for, 251–254
  verbal tactics for, 263–265
  vs. bargaining, 252
  win/win outcome for, 266
negotiation team, 258–259
Nelson, Daniel, 210
networking, 15, 389
noncompliance, 43–44
  response to, 40–54
  see also intolerance for noncompliance

obesity, 373
objectives, of negotiation, 267
Oncken, W., on time management,
  21
organizational design, 221–249
  action plan for, 240–242
  after merger, 391
  see also integration
organizational politics, 93

organizational power, 93
Organizational Power Audit, 110–113
organizational pressure and leader-
    ship style, 192
orientation, in group process, 338
overweight, 368–369, 373

paper-flow system, 24
partial reinforcement, 119–120
participative management, 186–188
People Express, 238
perception, 162–164
    principles of, 164–169
    selective, 169
performance appraisal, 130–135
    as behavior modifier, 125–126
    limitations of, 133
personal goals, 387
personality
    and environment, 66–67
    and leadership style, 192
    Type A, 44–46, 64
    Type B, 46–47
Personality-Environment Match, 67,
    77
personal power, 90
personnel, see staffing
Peters, Tom, *Thriving on Chaos*, 340
physical state, 65
    and perception, 164–165
planning, in negotiation, 257
political tactics, 97, 98–101
politics, 93–97
positional power, 90–91
power, 41–42, 82–115
    action plan for, 102
    impact of, 86–87
    meetings and, 335
    and motivation, 204
    organizational, 93
    potential vs. actual, 84
    prescription for, 97, 101
    soft vs. hard, 184
    sources of, 89–91
    and subordinates, 89

use of, 91–93
power action plan, 115
power audit, 88, 103–104, 390
pressure
    to conform, 332
    and leadership, 190–192
priorities, 23, 67
proactivity, 347
problem attributes, and leadership,
    190
process integration, 229–230, 234
project implementation profile, 321–
    330
    model for, 303–309
project life cycle, 309–312
    strategy in, 320
project management, 302–330
    client acceptance of, 307–309
    client consultation in, 306
    communication in, 308–309
    feedback in, 308
    mission in, 305
    model for, 319–320
    personnel in, 306–307
    schedule in, 306
    strategy and tactics in, 311–319
    troubleshooting in, 309
pseudo-entrepreneurial companies,
    349
punishment, 49

quality circles, 334

recruitment, 290–291
referent power, 90
reflection, 25
reinforcement, 119
    partial, 119–120
    timeliness of, 133–134
relaxation, 68, 69
responsibility, and motivation, 206
resumes, 291
rewards, 121
    and motivation, 215
    power from, 91

rights, assertive, 205
role overload, 12
Rosenman, Ray, 45

satisfaction, negotiation and, 256
security, and entrepreneurship, 345
selection interview, 170, 286, 292,
    299–301
selective perception, 169
shaping, 120–121
shareholder manager, 185
Silver, David, on valuation, 352–353
Skinner, B.F., 119
social facilitation, 333
Social Readjustment Rating Scale, 65,
    75–76
socioemotional leadership, 336
Sources of Power Audit, 107–109
specialization, groups and, 333
staffing, 285–301, 401–402
    hiring decision in, 293
    in project management, 306–307
    recruitment in, 290–291
    selection interview in, 170, 286,
        292, 299–301
stereotypes, 167–168
Stevenson, Howard, on entrepre-
    neurs, 346
stock ownership, 389
strategy, in project management,
    311–319
stress, 55–81
    definition of, 59
    life change and, 64–65
subliminal issues, 169
Subordinate Power Audit, 89, 105–
    106
subordinates,
    delegation and, 19–20

power and, 89
success, and entrepreneurship, 345

tactics
    political, 97
    in project management, 311–319,
        320–321
target behavior, 123
targets, in negotiation, 256
task leadership, 336
team player, 96
telephone, as interruption, 22
third-party intervention, 277–278
Thomas, Kenneth, on power, 92
Thriving on Chaos (Peters), 340
time, ways of saving, 18–26
time management, 9–39
    action plan for, 37–39
    daily log for, 16–17, 30–33
time pressures, and group decision-
    making, 332
tolerance, mismanaging, 46–47
top management, project support
    from, 305
Type A personality, 44–46, 64
Type B personality, 46–47

unstable organization, 233–234

valuation, of business opportunities,
    352–355
values, and perception, 166
visual aids, for meetings, 336

waist-to-hip ratio, 372–373
Wass, D.L., on time management, 21
weight control, 372, 373–374
weight loss, 371, 375
    exercise and, 376–377